Practical Enterprise Risk Management

How to optimize business strategies through managed risk taking

Liz Taylor

KoganPage

LONDON PHILADELPHIA NEW DELHI

First published in Great Britain and the United States in 2014 by Kogan Page Limited

2nd Floor, 45 Gee Street
London EC1V 3RS
United Kingdom

1518 Walnut Street, Suite 1100
Philadelphia PA 19102
USA

4737/23 Ansari Road
Daryaganj
New Delhi 110002
India

www.koganpage.com

© Liz Taylor, 2014

The right of Liz Taylor to be identified as the author of this work has been asserted by her in accordance with the Copyright, Designs and Patents Act 1988.

ISBN   978 0 7494 70531
E-ISBN   978 0 7494 70548

British Library Cataloguing-in-Publication Data

A CIP record for this book is available from the British Library.

Library of Congress Cataloging-in-Publication Data

CIP data is available.

Library of Congress Control Number: 2014004439

Typeset by Amnet
Printed and bound in India by Replika Press Pvt Ltd

CONTENTS

Foreword by Steve Fowler vii
Foreword by Mrutyunjay Mahapatra x
Acknowledgements xii

01   Introduction 1

Outline 1
Business is about taking risk 2
The difference between taking managed and unmanaged risks 5
Benefits of well-managed enterprise risk management 7
The myths about risk 8
Capacity to take risk 12
Questions for senior management and the board to ask 13
Notes 14

02   About enterprise risk management 15

Outline 15
Risk management 16
Implementing the programme for ERM 20
ERM – the process 22
Essential attributes of ERM for delivering value and capacity 23
Top level leadership in ERM 24
Identifying risk: types of risk, risk lists and taxonomies 26
Evaluating and prioritizing risk 29
Governance, risk and compliance 36
Questions for senior management and the board to ask 37
Notes 38

**03   Risk as an opportunity/threat to objectives
and value drivers** 39

Outline 39
Risk – opportunities and threats 39
Risk as uncertainty 43
Threat and opportunity management 45
Dealing with threat 45
Dealing with opportunity 47
Differentiating between objectives, strategic goals and value drivers 51
Questions for senior management and the board to ask 57
Notes 57

04   Implementing an ERM programme 59

Outline 59
Establish the foundation – the operating model for ERM 59
Documentation for ERM 62
Language, oversight and governance 63
Building capabilities: assess and develop responses and capabilities 66
Improving capabilities: monitoring and communication 68
Questions for senior management and the board to ask 70

05   Risk attitude, risk propensity and risk appetite 73

Outline 73
Risk aversion versus risk hungry 73
Applications of a risk appetite tool 76
Risk capacity versus tolerance 77
Developing risk appetite frameworks 78
The risk of not taking a risk 82
Risk appetite and value drivers 83
Organization behind the setting of risk appetite 88
Examples of risk appetite statements 90
Questions for senior management and the board to ask 93
Notes 95

**06   ERM culture, blame, boundaries and elephants
in the room** 97

Outline 97
ERM cultures and the blame culture 98
Using risk appetite as a tool to destroy the blame culture 99
Managing risk 101
The link between managed risk taking, mice, Maslow and Herzberg 104
The elephant in the room and conduct risk 108
In the public interest 113
Questions for senior management and the board to ask 114
Notes 117

07   Embedding and integrating ERM 119

Outline 119
What does embedding mean? 119
Main aspects of embedding ERM 121
A 16-step plan for embedding ERM 128
The three lines of play 130
Questions for senior management and the board to ask 136
Notes 138

08   Maturity in enterprise risk management 139

Outline 139
How risk maturity enables managed risk taking 139
Action plan for measuring and tracking performance 143
Questions for senior management and the board to ask 152
Notes 153

09   Resilience and sustainable habits 155

Outline 155
Business continuity management 156
The role of senior management 161
Corporate social responsibility 166
Questions for senior management and the board to ask 172
Notes 174

10   Learning and communication 177

Outline 177
The learning habit 179
ERM information systems 188
External communication 194
Questions for senior management and the board to ask 194
Notes 196

11   Conformance, performance, roles, responsibilities and regulations 199

Outline 199
Managing conformance versus performance 200
The role of boards in ERM 200
Governance for ERM 203
The role of internal and external audit in ERM 208
Compliance requirements for risk management: various countries and industries 211
Questions for senior management and the board to ask 220
Notes 222

12   Deliverables from quantitative ERM approaches 223

Outline 223
Measuring and valuing 223
Models for valuing risk and capital 229
Own risk and solvency assessments – a useful model 232
Stress testing and reverse stress testing 235
Risks that cannot be valued 239
Questions for senior management and the board to ask 240
Notes 242

13   Simple, elegant ERM tools for senior management 243

Outline 243

The triangle of risk – trigger, environment, strength or weakness 244

Using cause and consequence analysis to transform risk approach 249

Macro and micro risk management 252

Questions for senior management and the board to ask 253

Note 254

14   ERM and performance management synergies 255

Outline 255

Risk management alignment within the organization 256

Performance management 256

Performance management methods 258

Questions for senior management and the board to ask 263

Notes 264

15   The key strategic questions for senior management and boards to ask themselves 265

Outline 265

Recognizing the risks *of* versus the risks *to* the strategic plan 266

The key strategic questions 268

Summary 281

Appendix 1. Examples of corporate governance and ERM regulations 283

Appendix 2. The main principles of the UK Code of Governance, October 2012 285

Appendix 3. Summary COSO guidance 287

Appendix 4. Case study: Applying a more granular mathematical model to a risk for a non-financial organization 291

Appendix 5. Capital and risk considerations for US insurers, from NAIC ORSA Guidance 294

Appendix 6. Sample terms of reference for a board risk committee 297

Appendix 7. Example of roles of CRO and ERM team 302

Further Reading 305

Index 307

FOREWORD
Steve Fowler

Business has always been inseparable from risk and opportunity – indeed, risk taking in order to achieve opportunity is the very essence of all business.

In recent years though, perceptions of the negative side of risk seem to have reached a whole new prominence, sometimes to the detriment of nimble, judicious and skilful risk taking. How often has the image of the fluorescent-jacket-clad risk official been used synonymously with the idea of risk aversion or failure to compete? How often have we read that some unexpected or improbable event just has to be someone's 'fault'?

Never has risk seemed so negative, unrelenting, immediate, diverse or potentially devastating – or at least, that's the perception painted by many of our media, particularly in the Western world.

Too many failed businesses have been found afterwards to have overly focussed on the negative risks that are in the news this month. Instead of this approach – so-called 'risk management by media' – they should be guided by their own strategic objectives.

Effective risk management offers true strategic advantage. It must never become a technical discipline peddled by software-obsessed technocrats whom nobody understands. Instead, it has to be a strategic and people-focussed discipline, with strong elements of financial and statistical competence, coupled with a good grasp of history, futurology, psychology, sociology and common sense all thrown in for good measure.

Today's world is indeed infinitely more complex and interconnected than that of our parents or grandparents. We are truly living through so-called VUCA – volatile, uncertain, complex and ambiguous – times, and we need a guide to help us on that journey. Liz Taylor, in this highly accessible book, is that guide.

In the book, Liz sets out to cover everything one needs to know to develop and apply broad business-focussed, or 'enterprise', risk management (ERM) in a very practical and easily comprehensible way.

Starting with the concept of ERM as a fundamental business discipline, as Liz says in Chapter 1, risk is often misrepresented, not just in the media, but in the boardroom too. Life's uncertain by its very nature, 'stuff happens' and evidence can often mislead us. Should we worry about everything, and anyway, can we do anything about much of it, anyway? Getting the balance right in these areas is critical to sustainable business success.

Chapter 2 describes how to 'do' ERM – the main principles and processes involved – and the critical importance of leadership. With the wrong 'tone at the top' and inadequate risk/reward structures, as so many financial services companies have found to their cost in recent years, the best risk processes in the world will always fail, no matter how well documented they are.

Liz moves on in Chapter 3 to look in detail at that all-important balance between negative risk and positive opportunity: value creation and value protection matter equally to modern businesses.

Having mastered how to implement ERM processes, Chapter 4 then deals with how to establish an ERM programme, the importance of a common risk language across a firm, effective oversight and the key area of building risk management capability. The latter matters both at the professional end of the spectrum and throughout business leadership teams more generally. Within the risk management function itself, the world is moving towards increasingly common standards for measuring educational achievement and experience, as is already the case in the longer established professions such as law, engineering and accountancy.

In Chapters 5 to 8, Liz then defines and describes the important concepts of risk appetite, risk culture and risk maturity. These powerful tools are invaluable techniques for implementation of a true risk-focussed business strategy at board level.

Whilst most of this book discusses how to identify, measure and treat risk, Chapter 9 takes a useful excursion to cover planning for both known and unknown eventualities. Often thought to be the preserve of the IR or facilities function, business continuity planning is at its most effective when fully integrated into a contiguous risk and resilience management programme. Equally important in today's increasingly ethically-focussed world, is coverage of how corporate social responsibility programmes integrate with planning in this area.

Chapter 10 completes this excursion by covering how organizations can best learn from past incidents and how a risk management learning culture can be created and nurtured. Seventeen years after the Challenger Space Shuttle failure, NASA experienced the failure of the Columbia vehicle – for exactly the same reasons as that earlier disaster. More recently BP's Macondo well disaster in the Gulf of Mexico demonstrated many of the same root causes as the same company's Texas City oil refinery fire only a few years earlier. The one thing we learn from history is that we do not always learn from history....

Chapter 11 covers the role of the board in risk management, the concept of GRC – governance, risk and compliance, the respective roles of audit and risk committees and the three lines of defence model. It also provides a useful summary of the main compliance regimes currently in use across the world, from Dodd-Frank and COSO, through King III, EU corporate governance regulations and the primary Asian governance regimes, to Solvency II and Basel III.

The next three chapters of this book cover performance management, risk and capital assessment, stress testing and include an invaluable summary of the main tools and techniques used for risk assessment, measurement and treatment.

Each chapter in this book is concluded by useful questions for senior management and boards to ask, and this in turn is supported by a final chapter covering the integration of risk and strategic planning.

The text provides invaluable guidance in all the most important risk areas for businesses to keep sight of, from boardroom governance, through cyber risk, natural disasters, projects, political, treasury and people risks, and other operational risks, to shifts in areas of competition.

Whilst simple and straightforward risks are arguably easy to identify, quantify and understand, there are three areas in particular where I'd suggest companies should devote more attention:

Firstly, high impact, low frequency events. These are the so-called 'black swans': those things you'd never think of, nor expect, to happen. Yet paradigm shift is very real and remarkably commonplace – think of how MP3 files have replaced LPs, cassettes and CDs, or how hybrid vehicle drives now threaten established internal combustion technologies in the same way that these replaced steam and horse power. There is no substitute here to stretching the imagination, networking far and wide, and thinking the unthinkable.

Secondly, interconnections between risks. Most firms will review their supplier risks but how many really devote time to looking at their customer risks, or indeed the risks posed by their suppliers' suppliers? The 'extended enterprise' has truly come of age, and businesses must adjust their risk management strategies accordingly. At a global level, interconnectivity between economies is increasingly recognized to be not just a driver for global growth but also a major systemic factor in the risk of potential global fiscal meltdown.

Finally, culture, compensation and fraud continue to be major drivers of value loss in firms. How many of us wake up each day to ask 'who's next?' when it comes to reputation loss? Business today is much more closely scrutinised. Those who don't treat their customers and staff well, and explain what they're doing and why, will expect their reputations to be trashed tomorrow on Twitter. Today's grumble is tomorrow's front page news.

Practical enterprise risk management has come of age as a key business technique. Having a comprehensive and interlinked strategy in this area is, de facto, a necessity for not just major multinational enterprises but, scaled accordingly, for firms in every sector, every size and every part of the world. This book should form your guide.

Steve Fowler

Strategic Advisor to the Board
The Institute of Risk Management

Principal, Amarreurs Consulting

FOREWORD
Mrutyunjay Mahapatra

The world of risk management has changed and expanded manifold since Peter Bernstein wrote his seminal book on risk, *Against the Gods*, some 20 years ago. One of the complexities of risk management, that all of us have to deal with today, is the integral view of risk. As senior managers, all of us know that it is not enough to understand what the market risk, credit risk or operational risk our companies are facing is. Far more important is the interplay of risks and how we look at the full picture and not at a 'silo' picture, because the silo view has proven to be the greatest risk for many enterprises, which have either perished or struggled in the recent past.

Having read very many of the significant books on risk management, Liz Taylor's *Practical Enterprise Risk Management* is undoubtedly the best that I have come across so far. It brings to the fore not just the importance of the integrated view of risk, but also provides an abundance of practical tools and models, that can immediately be put to work in real-life situations.

Rhoda Byrne, in her book *The Secret Hero* writes 'Courage comes from performing fearful acts'. This is what we do every day in business. We take courageous steps in management and strategy, in spite of the fearful thing called 'risk' being present in whatever we do. Liz Taylor, in her book, deals admirably with this important and crucial concept of risk management not being just about threats. It is also about opportunities, and risk management devoid of integrated opportunities management is shallow.

In this book, the reader is helpfully guided, for a risk appetite statement is never divorced from the elegant model of enterprise risk and neither are profitability, business efficiency and competitive advantage considered isolated from the design, structure and implementation of good ERM.

Contemporary, comprehensive and current in its content, the book deals amply with the risks relating to corporate governance, conduct risk and personal ethics as part of risk culture and measurement of 'maturity' of an organization's ERM.

People form the foundation of any company. Therefore, successful ERM must integrate people policies and performance management into risk management. Liz Taylor, in a succinct and persuasive manner has brought in ideas like Six Sigma and TQM to inform and instil learnings from many fields into ERM.

Readers will appreciate the organization of individual chapters of the book, where, after discussion of concepts, a set of questions are posed for the senior management and the board on the chapter's contents so that the practical aspects always remain in focus and a self audit can take place simultaneously!

To quote Peter Drucker, 'One cannot manage change, one can only be ahead of it'. *Practical Enterprise Risk Management* definitely helps one in staying ahead of the changes in risk management.

Mrutyunjay Mahapatra

Regional Head, UK
State Bank of India

ACKNOWLEDGEMENTS

My grateful thanks to the following for their peer reviews:

Alex Dali; G 31000, Paris

Alex Hindson: Amlin plc, London

Artak Baghdasaryan: Central Bank of Armenia

Bill Ford: Privately Held Insurance, United States

Fiona Easton: Perth and Kinross Council, Scotland

Joe Clowes: Liz Taylor Risk Consulting, Devon

Mark Ferraro: Kinne Associates, North Carolina

Michael McCann: Auckland City Council, New Zealand

Nick Kay: Imperial College London

Richard Anderson: Crowe Horwath Global Risk Consulting, London

And thanks to all those from whom I have learnt, continually learn and will learn more about the journey of risk management.

Introduction

Outline

Taking managed risk can be exciting. It can open doors to more growth and more opportunities for innovation. Business and enterprise is about taking chances, just as life is about making difficult choices. Enterprise risk management should be a framework to enable difficult decisions to be made in a managed and structured way so as to maximize the opportunities for success and minimize the threats. We call this 'risk-based decision making'.

There are many myths about risk with perhaps unwarranted attention on those events that are extremely unlikely but with a large impact, and emerging risks that are more likely to be differing impacts of risks or differing causes of risks. There are also widely varying perceptions of opportunity and threat, which can lead to misconceptions about the real issues at hand; this in turn can constrain the process of innovation and even put the business in jeopardy.

> Enterprise risk management should be a framework to enable difficult decisions to be made in a managed and structured way so as to maximize the opportunities for success and minimize the threats.

In this introductory chapter we explore how businesses can use threat and opportunity management to enhance business strategies and how senior management can use the organization's capacity to take risks to enhance successful performance and innovation.

Business is about taking risk

Organizations of all types and sizes face internal and external factors and influences that make it uncertain whether and when they will achieve their objectives. The effect this uncertainty has on an organization's objectives is 'risk'.[1]

Life does not exist without uncertainty and the effect that uncertainty has on our objectives; imagine a world without aeroplanes, trains or cars? There are no sophisticated hospital procedures or lifesaving drugs, no internet, telephones or computers; no books or kitchen devices; no stock markets, stock traders or commodities; no electricity generation, gas distribution or coal mining. All these industries and products have grown in an environment where the risks to the developer and distributor were uncertain. The consequent impacts of the uncertainties on the wider public were almost unimaginable. Yet chances were taken, losses were sustained, but the consequent benefit to the businesses and enterprises involved, and to wider society, were arguably such that the risk was worth taking. Without some understanding of risk and its components, particularly the mathematics behind risk and uncertainty, life today would be quite different.

> The revolutionary idea that defines the boundary between modern times and the past is the mastery of risk: the notion that the future is more than a whim of the gods and that men and women are not passive before nature... by showing the world how to understand risk, measure it and weigh its consequences, they [the thinkers] converted risk-taking into one of the prime catalysts that drives modern Western society... the transformation in attitudes towards risk management unleashed by their achievements has channelled the human passion for games and wagering into economic growth, improved quality of life and technological progress. (*Against the Gods: The remarkable story of risk*, Peter L Bernstein)

The threat of loss of or reduction in quality of life could be deemed to be a risk that is not worth taking. Yet if we engage workers openly in the threat assessment and the transaction of appropriate remuneration and protection, we may be surprised how many people are prepared to work in 'dangerous' environments and accept that some threat is inherent in what they do, provided that the employer has managed the threat to as low a likelihood as could reasonably be expected.[2] The key here is the amount of control that the worker has in the decision making and the fair and open exchange between the employee and employer.

What is unacceptable is a threat that is imposed on a worker or bare-faced negligence or obfuscation of the real danger to life and limb. Equally bad is excessive caution or being 'risk averse'. In the UK, the Royal Society for the Prevention of Accidents maintains that:

> People who may be excessively 'risk averse' (for whatever reason) may prescribe safety measures which are wholly disproportionate… arguments that risks, however small, are unacceptable can be used as a device by those who oppose change or as a convenient excuse for banning things or not taking action.[3]

Sometimes those practising risk management, and other professionals who are responsible in some way for risk management, forget that managed risk must be taken for business to survive and to thrive. Yet at other times wholesale chances are taken without due regard to the capacity of the organization to take the consequences of not balancing capacity against exposure.

The strictures of the risk frameworks, processes, lists and bureaucracy can wrap the business in complicated agonizing knots. Risk, governance and compliance together can present a frightening array of hard-to-follow processes and results and unfathomable language and jargon. That is not to say that these are not important. They are. But they need to be translated into simple, elegant tools and knowledge systems for the board to be able to make sensible, life-giving risk-managed decisions for the business and for the stakeholders in a managed context (see Chapters 2 and 13 for practical tools).

CASE EXAMPLE

A risk professional invited a board of directors in a financial services company to radically change the way they offered their products, to remove the customers' limits for individual transactions and radically overhaul the 'approval' process for those transactions. The board's initial reaction was disbelief and rejection. However, having proved to them, with their own data, that the most profitable transactions were those of higher value and that they could wrap around the higher transactions an increasingly in-depth approval process, they became more interested. They were then shown a process of linking sales people's remuneration to profitability rather than volume, and they became excited. The final clincher was when the projections for growth of volume, reduced operating cost and increased profitability were shown. The deal was on.

Some months after the changes were implemented it was evident that this financial services business had increased its profitability faster and more steeply than those forecasts. Taking more managed risk had become exciting, opening doors to more growth and more opportunities for innovation.

The result of unbridled and complex risk management is that the board members break free of the process and do their own thing. Strategic decisions are made regardless of possible impacts or, worse still, the process is bent to make the analysis fit the desired result. Risk management is relegated to that process that the rest of the business should or must do and strategic threats that can damage the whole enterprise are sometimes taken without proper diligence. There is often a layer of self-delusion when the board think that a risk is being managed within its given risk appetite and capacity, when in fact the reality might be far from that.

> [while] directors are savvier about strategy than in 2011, [they] still struggle to get their arms around risk management, ... risk management is still a weak spot – perhaps because boards (and companies) are increasingly complacent about risks.... This is the one issue where the share of directors reporting sufficient knowledge has not increased: 29 per cent now say their boards have limited or no understanding of the risks their companies face. What's more, they say their boards spend just 12 per cent of their time on risk management, an even smaller share of time than two years ago. (Extract from McKinsey report, August 2013[4])

There is a whole world of difference between taking managed risk and taking unmanaged risk. Taking managed risk requires a programme to bring about openness and transparency about the opportunity or threat involved. There also needs to be a clear and truthful accounting of the value in the business – whether that is capital, reputation or liquidity. Taking unmanaged risk might well be where the senior management think that the risk is being managed (who would admit to it not being managed?) *but it is not managed* until there is a proper programme applied to the decision making – but that doesn't have to slow the process up if there are simple, elegant tools for senior management to wield when making risk-based decisions.

Risk presents opportunities and/or threats. Both need to be evaluated carefully and balanced against each other and then considered against the organization's capacity and willingness to take risky decisions. Does that require complex systems? You bet. But these systems and processes need to operate behind the scene and be translated into real, clear and clever information on which the board can make informed and successful decisions, and so that the board can seize and maximize opportunities. Given these tools and the capability to wield them, the board can then engage in exploring opportunities for the taking of more managed risk within the organization's capacity.

This is what Volvo said about taking managed risk in the notes to its 2011 accounts:[5]

> Risk may be due to events in the world and can affect a given industry or market. Risk can be specific to a single company. At Volvo work is carried out daily to identify, measure and manage risk – in some cases the Group can influence the likelihood that a risk-related event will occur. In cases in which such events are beyond the Group's control, the Group strives to minimize the consequences.

But there is nothing in the statement about how it seeks to enhance opportunities or activities that can open up new markets or innovation, nor indeed is there any overt consideration in this statement about the capacity to take threats and opportunities.

The difference between taking managed and unmanaged risks

Taking a managed risk means knowing the facts about the opportunity or threat that is presented, and knowing that the resources are available to cope if the worst threat or most extreme opportunity transpires. Taking an unmanaged risk means that we are plunging into the realms of the unknown and taking chances that could result in problems for the business.

When making a decision about an opportunity, a board is influenced by a multitude of factors. Some are external such as competitor pressure, current market positioning, state of and changes in the market, speed of change in the market, environmental factors, regulatory pressures and customer demand. Others are internal including capital availability, preferences, skills, capability and capacity. There are also influences from the particular preferences of the board, the way in which decisions are made, style of decision making and propensity to take opportunities or avoid threat.

Faced with such a multitude of factors, without adequate information and data, decision making can be muddled and often the board will revert to their common style with either one party making the decision and all agreeing with it – groupthink[6] – or delaying the decision until more information or data comes to light. Neither of these ways of making decisions is healthy and can result in the taking of unmanaged risks. The board should be able to take a balanced and realistic view of the threat against the opportunity.

Doing a SWOT analysis (see Chapter 3) is extremely useful for understanding and decision making for all sorts of situations in business and organizations. An acronym for Strengths, Weaknesses, Opportunities and Threats, the headings provide a good framework for reviewing strategy, position and direction of a company or business proposition or idea. However, these analyses are inherently flawed unless conducted realistically with adequate information and data. The key here is the realistic evaluation of the strengths, weaknesses, opportunities and threats. In a complex multinational business spread across many countries and many product/service lines, it is even harder to get a good handle on the facts as opposed to the fiction. The board may call for the risk experts to conduct a risk analysis. This will be based, normally, on the 'threats' alone and will not take into account the strengths, weaknesses and opportunity evaluation, even if there is a sophisticated and mature risk management team with quantitative as well as qualitative skills. This often means that the risk analysis is ignored because it is only one corner of the picture.

But how does a board gather the relevant information and data, and how do they know when there is enough information and data? Sometimes a decision has to be made on inadequate information and data, particularly if there is a rapidly changing situation and the opportunity has to be seized. The simplest logic is to evaluate the maximum impact of the threat upon the objective, whether in terms of capital required, reputation damage, loss of life, loss of information, regulatory breach or other value driver (see Chapter 5 on risk appetite) and match that against the capacity of the organization in terms of the objective and value drivers, if known. This is all easier said than done in a complex organization but unless one knows one's capacity to sustain loss, any decision made can expose the organization to failing to achieve the objectives. Failing to evaluate impacts, even on an approximate basis, will result in unmanaged risk taking and decisions that are wrong.

Benefits of well-managed enterprise risk management

An organization that embraces enterprise risk management (ERM) and inculcates it into its culture will enjoy a number of benefits; innovation will be easier to embrace and the organization will be swifter to respond to market changes and be able to seize opportunities as they arise. People will work to their maximum potential and the organization is more likely to be an employer of choice, with lower staff turnover, lower absenteeism and attracting high calibre people who are committed to helping achieve the corporate objectives and demonstrating the organization's values and culture in everything they do. The reputation of the organization is more likely to be robust and strategic decision making would be based on sound intelligence about the threats and the opportunities.

A *Harvard Business Review* report[7] on the role of directors and senior management and their requirements for knowledge about risk, stated:

> Sometimes the process itself breaks down. 'As an academic, it often surprises me that, even today, board members and CEOs are not on the same page and are not having that conversation about risk as an element of corporate strategy,' said Paul Walker, Zurich Chair in Enterprise Risk Management at St John's University. Sometimes the information that board members receive is less than the unadorned truth.
>
> 'Last year, I was speaking on this subject,' he said, 'and someone at a very large organization came up to me and said, "We clean it up before it gets to the board; we cleanse it, we sanitize it, we delete things."
>
> 'The good news', Walker said, 'is that board members themselves are asking questions. Board members have said to me, "We've got to get better in doing that." Some of the complaints I get from boards are that they don't get strategy risk information on a timely basis. So they can't really help the executive team make the right decision, because they feel rushed in some of these situations. Or they see ERM leaders who talk about ERM, but they don't seem to think broadly enough and they don't do deep dives, and they don't connect the dots. Or I've heard board members say to me, "You say you're doing ERM, but from our perspective, it looks a lot like silo risk management." So they want organizations to try to connect the dots a little bit more, because there's a lot of value in doing that'.
>
> Walker goes on to say, 'The Chief Risk Officer must dispel a common image as a person who says no to ideas, and must demonstrate the value of the metrics and other tools at their disposal, often to sceptical officials.' Walker cited a

recent conversation with a chief strategy officer whose 'biggest criticism of ERM was, "I need something that's actionable. You tell me what the risk is, but how do I act upon that?" So we've got to be ready for those difficult questions and have the solutions as well.'

It is more likely, with good ERM, that the organization would avoid potential future rating agency downgrades and increased cost of capital. Many rating agencies have incorporated ERM into their methodologies. As these rating agencies' expertise in evaluating enterprise risk management grows, the requirements for stronger risk management competency will most likely become an expectation. The personal liability of board members can be minimized as can the risk of criminal charges against senior officers for failure to act reasonably in making their compliance certifications about the adequacy of internal controls and enhancers over financial reporting. ERM also reduces volatility of outputs by lowering the effect and reducing the likelihood of negative events. This has a knock-on effect on stakeholders and ultimately provides better financial stability for the whole of the economy.

Regulators have increasing expectations for effective ERM. They expect organizations to use the framework for the broad spectrum of risks and to demonstrate the effectiveness with outputs. Public, non-profit and government entities are often required to perform risk-based management assessments. Projects are more likely to be implemented on time, on budget and to specification with the application of good risk management.

The myths about risk

Black swans

The black swan theory or theory of black swan events is a metaphor, based on the concept that most people thought that all swans were white until the first black swans were spotted in Western Australia in 1697. The theory describes an event that comes as a surprise, has a major effect, and is often inappropriately rationalized after the fact with the benefit of hindsight.

The theory, developed by Nassim Nicholas Taleb in his book, *The Black Swan: The impact of the highly improbable,* explains:

- The disproportionate role of high-profile, hard to predict and rare events that are beyond the realm of normal expectations in history, science, finance and technology.

- The non-computability of the probability of the consequential rare events using scientific methods (owing to the very nature of small probabilities).
- The psychological biases that make people individually and collectively blind to uncertainty and unaware of the massive role of the rare event in historical affairs.

Black swan events have become common parlance for those events that have a low likelihood but enormous impact. These are the most difficult events to predict and prepare for, and most often are outside the control of the organization, but which can be prepared for on a contingency basis.

Predicting the unpredictable is fast becoming the trend among risk consultants. Further, the regulatory requirements for banks under Basel III and European insurance and reinsurance companies under Solvency II are such that the organization must take some time to think about the unpredictable risks and to consider and set aside the capital required to fund such risks over time, using a number of different models, and then stress testing and reverse stress testing to see if the capital is adequate (see Chapter 12 for more information about this approach).

One of the best ways to consider the unpredictable risks is to scenario test them in a 'break the bank' reverse stress test. This requires the organization to consider those events that could combine to make the organization unviable. The myths surrounding this are numerous. Reverse stress testing does not help us predict the unpredictable just as it does not help us to predict the cause of major failure, but it does help us to predict other threats that we've not thought about and their *impacts*. It also helps the organization understand those impacts in terms of the resilience (see Chapter 9) of the organization to respond to severe impacts.

Emerging risks

The myths about emerging risks are also numerous and would have us believe that there are all sorts of threats that can come and bite us when we least expect. Early in 2013 a large insurance broking house stated that emerging threats were: 'From extreme weather volatility to discriminatory health plans, or the unintended consequences of cost cuts in the mining sector.'

Yet, these are new and unpredictable causes of predictable impacts, or new and unpredictable impacts of known causes. They go on to describe increased incidents of earth tremors from fracking (hydraulic fracturing of rock to obtain gas or other hydrocarbons), mis-selling of products, missing the next emerging market, cyber-attacks, environmentally unfriendly supply chains, extreme weather, running afoul of the US Foreign Corrupt Practices Act, rising costs in mining, 'no fault' clinical trials, ERM abandonment, directors in the dock for regulatory risks, discriminatory medical plans, local captives compliance, Euro referendum, Euro breakdown, Africa-based terrorism and reputation harm by social media, amongst others. But do those 'emerging' risks matter to the board? Well actually, many of them present opportunities and threats and above all they are arguably new causes or increased accelerants to known causes. The *impacts* of these are what need to be reviewed by the board. So if we concentrate on the impacts of known risks, we can adapt our response mechanism to the unknown risks.

Perception of risk

The concept of risk is often misrepresented to the board and can result in one of three things:

1 Obfuscating the true situation – drowning management with impenetrable jargon and nonsense statistics.

2 Exaggerating the real risk and demanding more resource than is really needed.

3 Lulling the board into a false sense of security.

The following has been adapted for senior management in business from *A Worrier's Guide to Risk,* developed by David Spiegelhalter, Winton Professor of the Public Understanding of Risk at Cambridge University, in collaboration with the Risk Research Council. The original text spoke about risk in the sense that it affects people personally. We have adapted the theme for business, using the example of debt management.

Life's uncertain – we don't always know what will happen

1 *Uncertainty can be fine.* Would we want to know exactly how and when the business will fail due to 100 per cent unrecoverable debts? How much time and energy should we spend on trying to forecast *all* our debts going into default at the same time? Does there come a time when we just need to accept that risk is present in the

business? How do we determine between those risks we just can't do anything about and those that we can?

2 *Stuff happens.* The overall pattern of events can often be predicted surprisingly well but not the detail. We can make a good guess at the number of bad debts next year, but not who will default or by exactly how much.

3 *Rare events are more common than we think.* There are so many possible rare events we know some will happen but not which ones. If we anticipate 200 'one in every 200 year events' on average one of those will occur each year (and more than one might occur in one year).

Evidence can mislead us – we often can't see the full picture.

4 *Jumping to conclusions.* The media reports business failures that make a good story – don't assume the amount and type of business failures reported reflects true business failure rates that will affect our debt recovery rates.

5 *Runs of good/bad luck happen.* Reduced debt defaults in one part of the business might not be as a result of good debt risk management, it might be just good luck. Evidence is needed to prove that good debt risk management is responsible for the change in data.

6 *The past is past.* Things change, and as the financial firms always say and the credit crunch has proven, 'past performance is not necessarily a guide to future performance'. Do not rely entirely on debt management models that are based on past data unless there is proof that the data is sound enough to predict the future and that the data can anticipate all the changes the future might bring.

What about our business – should we worry?

7 *Are we bothered?* How does the economic situation relate to our business's circumstances? Bad debt is a severe threat to undercapitalized and poorly risk-managed businesses. If we have good intelligence, good risk management and good capitalization for the business, we should be able to weather the storm. If we over-manage the risk, set aside too much capital or too much resource, we might just bring about massive problems for the business by

not being able to use that capital or resource for innovation and developing the business further.

Can we do anything about it?

8   *No? So don't worry about things we can't change.* The asteroid that will destroy the earth and cause multiple bad debts may be on its way.

9   *Yes, but…* If the asteroid arrives, the chances are that our business will also be destroyed. So only plan for and manage those *realistic* risks that could affect the business.

10   *They would say that, wouldn't they?* Reflect on who is bringing us the news about the risk. Is it in their interest to create fear and uncertainty? What's in it for them?

11   *What are we not being told?* The full story is about the opportunities as well as the threats. While we may be being presented with reams of doom and gloom scenarios, what are the opportunities for the business, what is the context for the doom and gloom scenario?

12   *Size matters.* A big increase in a very small risk may not be important – twice almost-nothing is still almost-nothing. So if we are presented with statistics that state that the threat of increased bad debt is increased by, say, 50 per cent, is that 50 per cent of a very small number or of a significant number?

The key point is to get the 'balance' right for the business.

Capacity to take risk

We have used the expression 'capacity' with regard to the ability to take risk. Some would argue that a more proper expression would be 'appetite'. ISO 31000 avoids all reference to 'appetite' describing it as 'the level at which risk becomes acceptable or tolerable'. However from a strategic viewpoint for the board, the starting point has to be capacity rather than acceptability or tolerance. Within this book we put forward an argument that risk appetite is a combination of *capacity* to take risks and the willingness or *tolerance* towards the taking of risks (see Chapter 5 on risk appetite).

In financial institutions, 'capacity' would be defined as capital, yet capital can be eroded by lack of goodwill and good reputation; one could regard the effect of loss of confidence on banks as a good illustration of this. Public bodies would define capacity in terms of their resources to meet demand. For both public and private enterprises capacity might be defined as:

$$\text{Capacity} = \text{assets} + \text{people} + \text{knowledge} + \text{goodwill}$$

If one could value people, knowledge and goodwill on the same basis as assets, there might be the basis for a mathematical formula.

It can be seen therefore that if the threats exceed capacity, the organization is in trouble. Conversely, if the capacity exceeds the threats by a good margin, there is opportunity to take more managed risk. We will explore some of this in more depth in the chapters to come.

Questions for senior management and the board to ask

(Including model answers based on best practice – at a high maturity level.)

Do we know the difference between taking managed risk and taking unmanaged risk?	The board and senior management should be very clear about the difference and should be open to scrutiny about the way in which they make decisions.
Do we have simple, elegant tools to enable us to make risk-based decisions?	The board and senior management should be able to use simple risk management tools on the level of unconscious competence – they do it without thinking about it.
Do we consider our perception of threats and opportunities collectively as a board?	The board and senior management should discuss risk perceptions and be open to external measurement of the different risk perceptions, perhaps through psychometric testing.

Do we pay enough or too much attention to the unlikely but high-impact threats that might sink the business?

The board and senior management should frequently ask questions about the high-impact risks even if they are unlikely.

Are we spending too much time on predicting emerging threats when we could just adapt our current responses to existing threats?

It is better to concentrate on the known threats on a regular basis, but occasionally request a horizon scan of what can change the causes or impacts of the known threats.

Do we separate our understanding of threats and of opportunities and adapt our management processes accordingly?

Risk is either a threat or an opportunity, and sometimes it is both. The board need to address both sides of risk and adapt their management processes accordingly.

Is the capacity of the organization to take risk evaluated so that we can enhance successful performance and innovation?

Capacity can be called many things, but it does need to be defined and then balanced against the risks being taken in the organization.

Notes

1   From ISO 31000:2009 Risk management – Principles and guidelines.

2   ALARP – As low as is reasonably practicable.

3   http://www.rospa.com/resources/Info/rospa-safety-guide.pdf

4   http://www.mckinsey.com/Insights/Strategy/Improving_board_governance_
    McKinsey_Global_Survey_results?cid=other-eml-alt-mip-mck-oth-
    1308&goback=.gde_960187_member_265076485#!

5   http://www3.volvo.com/investors/finrep/ar11/eng/risksanduncertain/pops/
    printable/31_risker_och_osakerhetsfaktorer_eng.pdf

6   Groupthink is a psychological phenomenon that occurs within a group of people, in
    which the desire for harmony or conformity in the group results in an incorrect or
    deviant decision-making outcome. Group members try to minimize conflict and
    reach a consensual decision without critical evaluation of alternative ideas or
    viewpoints, and by isolating themselves from outside influences.

7   http://www.ferma.eu/wp-content/uploads/2013/08/leadership-and-risk-
    management-executive-summary.pdf

About enterprise risk management

Outline

Enterprise risk management (ERM) is the application of risk management (which is a natural decision-making process) to all aspects of the enterprise. It encompasses all aspects of risk management that are practised in the organization but sometimes under other guises or names.

The ERM programme sets out the way in which and how it will be established, and the process sets out what will occur to make it happen. As part of the process, unless we get the context right with respect to the goals or objectives, we might be spending a great deal of time and energy looking at aspects of risk that are not crucial to the organization. So the starting point for the ERM process is to ask: 'What are we trying to achieve?'

Risk lists or taxonomies help us to make sense of the many types of risks, and evaluate how they are linked. Evaluating and prioritizing risks is crucial for making managed risk-taking decisions.

When dealing with threat separately from the opportunity, we examine ways of dealing with opportunity as well as the threat. While risk is normally determined as a combination of likelihood and impact, there is a third aspect, which is about how close the risk is, or its proximity, which helps us to know 'when' the event or impact is likely to peak.

ERM is often combined with governance, through either practice or legislation, and compliance is sometimes wrapped in with risk and governance to create a holistic approach. We explore the pros and cons of this combination as it could lead to overload of the bureaucratic burden.

FIGURE 2.1   Advantages of solid enterprise risk management

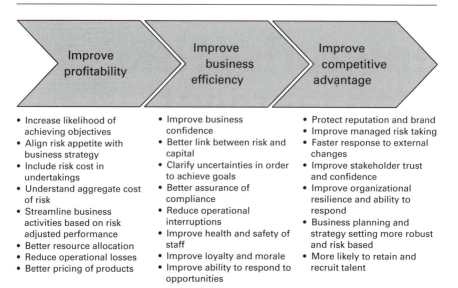

Improve profitability	Improve business efficiency	Improve competitive advantage
• Increase likelihood of achieving objectives • Align risk appetite with business strategy • Include risk cost in undertakings • Understand aggregate cost of risk • Streamline business activities based on risk adjusted performance • Better resource allocation • Reduce operational losses • Better pricing of products	• Improve business confidence • Better link between risk and capital • Clarify uncertainties in order to achieve goals • Better assurance of compliance • Reduce operational interruptions • Improve health and safety of staff • Improve loyalty and morale • Improve ability to respond to opportunities	• Protect reputation and brand • Improve managed risk taking • Faster response to external changes • Improve stakeholder trust and confidence • Improve organizational resilience and ability to respond • Business planning and strategy setting more robust and risk based • More likely to retain and recruit talent

Risk management

Since the mid-1990s enterprise risk management has emerged as a concept and as a management function within organizations. Its emergence can be traced to two main causes: survival and regulation.

There were a number of high profile company failures due to (in retrospect) preventable causes. Shareholder value models were increasingly playing a greater role in strategic planning and early strategic planning models paid insufficient attention to risk. Modern strategic planning models are based more on shareholder value concepts, which draw their inspiration from the finance theory where risk has always played a central role.

The main benefit of enterprise risk management is that it increases an organization's chance of survival. More important for senior management, it enables them to see improvements in profitability, business efficiency and competitive advantage; see Figure 2.1.

Risk management has been around for decades, in the sense that it is about managing threats. Every CEO and senior manager has exercised risk management on a daily, almost minute-by-minute basis. Even the process of getting to work requires risk management skills and expertise. The process of risk management involves asking the following questions:

1 What do we want to achieve?

2 What can stop us?

3 How big is it?

4 How likely is it?

5 What do we do about it?

If we think about our last journey into the office we probably went through a thought process along the lines shown in Table 2.1.

That instinctive process is at the root of risk management. It seems simple enough when looked at from a single person's viewpoint, but can become more complex when we begin to look at the collective risks for more than one person; see Table 2.2. There will also be different viewpoints as we address the questions to different audiences. There is therefore a need for a framework for asking the five questions for risk management across complicated organizations to make sure that there is a common language and common approach towards managing risk.

Traditionally (and indeed it still is in many organizations) risk management has been about dealing with threat and keeping it focused on operational risks to the business such as health and safety, product damage, loss of assets and so on. There's nothing wrong with that; in fact it is important for the survival of an organization. However, we've already established that risk can be a threat and/or an opportunity and risks exist in other aspects of the business that have not traditionally had a risk management focus on them. Thus an enterprise-wide approach to risk management becomes enterprise risk management.

The difference between risk management and ERM

ERM is about applying the risk management programme and processes to *all* aspects of the organization and widening the concept from just reducing threat to embracing managed risk taking to achieve maximum increase in value. That means using risk-based decision making and applying it to all of those aspects that contribute to achieving objectives and increasing value, whether it's about enhancing growth, increasing return or improving quality. ERM also requires recognizing that risk is both a threat and or an opportunity (see Chapter 3).

ERM embraces all forms of risk management in the organization, even if they might not be called 'risk management'. We show it in Figure 2.2 as the helm of a ship where the CEO is the helmsperson and each of the elements of the ERM process enable him or her to steer the ship in the right direction.

This doesn't mean that the ERM team should take responsibility for all areas of risk management; ERM should be managed on the basis that everyone in the organization takes responsibility for their own area of threats and

TABLE 2.1 Risk analysis of getting to work

	Getting to work		
What do we want to achieve?	**I want to get to work on time and in one piece**		
What can stop us?	**Cause 1:**	**Cause 2:**	**Cause 3:**
	An accident on the road so the traffic was bad	My car breaks down	My other half went to work with my car keys
How big is it?	Shouldn't hold me up for longer than 30 minutes, so not a problem as I don't have any urgent meetings first thing	Would be a big impact depending on where I break down	Would be a big impact
How likely is it?	Pretty likely – happens at least two days out of five	Unlikely, as I have the car maintained by a good firm	Unlikely, it's not happened before
What do we do about it?	I always leave for work with 30 minutes in hand.	I always make sure my cell phone is well charged and I have a number of cab firms on short dial.	We have a system of leaving all our keys on a hook in the kitchen (but safe from thieves) and my keys have a special fob that makes it distinct from the other keys

TABLE 2.2 Risk analysis of business survival

	Business survival		
What do we want to achieve?	**The business must remain robust and able to pay the shareholders' expectations, as well as service the long term debts**		
	Cause 1: according to the Finance team:	**Cause 2: according to the HR team**	**Cause 3: according to the Marketing team**
What can stop us?	We run into a liquidity problem	We lose staff who are key to the running of the business, and can't replace them within a reasonable length of time	Our marketing campaign is a flop and brings about a loss of reputation
How big is it?	Huge. We'd really struggle if our liquidity was to run into problems	Huge. If we lost certain people, the news would get out and we'd lose credibility in the market place	Medium. The market perception of our organization is high and we'd ride this one failure… but not another after that
How likely is it?	Unlikely, as we are currently well regarded by the banks, so we can always borrow more	Likely, we lost two people last week, and five more are talking about going.	Unlikely, all our other marketing campaigns have been successful
What do we do about it?	• Ensure that we maintain our AA rating • Track costs and revenue with close diligence • Report regularly on our capital and cash position	• Make sure we identify all people who are key to the organization • All those identified must have a succession plan • Succession plans tracked and reported regularly	• Only use agencies that we trust absolutely • Rigorously trial the campaigns before launch

FIGURE 2.2 The hub spokes and wheel of types of risk management that make up the ERM programme

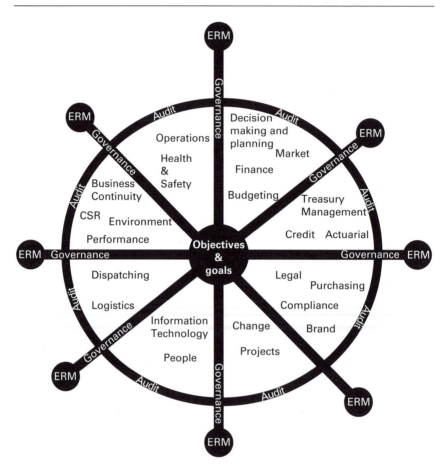

opportunities in the business, and the guardians of the programme and those enabling the programme to add value to the organization are the enterprise risk management team. The internal audit then challenges and provides assurance that the programme is fit for purpose and is being operated to provide best value (see Chapter 7 for more on the three lines of play/defence).

Implementing the programme for ERM

Any management discipline requires a programme or framework to be effective and effected. ISO 31000 refers to the programme for implementing ERM as a 'framework' (see Figure 2.3) but we prefer to call the overarching package a 'programme', as there are often individual 'frameworks' and policies

FIGURE 2.3 Programme for ERM

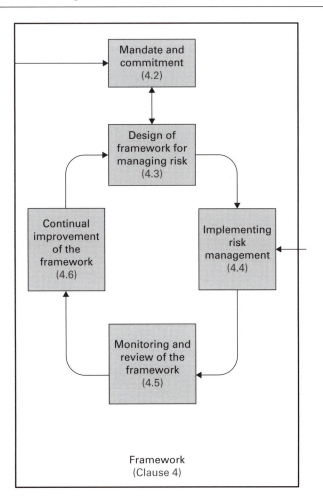

Reproduced from ISO 31000:2009

for the various types of risk management. This is particularly pertinent for larger and more complex organizations. In Chapter 4 we set out a suggestion for an overarching ERM programme incorporating an operating model that sits above and informs the individual frameworks and policies for risk management. This whole structure is therefore called a 'programme' for ERM.

The programme for implementing ERM is no different from any other management discipline that is based on the plan, do, study, act cycle:[1]

- There must be a *mandate and commitment*. There must be strong, rigorous and sustained support from senior management with strategic design and planning to ensure commitment and ownership at all levels (see Chapter 4 on governance for ERM).

- *Plan:* the design of the programme should address:
  - the internal and external context of the organization;
  - the drivers, intents, accountabilities and organization;
  - the way in which accountability is recognized with rewards and sanctions;
  - the way ERM is to be integrated into the organization and become a part of *all* activities that drive value and capacity;
  - the resources to be allocated including the people who will drive it and the training needed for all those accountable;
  - the communication mechanisms, both internal and external.

- *Do:* implementing ERM in the organization requires a programme for planning and timing of the implementation as well as how, in practice, the organization is going to exercise it.

- *Study:* monitoring and reviewing the programme – separately from reporting the outputs from the programme.

- *Act:* continual improvement of the programme based on the review of its effectiveness.

A more complete action plan for implementing the ERM programme is included in Chapter 4.

ERM – the process

The following is a summary of the basic principles of ERM (see Figure 2.4). There are many excellent detailed books on the subject and this is not the place to review the intricacies; we will just look at what it is that senior management need to know and do.

Enterprise risk management is about continuously asking the following questions:

- *Context* – What is the objective or goal we wish to review?
- *Identify* – What are the risks that are associated with that objective or goal?
- *Analyse* – What is the impact and likelihood (and the proximity or velocity – see later in this chapter for more detail)?
- *Evaluate* – what is the capacity and tolerance (see Chapter 5 on risk appetite) of the organization and which are those that need most attention?
- *Treat* – What do we do to deal with, or how do we respond to the risk?

FIGURE 2.4   Process for enterprise risk management

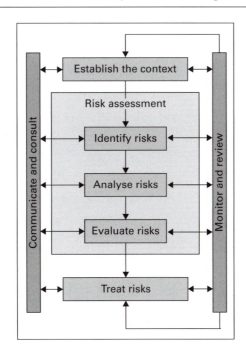

Reproduced from ISO 31000:2009

All of this is within a dynamic programme of monitoring, reviewing and communicating the inputs and outputs.

Essential attributes of ERM for delivering value and capacity

The further aspect that we explore is about using ERM to ensure that the capacity remains adequate at all times, even if the threats to growth, return and quality become larger than expected. In other words it's about asking whether the organization has enough capacity to cover things if the worst happens.

Figure 2.5 summarizes an approach to ERM that will enable increasing value by increasing growth, return and quality and ensuring adequate capacity by three supporting columns for ERM attributes that need to be in place – design, structure and implementation.

The central and most important structural attributes are that ERM is proportionate, aligned, comprehensive, embedded and dynamic. Increasing

FIGURE 2.5   The three pillars of ERM: design, structure and implementation

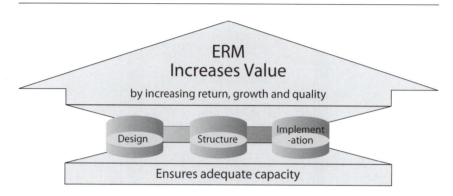

value in the organization through enhanced growth, increasing the return and improving quality is demonstrated through the following actions:

- Assessing the internal and external environments and adjusting our business accordingly, being transparent and inclusive, and using the best available information – *proportionate and aligned*.

- Managing financial and operational risks and exploiting opportunities on a systematic basis where risk management is integrated into the whole business – *comprehensive and embedded*.

- Assessing all financial and operational strategies in a holistic manner and on a continuous basis – *dynamic*.

Top level leadership in ERM

Many organizations have excellent ERM frameworks and processes, but fail in the application of leadership and the overall involvement of everyone in and around the organization. A good ERM regime can be completely scuppered by ignoring the requirements of customers or shareholders. Conversely a good framework and process where threats receive undue attention can ignore the need to recognize and maximize opportunities, so the opportunities fade into the background in the shadow of the threats.

The board and senior management are not exempt from practising enterprise risk management themselves. They must use risk-based decision

CASE EXAMPLE

(From website H2G2 commenting on the reports following the two space shuttle disasters; Columbia and Challenger.)

The Challenger space shuttle explosion was caused by frozen O rings; the rocket engine manufacturer warned of the danger of launching in extreme cold, but this fact was hidden in a myriad of other facts presented on page 167 of a PowerPoint presentation.[2]

On 1 February 2003, Columbia, the NASA space shuttle, disintegrated on re-entry into the Earth's atmosphere, killing the seven crew members and scattering burning wreckage over a wide area of the United States. The tragedy halted the shuttle programme for two and a half years while an investigation into the disaster took place.[3]

Later that year, the Columbia Accident Investigation Board published its report. It identified the principal cause as something which NASA had noticed during the shuttle's launch on 16 January, and which it made public on the day following the accident. One minute and 22 seconds after take-off, a piece of insulating foam had separated from the external fuel tank and collided with the vehicle's left wing. The damage to the wing's thermal protection wasn't apparent during the Orbiter's mission, but in the heat of re-entry the aluminium airframe structure progressively melted until the aerodynamic forces caused it and hence the Orbiter to fail catastrophically.

The report went on to list a number of organizational causes and contributory factors for this accident, but one of these was somewhat unexpected. It blamed NASA's use of the software presentation tool, Microsoft PowerPoint.

making in their own offices as well as lead the process for the rest of the organization.

There are many examples of where enterprise risk management leadership from the top *could have* prevented events from happening. An example of this is described in the case example above.

Thus leadership in ERM from the top is not limited to telling everyone else to do it; there must be risk-based decision making at the top of the organization and a demand from the top for prioritized risk information so as to make good risk decisions.

Identifying risk: types of risk, risk lists and taxonomies

A list of prompts is used in risk identification to ensure that there is a holistic review of the threats and opportunities that might threaten or enhance a particular strategic goal or value driver. Without a list there may be too much emphasis on some threats and opportunities and gaps where some areas are not considered. For example, a finance-driven group who are conducting a risk assessment might mainly concentrate on financial aspects, health practitioners might tend to concentrate on clinical threats, and project managers on project threats and opportunities.

The advantage of a risk taxonomy or risk classification system as opposed to a straightforward risk list is that connections between interrelated risks can be made. This enables a more valid prioritization of the most important threats and opportunities and recognition of the themes that are relevant to the organization.

In December 2012, the Economist Intelligence Unit conducted a global survey, sponsored by KPMG International, of more than 1,000 senior executives from the corporate suite or board (C-suite).[4] One of the questions asked was: 'Which of the following issues pose the greatest threat to your industry?' The results are shown in Table 2.3, with the percentages showing the most important risks (more than one risk could be selected in this survey). The second largest item in the list was 'reputation'. However, reputation risk doesn't appear in many risk lists, because reputation risk isn't really a risk at all: it's a consequence or impact of many of the other threats and opportunities.

Any event that has a positive or negative impact on the organization can change the reputation of the business for better or for worse. We can have a specific business strategy to deal with reputational impacts, but that will end up as our risk strategy, as we will soon work out that many if not all of the strategic, operational or project risks to the business could have a reputational impact (amongst other impacts).

The reputational effect of risk events has a habit of taking on a life of its own after the occurrence. What started with a fatal explosion subsequently resulted in years of continuing uncertainty for BP, loss of jobs and major costs as people sought compensation for their apparent (and sometimes non-existent) losses.

Many organizations order the risks to an organization in a form of risk classification system (see Figure 2.6):

- *Strategic risks* include risks from: reputational damage (eg, trademark/brand erosion, fraud, unfavourable publicity) competition, customer wants, demographic and social/cultural trends,

TABLE 2.3 Principal risks; KPMG survey

	%
Regulatory pressure/changes in regulatory environment	49
Reputational risks	41
Credit/liquidity risks	34
Geopolitical risks (EG Eurozone crisis)	32
Supply chain disruption	28
Information security/fraud	17
Disruption of technology	17
Data governance and quality	13
Legal	12
IT infrastructure	11
Social media	9
Natural disasters	9
Climate change	7

technological innovation, capital availability, and regulatory and political trends.

- *Financial risks* include risks from: price (eg asset value, interest rate, foreign exchange, commodity), liquidity (eg cash flow, call risk, opportunity cost), credit (eg default, downgrade), inflation/purchasing power, and hedging/basis risk.
- *Operational risks* include risks from: business operations (eg, human resources, product development, capacity, efficiency, product/service failure, channel management, supply chain management, business cyclicality), empowerment (eg, leadership, change readiness), information technology (eg, relevance, availability), and information/business reporting (eg, budgeting and planning, accounting information, pension fund, investment evaluation, taxation).

CASE EXAMPLE

(Quote from *The Washington Times*, 8 August 2013, regarding the
Deepwater Horizon oil spill.[5])

The Deepwater Horizon oil spill was an oil spill that began in April 2010
in the Gulf of Mexico on the BP-operated Macondo Prospect. It is considered
to be the largest accidental marine oil spill in the history of the petroleum
industry. Following the explosion and sinking of the Deepwater Horizon oil rig,
which claimed 11 lives, a sea-floor oil gusher flowed for 87 days, until it was
capped on 15 July 2010. The total discharge is estimated at 210 million US gal
or 780,000 m^3.

On Wednesday 7 August 2013, a federal judge ruled that BP must pay $130
million to a court administrator to disburse among those who claimed they were
injured from the 2010 Gulf of Mexico oil spill.

BP had fought the fees, calling them 'excessive costs', one attorney for the
company said, Reuters reported. But US Magistrate Judge Sally Shushan in
New Orleans found differently. She called it 'unreasonable' that BP would halt
its payments to claimants – payments that have already surpassed $560 million
since June 2012, Reuters said.

BP didn't comment on the judge's ruling. But the company's main argument
is that a fee schedule worked out in 2012 during settlement talks with Gulf-area
businesses and residents is unfair. The total amount the company could end up
paying, when all's said and done, is $1.5 billion, a BP finance director predicted,
Reuters reported.

On top of that, BP said, much of the fee money has been paid for fraudulent
claims. In all, BP faces about $42.4 billion worth of charges that are related to the
April 20 2010, drilling rig explosion that killed 11.

- *Hazard risks* include risks from: fire and other property damage,
  windstorm and other natural perils, theft and other crime, personal
  injury, business interruption, disease and disability (including work-
  related injuries and diseases), and liability claims.

The main disadvantage of using a risk classification system is the implication that each of the areas of risk are equal, whereas in reality they are not
and vary enormously from one industry to another.

FIGURE 2.6 Example of a risk classification system

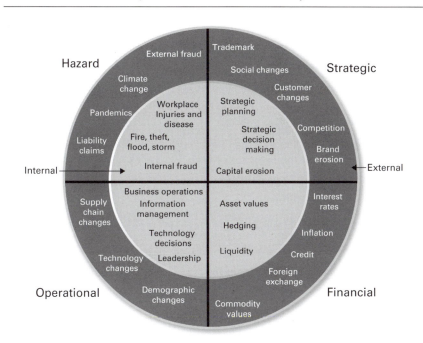

Evaluating and prioritizing risk

Risk professionals spend enormous amounts of time in developing risk evaluation frameworks and processes measuring likelihood and impact. On the other hand, actuaries develop complex processes and calculations to measure what they believe to be the real risk. (In Chapter 12 we explore more about the two approaches.) For senior management, the principal requirement is whether the prioritization process gets down to the nitty-gritty of the real threats and real opportunities to the organization and whether this translates into useful intelligence that will help with risk-based decision making.

Proximity or velocity of risk

The ERM process states that risk is a combination of impact and likelihood. This works in part but is increasingly understood to be missing a third element – the proximity or velocity of risk or 'when is it at its peak'. This means that in the process of identifying opportunities or threats the organization needs to take into account the timeframe at which or in which the event or impact may transpire.

Consider a risk analysis that has identified threats and opportunities for the business planning period; that may be for the next three years. The list of threats and opportunities could include political, economic, social, technological, legislative, environmental uncertainties that may occur in the next three years. However, if the business is launching a new product against which an analysis for the business planning period has been performed, this analysis might not spot a key weakness in the product's effect on the enterprise's reputation in the longer term.

Predicting the way in which a threat or opportunity might peak is especially useful in project management where there are crucial junctures when, if a threat transpired or an opportunity occurred, it would make more difference than at other times.

This example helps us understand that trying to predict the timing of the threat can allow us to plan in advance what our response might be. Having planned that response, if our timing is wrong, then we are better positioned to accelerate or slow down the response.

Recording and reporting risks

Most organizations use a risk register, list or system for recording threats; however, they are normally just recording threats rather than threats *and* opportunities. If the risk list is just recording threats, then it should be renamed as a threat list.

Let's look at the case of a business that undertakes medical research using animals. It has regular intrusions by political activists who have, over the last three years, undertaken a specific campaign to close the business down. It has good 24-hour security, supported by the local and national police who are targeting the political activists and already have imprisoned two of the leading activists. There are periodic noisy demonstrations at the entrance to the facilities but none has yet turned violent, or interfered with business.

The most severe threat identified is that of the political activists attacking the business through its people. Already two members of the board have received threats against their homes and family. It is only a question of time before these threats turn into direct action, and other senior management, suppliers and customers become involved. All senior management have been put on alert, and have had security reviews by the police. Most have had additional security installed at home, with panic buttons. Children, particularly younger children, have not yet been made aware of the threats. We know that the threat is serious from studying the methods used by this political group on other organizations – direct action is possibly going to happen, and it's going to have enormous consequences for the families involved, but we don't know *when* it's going to happen.

There is a pattern that the political activists follow, but we need to know at what point senior management are going to need round-the-clock protection for them and their families. So research is undertaken to provide some level of understanding of how this threat might develop. From the research into the activities of these people, and anticipating when the two leaders might be released on parole, a chart is drawn up with the help of the specialist police unit; see Table 2.4.

We can get even more predictive by looking at the combinations of proximity or velocity (When is the risk likely to peak?) and different impacts (How badly is this going to affect our families?) then making the plans based on that further analysis; see Table 2.5.

TABLE 2.4 Forecast of changing likelihood for an event over time

Timescale	Likelihood (%)
Quarter 1	1
Quarter 2	2
Quarter 3	5
Quarter 4	20
Quarter 5	30
Quarter 6	40
Quarter 7	40
Quarter 8	10

TABLE 2.5 Matching changing impacts to changing likelihoods over time

Timescale	Likelihood (%)	Likely impact to senior management and families	Possible action
Quarter 1	1	Business as usual	Continue with current controls/enhancers
Quarter 2	2	Business as usual	Continue with current controls/enhancers
Quarter 3	5	Business as usual	Continue with current controls/enhancers
Quarter 4	20	Threats spread to next layer of management, website lists all targets with details of home addresses and telephone numbers, phone calls start to homes	• Families of snr mgmt to be briefed and given security advice • Post and phone calls to be intercepted • New cell phones issued to all with trackers on them • CCTV booked to be installed • Schools informed
Quarter 5	30	At Snr Mgnt homes; Graffiti, low level damage	• 24 hour security service for all senior management • CCTV relayed live to police • Police attempt to have the activists' website taken down

Quarter 6	40	Broken windows, damage to gardens, pets stolen or killed	• Families most at risk are sent away to relatives • Armed security for senior management provided • Additional security provided at schools
Quarter 7	40	Garden sheds set alight, family graves desecrated, snr mgnt followed to business meetings and threats made in earshot of customers	• Police make arrests • More families move out to stay with relatives or take long vacations • Cell phones changed again • Additional checks amongst staff as to who is colluding with the activists
Quarter 8	10	Management and families shaken up, severe depression and anxiety, some might quit the business,	• Families move back and repairs effected • Counselling provided • CEO and chairman hold a gathering for management and families to make them feel loved and wanted • Children presented with medals for their bravery

While it is important to record the threats and opportunities, senior management should beware of the complacency and lack of energy that can set in once the risk list is written. The same applies to systems: they too can constrain a risk-based decision-making process because once it's written down, people tend to forget about it.

Few lists will record the proximity or velocity, and at best will be able to record if the threat or opportunity is increasing, reducing or remaining the same. An additional field could be coded to record the anticipated timeframe in which the threat or opportunity will reach its peak, or better still show the changing likelihood and impact at specific points in time (over one, two, five, 10 and 20 years, and so on). Worse still is the risk list that is brought out for review by senior management in its full detail – pages and pages of it![6]

A better solution is for the risk register or list to be kept as a record of the performance of the threat or opportunity, its controls/enhancers and so on, and for senior management to be presented with a summary of the salient points on one page. This could be in the form of a dashboard or a risk map, reporting on the impact of threats and opportunities over three years; see examples in Figure 2.7 and Table 2.6.

Using this kind of intelligence, one might be drawn to one risk in particular, perhaps that of credit/liquidity: while it presents a threat of minus

FIGURE 2.7 Graphic representation of risks that are both threats and opportunities

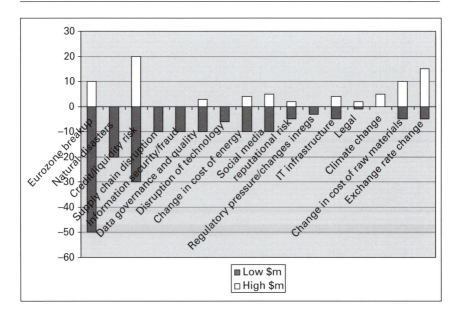

TABLE 2.6 Data for risks that have both positive and negative values

Risk over next three years	Max Impact		
	High $m	Low $m	Net cost
Eurozone breakup	10	−50	−40
Natural disasters	0	−20	−20
Credit/liquidity risk	20	−30	−10
Supply chain disruption	0	−10	−10
Information security/ fraud	0	−10	−10
Data governance and quality	3	−10	−7
Disruption of technology	0	−6	−6
Change in cost of energy	4	−10	−6
Social media	5	−10	−5
Reputational risk	2	−5	−3
Regulatory pressure/ changes in regs	0	−3	−3
IT infrastructure	4	−5	−1
Legal	2	−1	1
Climate change	5	0	5
Change in cost of raw materials	10	−5	5
Exchange rate change	15	−5	10

$30 million it also presents an opportunity of $20 million. Senior management can then ask questions about how well the risk is being managed so as
to minimize the downside and maximize the upside.

Governance, risk and compliance

One direction that some organizations take, particularly organizations in
the United States that are driven by Sarbanes Oxley (SoX) and COSO (see
Chapter 11 and Appendix 3 for more information), is to link or even combine ERM with governance and compliance, or GRC. Figure 2.8 shows very
broadly the links and relationships between the three areas.

The argument in favour of combining the approach to all three areas
is that it avoids duplication and gaps in approach. It also reduces the cost
of running separate teams and improves the efficacy of each of the three
areas. The counter-indication is that it can create an unwieldy and even
more impenetrable maze of bureaucracy so gaps might be even more likely.
Much depends on the size and complexity of the organization.

Following recent high-profile failures, the scope of corporate governance
has widened to embrace the risks that a company takes. Directors are now
increasingly required to report on their internal risk control and enhancer
systems, either through voluntary codes or by legislation.

FIGURE 2.8 Relationships between governance, risk
management and compliance

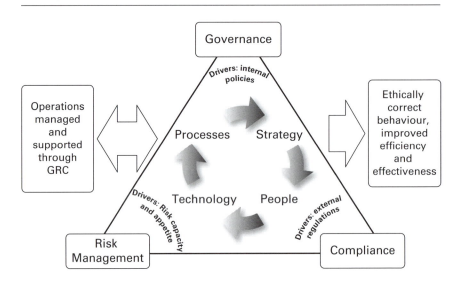

CASE EXAMPLES from Barings and Bugatti

Barings Bank, founded by the Baring family in 1762, was the oldest merchant bank in London. It collapsed in 1995 after one of the bank's employees, Nick Leeson, lost $1.3 billion due to speculative investing, primarily in futures contracts, at the bank's Singapore office.

The Bugatti marque had produced cars since 1909. The death of Ettore Bugatti in 1947, who had outlived his son Jean Bugatti who died in 1939, ensured there was not a successor to lead the factory. The company struggled financially, and released one last model in the 1950s before eventually being purchased for its aeroplane parts business in the 1960s. In the 1990s, an Italian entrepreneur revived it as a builder of limited-run exclusive sports cars. Today, the name is owned by German automobile manufacturing group Volkswagen.

Questions for senior management and the board to ask

(Including model answers based on best practice – at a high maturity level.)

Do we bring together all our risk management activities under one ERM programme?

Best practice is to have a common operating framework or model for all aspects of risk management under the umbrella of enterprise risk management and then to have separate risk management frameworks and processes for the various aspects of risk management.

Do we have a common language and framework for all our risk management activities?

The answer to this should be yes, we do have a common language and framework or operating model.

Are we clear about applying ERM to our value drivers and strategic goals?

It is absolutely critical that ERM is inextricably tied to the strategic goals and value drivers of the organization.

Do we have a good risk list or taxonomy that helps identify risks?	While this might feel like something for operational management, the board members must understand the risk list or taxonomy or appreciate that the links and interdependences between risks can create systemic risk for the organization and its wider stakeholder environment.
Do we manage opportunities as well as we manage threats?	Yes, we manage them equally well.
Do we understand the proximity or velocity of threats and opportunities as part of our ERM process?	The board have to demand that this information is provided to them as part of the regular dashboard reporting and is taken into account when calculating the risk and capacity of the organization.

Notes

1 First proposed by Deming in the 1950s; see https://www.deming.org/theman/theories/pdsacycle

2 http://spaceflight.nasa.gov/shuttle/archives/sts-107/investigation/CAIB_medres_full.pdf

3 http://h2g2.com/entry/A39477090

4 Author's note: The results of this survey, with 49 per cent of respondents maintaining that regulatory pressure/changes in regulatory environment were a large threat, beg the question as to which industries were included. It is largely banks, insurance companies and utility organizations that are concerned that regulatory pressure could prove threatening to the whole organization.

5 http://www.washingtontimes.com/news/2013/aug/8/bp-pay-130m-fee-oil-spill-injuries-judge-rules/

6 Author's comment: Often the risk register constrains the energy and vitality of a risk-intelligent organization, particularly if there is a poorly developed risk system into which the risk information is shoe-horned and then sits there to fester in a static environment until a risk professional comes along to breathe some life into it.

Risk as an opportunity/ threat to objectives and value drivers

03

Outline

In seeking to achieve objectives by looking with clarity at risk, it can be seen that some risks are threats and some are opportunities. Others can present both threats and opportunities, or we could turn a threat into an opportunity by doing different things. Conversely, we can turn an opportunity into a threat if we don't handle it right.

When identifying and managing threats and opportunities to the organization, we must apply them closely not only to the strategic goals of the organization, but also to the things that drive value in the organization, such as knowledge, capital, cash flow and liquidity, people and assets.

Risk – opportunities and threats

When we talk about taking more managed risk, we mean those risks that present opportunities as well as threats. These might include:

- interest rates;
- demand for services;
- the climate;

- financial market;
- demographics;
- commodity values;
- inflation;
- competition;
- technological advances;
- supply chain;
- workforce;
- regulations.

Each of these can present opportunities, but they can also present threats if they are not predicted, recognized and responded to. Even bad press can be turned into an opportunity if it is handled right by taking control of the story and taking control of the timing of the story.

There are other types of risk that mainly present a threat. Examples of these might include:

- Financial loss caused by an event – this could be loss of a plant, facility or investment, or a counterparty credit default.

- Loss of life, injury or damage to people, whether employees, customers or members of the public.

- Political unrest in export markets.

Extract: COSO ERM executive summary[1]

COSO: Enterprise Risk Management – Integrated Framework

Events – Risks and Opportunities

Events can have negative impact, positive impact, or both. Events with a negative impact represent risks, which can prevent value creation or erode existing value. Events with positive impact may offset negative impacts or represent opportunities. Opportunities are the possibility that an event will occur and positively affect the achievement of objectives, supporting value creation or preservation. Management channels opportunities back to its strategy or objective-setting processes, formulating plans to seize the opportunities.

These normally do not obviously represent opportunities, although it could be argued that there is an opportunity to avoid and or manage these threats to a minimum. The primary consideration for threats is the organization's ability to exercise control. This will entail all the usual risk management processes including identification, evaluation and response. The primary consideration for opportunities is the organization's ability to take risk.

Figure 3.1 explains that managed risk-taking behaviours start from the strategic level in the organization, where the measurement is about shareholder value. This is because value creation or opportunity is the primary focus. Conversely, at the operational or project level of the organization, the primary focus is about exercising control over the threats, or value protection.

The treasury department, the credit team and the actuarial team have approaches that recognize opportunities whereas audit, IT, health and safety, environmental, dispatching, logistics, legal, project management, risk and business continuity departments mainly tend to concentrate on threats. A true ERM team needs to weave and internally sell a framework and language that speaks to all of these professionals so they act in a coordinated manner to maximize opportunities and minimize threats.

FIGURE 3.1 Approach to risk from top down to bottom up

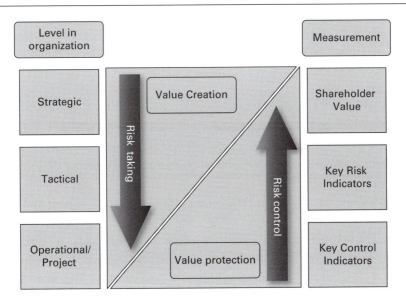

Adapted from IRM Risk Appetite and Tolerance Paper

Risk as both opportunity and threat

Have we ever flipped a threat into an opportunity? Consider a young child on a train. Her face suddenly puckers up, she holds her breath and we just wait for the explosive percussion of the howl. But the father sees what's happening, reaches for his phone and offers it to the girl to distract her from whatever she was about to get all upset about. The child's face turns to one of pure joy, the pucker turns into a smile and the redness in the cheeks subsides as she reaches her sticky hands towards her father's phone. Threats can be like that. If we see it coming down the line and have the means to do something about it, we can flip it into an opportunity.

Some opportunities can also turn into threats if not managed properly.

Cloud computing can present an opportunity and a threat. Cloud computing can mean many different things to different people; for many organizations it seems to be more of a threat than an opportunity. The perceived threat comes from the idea that the organization's most precious assets can be located in a data centre hundreds or thousands of miles away, far from the reach and the control of the organization.

Cloud computing is a catch-all term that can cover many technologies, such as managed service providers, application service providers, hosted servers, hosted storage technology, hosted security solutions and other services and technologies. A typical business can combine a few of those services to build a complete hosted solution that eliminates most of the traditional networking hardware found in a business. So the opportunity from cloud computing, for the organization thinking of using it, is that it can massively reduce cost in terms of not having to have huge amounts of hardware. It eliminates the time spent in backing up, and it can reduce downtime from lost data.

These three examples of how a risk can present both an opportunity and a threat enable us to begin to move from a traditional 'risk is negative' thought pattern, to one that recognizes that risk can be *both* an opportunity and a threat. Some risks can present either opportunities or threats, such as the actions of a market. The shares can go up in value, or decrease in value. Interest rates can go up or go down. Each action of the market or interest rates (whether up or down) is mutually exclusive of the other. The organization can prepare a response for these aspects where one action is exclusive of another by being intelligent about its exposure to these events. Some really smart organizations ensure that they win regardless of the movement because of the portfolio of businesses that they are in, or because of the way in which they structure their threat controls and opportunity enhancers.

CASE EXAMPLE Minimizing threats in demolition

A six-storey silo of grey concrete had towered gloomily next to a busy road for over 50 years. It had been long due for demolition and, finally, management decided that it was time to tackle it.

In the planning phase for the demolition, management were very concerned about the injury, damage and possible interruption to people, neighbouring businesses and roads. There seemed to be so many threats to discuss that the risk seemed to be taking the conversations round in circles.

The risk manager suggested that, to minimize the threat, the demolition should become a public event and the local people should be invited to witness the toppling of this mighty landmark. A lottery was set up, inviting people to take free tickets to see who would win the right to 'press the button'. The event became even more of a spectacle when the winner of the 'lottery' turned out to be a disabled child in a wheelchair. People came in their thousands to watch this landmark behemoth being extinguished in a modern day 'David and Goliath' adventure.

Taking note of all the appropriate precautions in discussion with the regulators and the risk team, the professional demolition team set out a wide boundary for the public to watch from a safe distance, they removed the interior of the building and all traces of noxious substances (there had been a considerable amount of asbestos), the road was closed and the button pressed. The building imploded creating an enormous cloud of dust. When the dust cleared, the building was a heap of rubble, it was no more and no one had been hurt.

The people returned to their homes and started clearing the dust from their cars and houses, but they were happy. 'David' had beaten 'Goliath', and the victory was to be celebrated. The busy road was re-opened six days later and the business that owned the silo prepared itself for the complaints and criticisms. There were no complaints, no criticisms and no adverse press. In fact there was a sudden stream of young and old applying for jobs at the company.

Risk as uncertainty

The central issue in risk from an ERM viewpoint is that it is uncertain. There are some things that are certain – we know about them.

CASE EXAMPLE   Large Hadron Collider

On 19 September 2008 the Large Hadron Collider (LHC) broke down in
the middle of a widely publicized experiment to create antimatter.[2] CERN,
the European Organization for Nuclear Research, restarted the LHC on
20 November 2009, despite having originally predicted a restart in early 2009.
The first particle collisions were observed three days later.

CERN had a communication plan that was about openness and transparency,
so the breakdown was very much in the public domain. It was reported widely
around the world. However, the overoptimistic restart time was managed
well, with regular updates and information being provided using all manner of
communication media, and CERN's reputation remains buoyant.

Risk is described as the effect of uncertainty on objectives,[3] where an
effect is a deviation from the expected – positive and/or negative. Objectives can have different aspects (such as financial, health and safety, and
environmental goals) and can apply at different levels (such as strategic,
organization-wide, project, product and process). Risk is often characterized by reference to potential events and consequences or a combination of
these. It is often expressed in terms of a combination of the consequences of
an event (including changes in circumstances) and the associated likelihood
of occurrence. Thus uncertainty is the state, even partial, of deficiency of
information related to understanding of or knowledge about an event, its
consequence or likelihood.

Traditional risk management looks at just the threat aspect of risk, yet
that's just one side of the coin as we can see from the case studies above.
Threat is also just one corner of the SWOT analysis (Strengths, Weaknesses,
Opportunities and Threats). Strengths and weaknesses are more about the
certainties in the organization – or at least they should be. The uncertainties
are the opportunities and threats.

SWOT analyses are useful but are inherently flawed unless conducted
realistically with adequate information and data. The key here is the realistic evaluation of the strengths, weaknesses, opportunities and threats. In
a complex multinational business spread across many countries and many
product/service lines, it is even more complicated to get a good handle on

the facts as opposed to the fiction. The board may call for the risk experts to conduct an analysis, which will be based, normally (even if there is a sophisticated and mature ERM team with quantitative as well as qualitative skills) on the 'threats' alone and will not take into account the strengths, weaknesses and opportunity evaluation.

Threat and opportunity management

So if general management have been using SWOT analyses for years, why has risk management only concentrated on the threats, and not both the opportunities and threats? And why doesn't the business have an expert 'opportunity' team – oh, perhaps that's the marketing department. What about the strengths team – well that is often the finance department. And the weaknesses team? Well, perhaps that's the HR department. But none of these teams is working on a joined-up basis looking at the missing parts. Why doesn't the HR department do a strengths and weaknesses evaluation of the skill and capacity of the workforce to respond to the opportunity, and the finance team do likewise? The marketing team might work with the risk team to work up a balanced view of the opportunities and threats and the operations team work on the physical strengths and weaknesses.

A few organizations are recognizing this gap and have reorganized the risk team to be the risk and opportunity team. This team will be imbued with the skills to evaluate opportunities as well as threats.

Dealing with threat

When dealing with risk, whether threat or opportunity, it is tempting for us to go straight for some options such as reducing the threat, increasing the opportunity and so on. However, there are some options that only senior management or the board can select and they need to be involved in the decision making before operational management get weighed down by the detail of dealing with a risk. These options are to:

1 terminate the activity that gives rise to the threat;
2 tolerate the threat;
3 transfer some of it by sharing the threat with others.

CASE EXAMPLES Lufthansa and Adidas

Lufthansa opportunity and risk management system[4]

'As an international aviation company Lufthansa is exposed to macroeconomic, sector-specific and company risks. Our management systems are constantly updated and enable us to identify both risks and opportunities at an early stage and act accordingly. Our proven risk strategy allows us to take advantage of business opportunities as long as a risk-adjusted return can be realized on market terms.

'The calculated management of opportunities and risks is an integral factor in the management of our company. Our risk management is therefore integrated into our business processes.'

Adidas Group[5]

'In order to further increase efficiency and effectiveness of the Group's risk management process, we implemented a Group-wide IT solution in 2011 which allows for systematic analysis and monitoring of risks and opportunities… In particular, we decided to place extra emphasis on more detailed assessment of risks and opportunities in the upcoming twelve-month period while at the same time maintaining transparency and awareness of risks and opportunities that may affect the Group in the medium to long term.'

Operational management are responsible for deciding on number 4 – how to treat the threat; the first three are strategic decisions that the board and senior management must be involved in.

ISO 31000 sets out the following seven options for dealing with risk, which we've matched against the four 'Ts' above:

1 Avoiding the risk by deciding not to start or continue with the activity that gives rise to the risk; *terminate*.

2 Taking or increasing the risk in order to pursue an opportunity; *take* (see the section on opportunities below).

3 Removing the risk source; *treat – prevent*.

4 Changing the likelihood; *treat – reduce.*

5 Changing the consequences; *treat – reduce.*

6 Sharing the risk with another party or parties (including contracts and risk financing); *transfer* some of the threat.

7 Retaining the risk by informed decision – *tolerate.*

When we consider whether we should treat the threat, we can think of the actions available in terms of 'prevent', 'reduce', 'detect' or 'respond'. Preventative controls are those that stop the threat from occurring in first place (such as removing the ignition source to prevent a fire). Reduction controls deal with reducing the likelihood and/or the impact. Detective controls are those that spot the threat arising or changing in terms of likelihood and/or impact. These detective controls might trigger a 'respond' or 'reduce' control (such as smoke detectors being the detective control, triggering a fire alarm for people to evacuate). Respond controls are the corrective controls that would mitigate the impact of the threat once it has occurred. If we relate these to an example of the market drying up, Table 3.1 shows how these controls might work with some pros and cons.

Dealing with opportunity

Having considered threats, of much more interest to the senior manager is how this relates to managing opportunities. We've presented the four 'Ts' of managing threats; here are the four 'Os' of managing opportunities:

- open up;
- own;
- obliged;
- optimize.

Figure 3.2 summarizes the actions for dealing with threats and opportunities.

Internal controls for opportunities as well as threats

The world of risk and corporate governance speaks in terms of internal controls and assurance. That is a great way to speak about how we deal with threat but is it really appropriate for talking about opportunities? You

TABLE 3.1 Working out the options for control of a threat

	Threat of market drying up: options for control		
	Reasons why we would use this	Explanation	Comments
Terminate	Get out of that market altogether	Deals with the threat	Might just lose us the business
Tolerate	Doing anything about the threat is too costly, or the threat is outside our control and terminating the activity is not an option	No outlay or investment needed to treat the threat	We need to ensure that we have adequate capital and alternative sources of income in case the market dries up altogether
Transfer some of the threat	Get someone else to share in the threat, such as contracting out the work, or take out insurance	Sharing a threat makes people take ownership of their part in the activity	Requires total honesty and transparency between partners. This means that the incentives for sharing must be in place – all too often there is a conflict of interest
Treat	Prevent	Stopping the threat happening altogether can save assets and time. We might create a viral marketing campaign to create more demand, or change the product to make it more appealing or to differentiate it in the market	Can sometimes be a costly, and ineffective option particularly if the causes of the threat are mainly outside our control (note: 'prevent' controls concentrate on the causes of a threat)

Reduce	Reduces the likelihood and/or the impact of a threat. We might boost an existing marketing campaign to create more demand, or slightly adjust the product to make it more appealing or to differentiate it in the market	Less costly than totally preventing the threat from occurring, this is most likely to be the preferred option
Detect	Measuring the rate at which the market is increasing or reducing should be relatively simple and low cost; we put in tracking measures for each of the possible causes of threat and measure them constantly or at appropriate intervals against our stated risk appetite	This control must be matched with a 'respond' or 'reduce' control; in other words, if things get worse, what's our plan for dealing with it? There's no point in putting in detective controls if we are not going to respond appropriately, that's like putting smoke alarms in an unmanned vehicle: no one is there to hear it
Respond	When the causes of the threat are mainly out of our control, the 'respond' controls are the ones that should be the most effective for the threat. The respond controls are triggered by our detective controls	Must be timely to have any effect; if triggered too late, the business might already be lost. Must also be of adequate intensity to deal with the threat

TABLE 3.2 Options for control of a threat and an opportunity

Threat	Explanation	Opportunity	Explanation
Terminate	Stop the activity that causes the threat to arise	Open up the opportunity	Take the decision to open up the opportunity eg by developing new markets or products
Transfer some of the threat	Get some other organization to share in the threat	Own our part of the opportunity	Take ownership of some of the opportunity eg through contractual means and or sharing the reward
Tolerate	Accept the threat as it is because there are no mitigation options available to us	Obliged	We are obliged to accept the opportunity as it is because there are no optimization techniques open to us
Treat (see Table 3.3)	Mitigate the threat using various mitigation techniques	Optimize (see Table 3.3)	Maximize the opportunity through various optimization techniques

do need some 'controls' for opportunities, to make sure they don't get out of hand and that you are not introducing threat alongside them. But control has a negative connotation, like putting the stopper on a bottle or tightening the levels of delegated authority.

Control implies discipline, authority, oversight, regulation, restraint, supervision and rules. The opposite to control, however, implies chaos, disorganization, mismanagement and neglect. None of the latter is appropriate for a business environment, even when we are trying to encourage people to take managed risk. So perhaps we should use internal controls for opportunities as well as threats but make sure that they do not constrain opportunities while providing oversight and discipline.

FIGURE 3.2   Diagram of responses to threats and opportunities

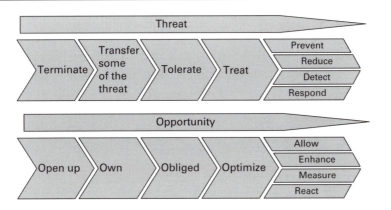

The internal control process is designed to provide reasonable assurance of three objectives:

1 Effectiveness and efficiency of operations.

2 Reliability of financial reporting.

3 Compliance with applicable laws and regulations.

However, organizational success is reliant on innovation as well as these objectives. So when talking about enterprise risks that are both threats and opportunities we need to speak in terms of controls and enhancers. Perhaps one day there will be a new term for this, the 'contrancer' – an action that controls threats and enhances opportunities.

Differentiating between objectives, strategic goals and value drivers

A risk can be an opportunity for one organization and a threat for another, depending on its objectives, value drivers and goals. There are two common mistakes an organization makes when looking to evaluate opportunities and threats: the objectives and strategic goals sometimes ignore those fundamental aspects of the business that provide value, and the business fails to relate the risk and opportunity management to the value drivers in the business.

A value driver is something that drives value in the organization. It might include some or all of the following:

● knowledge and people;

● capital and assets;

- cash flow and liquidity;
- brand and reputation;
- intellectual capital, company data, formulae and algorithms.

The starting point for managing risk is to work out what the context for the risk is. Many organizations start with their objectives or strategic goals, which has merit. However, what often gets left out is the risk to the value drivers, which might not appear within the strategic goals or objectives. Intelligent organizations recognize the importance of value drivers and shape their corporate goals, both short and long term around them; in that way the real threats and opportunities are constantly on the senior management agenda.

Examples of value drivers

Here we examine some value drivers: knowledge, capital, cash flow and liquidity, and reputation/goodwill.

Knowledge

People within the organization often hold key knowledge that makes the organization what it is. Retaining knowledge in the business is often overlooked; few businesses value 'handover' periods, or plan properly for succession. Many industries currently face a massive loss of knowledge as the 'baby boomers' born in the 1950s come up to retirement. In some sectors this presents an industry-wide fault line.

One such example is the nuclear industry where up to 20 per cent of the current senior management and nuclear experts across the world are coming up to retirement.[6] This was recognized in 2006[7] and some effort is being made to rectify this gap with graduate recruitment, but many nuclear organizations are faced with the prospect of hiring back their retirees as ongoing consultants.

Capital

This is commonly understood to be crucial to an organization's success and many organizations have good understanding of their capital position and its makeup. But is that matched to the capital requirement for the future state of the business? Are risks projected into the future, and stresses applied to those risks to calculate and plan the future capital requirement even if the threats are at their most extreme and the opportunities fail to transpire as planned?

Banks around the world are now subject to the Basel II and preparing for the Basel III Accord. This requires all banks to know in depth what risks they are currently taking and will take into the foreseeable future, and to ensure that there is sufficient capital to meet those threats and opportunities. Insurers and re-insurers in Europe are preparing for a regime called Solvency II. The principle of assessing and evaluating all present and future risks, and weighing them up against capital, common to both Basel II and Solvency II is good in concept and is a model that could and arguably should be adopted by all business concerns.

To have enough capital to meet one's risks is good logic but it misses the fundamental aspect of goodwill. When the US banks sold sub-prime mortgages[8] beginning around 2004, and then sold the sub-prime book to each other, they gave no consideration to the long-term sustainability of this in terms of the effect on their customers and the future loss of goodwill. There was no concept of balancing future risk and capital at that time. The rise in mortgage delinquencies and foreclosures resulted in the reduction in securities that were backed by the mortgages. (See Chapter 9 on conduct risk). This resulted in several major financial institutions collapsing in September 2008, with significant disruption in the flow of credit to businesses and consumers and the onset of a severe global recession.

Cash flow and liquidity

Some banks did not get involved in the sub-prime business, such as Morgan Stanley, but they took their eye off the ball with respect to cash flow and liquidity. The New York-based bank came close to running out of cash because of a run on its prime brokerage, the unit that finances hedge fund trades and holds its cash and securities. These loans also show the degree to which Morgan Stanley and other banks depended on such brokerage accounts for funding, even though clients could close them at short notice.

While no firm anticipated the full dimension of the financial crisis that arrived in 2008, Morgan Stanley began moving aggressively in 2007 to adapt the business to the new environment – reducing leverage, trimming the balance sheet, raising private capital and cutting costs. Here is the report of its 2009 annual meeting:[9]

> We brought down leverage significantly – from 32.6 times at the end of 2007 to 11.4 times at the end of 2008. We took down our balance sheet from about $1 trillion in 2007 to approximately $650 billion in 2008, reducing our exposure to legacy assets. This proved critical in navigating the most challenging market

TABLE 3.3 Mitigation and optimization techniques for threats and opportunities

Treating the threat	Explanation	Optimizing the opportunity	Explanation
Prevent	Stop the threat from arising by removing the things that will bring about the threat	Allow	Ensure that all the elements are in place so as to make sure that the opportunity can be taken
Reduce	Reduce the likelihood and or the impact of a threat	Enhance	Enhance the likelihood and or the impact of the opportunity by putting in place enhancement measures
Detect	Measure the rate at which likelihood and/or impact is changing	Measure	Put in place checks and measurements to see if the opportunity is arising, increasing and being taken at the expected rate
Respond	Minimize the impact of the event after it has happened	React	If the opportunity is not arising as fast as expected, or the rate of improvement slows down, a reaction might be to stop that slow down

shocks of last September and October. Today, we are maintaining prudent levels of leverage – carefully targeting our capital to those businesses that offer the most attractive risk-adjusted return.

Good will/reputation

Some major organizations put a value on their brand in their balance sheet. In many cases this is a tiny proportion of the true value of the brand and often the immense dependence on and power of the brand is only realized when it is gone (see Chapter 9 on corporate social responsibility). Table 3.4 is an extract from a report by Millward Brown.[10]

The companies concerned do not admit to anywhere near those amounts in their annual filings or reports. For example, Apple only claims $1.1 billion on its asset base in its 2012 filing of accounts[11] – compare that to the

TABLE 3.4 Top 25 brands by brand value, 2013

Rank	Company	Brand Value, 2013 (US$ million)
1	Apple	185,071
2	Google	113,669
3	IBM	112,536
4	MacDonald's	90,256
5	Coca-Cola	78,415
6	AT&T	75,507
7	Microsoft	69,814
8	Marlborough	69,383
9	Visa	56,060
10	China Mobile	55,368
11	GE	55,357

(continued)

TABLE 3.4 Top 25 brands by brand value, 2013 (*continued*)

Rank	Company	Brand Value, 2013 (US$ million)
12	Verizon	53,004
13	Wells Fargo	47,748
14	Amazon	45,727
15	UPS	42,747
16	ICBC	41,115
17	Vodafone	39,712
18	Wal-Mart	36,220
19	SAP	34,365
20	MasterCard	27,821
21	Tencent	27,273
22	China Construction Bank	26,859
23	Toyota	24,427
24	BMW	24,015
25	HSBC	23,970

$185 billion calculation in the table. Yet should there be a loss of confidence in any of these top brand companies, compounded by an inability to maintain market share, this could create a vortex of negative impacts resulting in possible takeover or, at worst, liquidation. To survive and continue to innovate, enterprise risk management in Apple – and others – must concentrate on customer focus including maintaining customer loyalty, ensuring the highest standards of service and innovation and offering products and services that make people's lives better.

Questions for senior management and the board to ask

(Including model answers based on best practice – at a high maturity level.)

Do we clarify those risks that are threats and those that might be opportunities as well?

The ERM operating model, the frameworks for all risk management areas and all the risk management processes, all address threats and opportunities.

Do we understand those risks that can be both opportunities and threats?

Yes, and we have arrangements in place to maximize the opportunities and minimize the threats.

Are we clear about those things that drive value in our organization as well as our strategic goals?

Yes, all our strategic and business goals are based on those things that drive value in our organization.

Do we make clear links between ERM, our objectives, strategic goals and our value drivers?

The starting point for our ERM focus is not only our objectives, strategic goals and value drivers; it is also our culture and philosophy.

Notes

1   http://www.coso.org/documents/coso_erm_executivesummary.pdf

2   http://indico.ific.uv.es/indico/conferenceDisplay.py?confId=776

3   In ISO 31000.

4   http://reports.lufthansa.com/2011/ar/combinedmanagementreport/
riskandopportunitiesreport/opportunityandriskmanagementsystem.html

5   http://www.adidas-group.com/en/investorrelations/corporate_governance/
risk_management/default.aspx

6   http://www.nei.org/News-Media/News/News-Archives/help-wanted-25000-
skilled-workers

7   http://www.iaea.org/Publications/Magazines/Bulletin/Bull492/49204216465.html

8   Subprime lending is lending money to people who may have difficulty
maintaining the repayment schedule. These loans are typically characterized by

higher interest rates, poor quality collateral, and less favourable terms such as variable or adjustable rates to compensate for higher credit risk.

9 http://www.morganstanley.com/2009annualmeeting/ms177557pr.pdf

10 http://www.millwardbrown.com/BrandZ/Top_100_Global_Brands.aspx

11 http://investor.apple.com/secfiling.cfm?filingID=1193125-12-444068

Implementing an ERM programme

04

Outline

There are many different ways to implement an enterprise risk management programme; this chapter provides a guideline that could be adapted to the needs of the organization. The first step is to establish the foundation for the programme for ERM. This requires a thorough understanding of the organization and its context as well as the reason for establishing the programme.

The direction and intent of the programme should include the need for a common language, proper oversight and governance, accountability, and the resources to be deployed. In building the capabilities to understand, respond to and harness the power of ERM, there are many things to consider, not least the ultimate requirements for ERM. That will determine the resources that are to be deployed and the investment that might be required.

The ERM process, communication and reporting mechanisms should all point towards improving sustainable competitive advantage. The road map in Figure 4.1 summarizes this.

Establish the foundation – the operating model for ERM

When designing an ERM programme, it is important to examine the internal and external context of the organization including the requirements of various stakeholders. By establishing the context, the organization articulates its objectives, and defines the external and internal parameters to be taken into account when managing risk. These internal and external factors

FIGURE 4.1 Road map for implementing enterprise risk management

Component of ERM	Establish foundation			Build capabilities			Improve capabilities		
	Establish context & stake-holder needs	Adopt common language	Establish oversight and governance	Assess risk and develop responses	Design and implement capabilities	Improve capabilities	Establish total cost of risk and capital required	Improve organization performance	Establish sustainable competitive advantage
External environment	✓	✓							
Internal environment	✓	✓	✓		✓				
Risk appetite	✓	✓	✓	✓	✓				
Objective setting	✓	✓	✓	✓	✓				
Event identification				✓	✓	✓			
Risk assessment				✓	✓	✓	✓		
Risk response				✓	✓	✓	✓	✓	
Control and enhancement activities				✓	✓	✓	✓	✓	✓
Information and communication						✓	✓	✓	✓
Monitoring						✓	✓	✓	✓

may be identified through a scan that can be used to shape the design of the ERM approach and process.

In conducting an internal and external scan, organizations may want to look at:

- Results of audits, evaluations, reviews or other documents that provide information on the organization's enterprise risk management, strategic leadership, values and ethics, integrated performance information, stewardship and accountability.

- Strategic planning documents such as the corporate plan, business unit performance report, report on plans and priorities, capital assets and functional plans.

- Input from affected and interested parties including key partners and other stakeholders.

- Key external scanning factors (social, economic, etc).

In addition to information collected during the scan, it is important to develop an understanding of the organization's willingness to accept the possibility of negative events and its openness to opportunities in the pursuit of an objective or outcome.

An organization's appetite for threat and opportunity varies with its culture and with evolving conditions in its internal and external environments. Risk appetite and tolerance can be determined through consultation with affected parties, or by assessing stakeholders' response or reaction to varying levels of risk exposure. Consideration may be given to the following elements to get an understanding of the organization's risk appetite and tolerance level:

- The organization's overall risk culture.

- How risk appetite may have influenced the design of existing tools (heat maps, risk assessment scales, escalation processes, etc).

- How the organization has reacted to past risk events and issues including the type and extent of risk responses, and employees' understanding of the risks taken by themselves, their team or group and the department.

- How stakeholders have reacted to past risk events and issues, and employees' understanding of the risk tolerances of key stakeholder groups and/or consultations with stakeholders on risk appetites.

- The operating model (ie, Acts and regulations, business unit and departmental policies, directives and guidelines, and levels of delegation of authority) as governing instruments generally articulate acceptable departmental practices and expectations in given circumstances.

● Other organizational information such as the organization's performance expectations and actual performance.

The internal and external scan could be documented in the ERM operating model.

Documentation for ERM

It is helpful, as in all management disciplines, to document the ERM programme in some manner, to facilitate the implementation as well as provide a means of communicating the approach to all stakeholders in order to ensure a common and clear understanding. Figure 4.2 shows the type of documentation that might be used for implementing ERM; Table 4.1 provides more detail. The flow of documentation is shown as a cycle because the annual report should include a review of the operating model, frameworks and processes. Good data underpins all of the processes for enterprise risk management, and therefore it sits in the centre of the cycle.

FIGURE 4.2 Supporting documents for embedding enterprise risk management

TABLE 4.1 Description of elements for the documentation of ERM

Element	Describes
Operating model	The overarching context for ERM within the organization
Framework and policy	What, how, who and why for each aspect of risk management; there may be many frameworks and policies for each of the types of risk management, or just one overall ERM set, in which case this could become the operating model
Risk appetite	Risk capacity and limits, key risk indicators
Risk register	The risks identified, owners, risk assessment
Operational documentation	• Technical documents • Key risk indicators and key control indicators • Records of risk assessments such as risk and control self assessments (RCSA) • Log of controls for threats and enhancers for opportunities • Investigation reports • Audit reports • Other operational documentation
Dashboard	The month-by-month performance against key risk indicators
Annual report	Overall performance of risk and capital
Data	The underlying data that informs the risk and capital management programme

Language, oversight and governance

A common language is crucial for establishing a long-lasting ERM process that encapsulates and provides structure to all the risk management processes in the organization. The ERM operating model, frameworks and policies are normally how this is articulated.

> Establishing and articulating the organization's direction for integrated enterprise risk management provides the high-level framework for further design activities.

The establishment and articulation of the organization's overall direction for integrated ERM, including vision, objectives and operating principles, supports this common language. This also ensures the successful integration of the ERM function into the organization. A clear articulation of the vision, objectives and operating principles could also help promote the creation and promotion of a supportive culture.

The organization should consider making a statement that clearly sets out its objectives for integrated risk management activities, and demonstrates a commitment to implementing integrated ERM throughout the organization. This statement may be a specific operating model, ERM policy or similar document but, in support of risk management as an integral part of the entire organization's structures and processes, it may best be included in existing corporate policies on the organization's objectives and commitments.

When establishing and articulating the overall direction for integrated ERM, an organization may wish to consider:

- The rationale for managing risk, including internal and external contexts.
- Links between the organization's mandate and objectives and the ERM objectives.
- The necessary and appropriate accountabilities and responsibilities for managing risks.
- The way in which conflicting interests are managed.
- Sanctions/incentives for poor/good risk-taking behaviour.
- The commitment to adequately resource ERM activities.
- The manner in which ERM will be integrated into the organization.
- Mechanisms for escalating risks and reporting on risks.
- Mechanisms for enhancing opportunities through ERM processes.

- The methods for reporting and measuring ERM performance.
- The commitment to review and update the ERM approach as appropriate, whether in response to a positive or negative event or based on an appropriate periodic cycle.

Aligning the enterprise risk management vision and objectives with corporate objectives and strategic direction helps make ERM meaningful and relevant to all employees.

The operating model, framework and policies set out the governance structure, confirming that the board and senior management are ultimately accountable for the implementation of enterprise risk management within the organization. Operational management, ERM team and internal audit accountabilities are established throughout the governance structure to ensure that key risks have been appropriately managed (identified, assessed, responded to, communicated, monitored, adjusted as required, and reported on), including assurance mechanisms.

In the design of an approach and process, clear enterprise risk management roles, responsibilities and networks should be defined at appropriate levels within the organization, relative to its size and complexity. In determining and documenting the appropriate accountabilities, organizations should consider:

- Specifying appropriate risk owners who have the accountability and authority for risks.
- Specifying appropriate risk control/enhancer owners who have the accountability and authority to manage risks.
- Ensuring the organization's governance structures support the required levels of accountability and authority for the risk owners and the risk control/enhancer owners.
- Identifying the appropriate structure for the development, implementation and maintenance of the ERM approach and associated processes.
- Communicating that all staff have a role to play in identifying and managing risks; establishing performance measurement and internal and/or external reporting and escalation processes.
- Ensuring appropriate levels of recognition, reward, approval and sanction.
- Providing assurance over the ERM programme, policy and application of those in the processes of enterprise risk management.

Building capabilities: assess and develop responses and capabilities

All staff should be provided with the training and other resources needed to ensure that they have the appropriate skills, competencies and experience to carry out their responsibilities. General competencies for staff involved in the design and implementation activities may include:

- Knowledge of an organization's overall management framework including roles, responsibilities, accountabilities, reporting structures and escalation procedures.
- Knowledge of the culture of the organization and the way in which other initiatives are implemented.
- Understanding of how to (and the skills to gain) ownership within each part of the organization.
- Ability to engage in discussions about risk.

Understanding of ERM and how to apply it to each area of responsibility

Regardless of the process used to design an ERM approach, there are several activities that are likely to occur at some point in the design process. They include:

- Developing an understanding of the organization and its context so as to identify factors that could significantly influence the design of the approach and process.
- Developing an overall ERM policy statement that is organization-specific and supported by senior management.
- Specifying accountabilities for ERM within the organization.
- Allocating resources for implementing and supporting ERM within the organization.
- Outlining a standard ERM process including common terminology.
- Implementing a range of measurements to report on the key success factors for the ERM programme.
- Establishing communication and reporting mechanisms for ERM.

Appropriate resources (people, partners, tools, etc) need to be allocated for the design, implementation and maintenance of the ERM approach and process as well as for the ongoing conduct of ERM activities. With respect to resourcing, upfront investments could be necessary for the initial phases of design and implementation. Start-up costs (time, attention, training, systems and communication) may be incurred until the practice becomes an integral part of organizational structures and processes. It may take time and effort to gain momentum, train managers and specialists, and establish good tools and processes. Once fully implemented, initial start-up investments can be re-allocated as appropriate.

There is no standard size or allocation of resources for integrated ERM activities. To assess the resource requirements for establishing and maintaining an ERM approach and process, it is important to identify the nature, adequacy and usefulness of existing organizational tools, techniques, people skills and expertise for managing risk to determine incremental requirements. Key resource considerations could include, among others:

- The people, skills, experience and competence necessary to design and implement the ERM approach and process throughout the organization, including determining the most appropriate approach and process, working with staff to embed ERM into their structures and processes, educating staff, putting tools in place, etc.
- The people, skills, experience and competence necessary to conduct ERM activities on an ongoing basis.
- The people, skills, experience and competence necessary to maintain the approach and process along with supporting procedures.
- The organization's existing processes, methods and tools (including systems and technologies) that can to be used for managing risk and capital.
- Incremental requirements with respect to processes, methods and tools (including systems and technologies) needed for managing risk and capital.
- Understanding of and the skills to gather the data, assess and analyse risk and capital.
- The skills to be able to assist senior management and indeed management at all levels in identifying and assessing risk.
- The necessary training programmes for the organization's staff to ensure a common understanding of and approach to ERM (eg common language and terminology).
- Any resource constraints that could require trade-offs during the development and execution of the ERM processes.

In the ongoing management of risks, specific attention should be given to the allocation of resources for risk response activities. While the identification and analysis of risks is much easier to embed into day-to-day decision-making activities, specific resources may need to be assigned to risk response action items. These resources should be at the appropriate level for the severity of the risk and should take into account any necessary trade-offs due to resource constraints. It is important to note that resource allocations should be aligned with the level of risk to be managed, with resources being focused on key risk areas as set out in the risk appetite statement.

Under the leadership of senior management, an organization may choose to express its risk appetite from the perspective of the organization as a whole or for different types of risks, which may then be applied to individual risks during the ERM process and inform the type and extent of risk response for a given risk. When starting out, it is important to note that risk appetite may vary between and even within organizations, and can be influenced by mandate, stakeholder views and organizational culture (see Chapter 5 on risk appetite).

Improving capabilities: monitoring and communication

Monitoring of the outputs of ERM aims to improve capabilities and to ensure that the objective for ERM is achieved. Key risk indicators are the focus for the tracking systems (see Chapter 5 on key risk indicators).

The communication of risk is only one factor in the monitoring of outputs but is a good driver for a focused and timely tracking process. Communication, consultations and reporting should involve external and internal stakeholders in order to successfully implement and conduct integrated ERM in an inclusive manner.

Establishing communication and reporting mechanisms provides a continuous means for keeping stakeholders informed of organizational ERM processes, practices and risk responses. It helps maintain momentum to ensure that risk interest remains strong. It involves generating and sharing relevant information among the right people, anticipating and responding effectively to public concerns and expectations, achieving understanding of risks, getting action (voluntary or otherwise), and the reciprocal: receiving feedback.

In the interest of openness and transparency, an organization should be able to provide interested stakeholders with a snapshot of its key threats and opportunities and what is being done to manage them at any time. Many organizations do this through a monthly, bi-monthly or quarterly dashboard. This summarizes the main changes that have taken place on the risk list, or risk register, and performance against the key risk indicators which in turn reports the performance against the risk appetite limits and thresholds.

As applicable, communication, consultation and reporting activities occur as an organization is establishing its approach and process and on an ongoing basis during all stages of the ERM process when practising integrated ERM. However, to ensure that the mechanisms necessary to support these activities are in place, plans for communication, consultation and reporting should be developed at an early stage.

The following are some elements to consider when identifying or designing the appropriate corporate infrastructure to ensure clear communication of risk issues, practices and procedures throughout the organization:

- the consultation with internal and external stakeholders in the design of the ERM approach and process;

- the communication of senior management commitment to and vision of ERM throughout the organization;

- the communication of key components of the ERM approach and their modifications in a timely manner;

- the communication of the ERM process and any modifications in a timely manner;

- the consultation with internal and external stakeholders during the ERM process (to identify and assess risks, to determine response strategies, etc);

- the communication and reporting of risk information (identified risks, response strategies, performance against key risk indicators, etc) resulting from the application of the ERM processes to the appropriate levels of the organizations at the right times to support decision making;

- the reporting of the effectiveness and outcomes of the ERM approach;

- the sharing of good practices and lessons learnt and the collaborative development of risk resources for continuous improvement;

- the use of existing reporting tools to report on risks; and

- the establishment of linkages with other governance and compliance areas within the organization.

There may be a communication strategy or plan to accompany the ERM approach and process. Communication practices should involve clear and simple messages to help ensure a common understanding of the information provided. It is good practice to have an annual report that summarizes the outputs from ERM, from which a review of, and amendment to, the ERM context and approach should feed.

Questions for senior management and the board to ask

(Including model answers based on best practice – at a high maturity level.)

Have we established the external and internal foundation for the programme for ERM?	Yes, there is an overarching operating model or framework for all aspects of ERM.
Does this include a thorough understanding of the organization and its context as well as the reason for establishing the ERM programme?	Yes, we have consulted with and had input from external and internal stakeholders.
Do we have a clear plan and framework for the documentation of ERM?	Yes, there is a joined-up plan for enabling all aspects of risk management to be incorporated under the one operating model for ERM.
Does the direction and intent for the programme include the need for a common language, proper oversight and governance, accountability and resources to be deployed?	Yes, the operating model for ERM ensures consistent language and approach where appropriate, a good oversight and challenge process to the governance structure for ERM, and the accountability for delivering the outputs for ERM.
In building the capabilities to understand, respond to and harness the power of ERM, do we take into account the ultimate requirements for ERM?	Yes, we are very clear about using ERM to enable us to deliver sustainable competitive advantage and we have some challenging goals and targets in that regard.

Do we adjust the resources that are to be deployed and the investment that might be required based on the requirement?

Yes, the overarching structure also allows us to re-deploy resources across different aspects of risk management within the ERM structure, to enable cross-fertilization of ideas and to ensure best use of resources where most needed. This also helps us to break down the silos between different aspects of risk management and to release innovation.

Do the ERM communication and reporting mechanisms all point towards the direction of improving sustainable competitive advantage?

Yes, the cycle of (weekly/monthly) dashboards from each of the risk management areas, which are then wrapped into (monthly/quarterly) ERM dashboards enables us to have a complete picture of our performance against our key risk indicators.

Risk attitude, risk propensity and risk appetite

05

Outline

Risk has a different meaning to each enterprise or individual because each has a different perception of the opportunity and the threat depending on their propensity to take risk or to avoid it. Enterprise risk management will not be seen as an essential part of releasing innovation until there is an overarching risk appetite framework that is scalable for each part of the organization, understood in the context of each business unit's goals and framed in a common language.

In this chapter we explore aspects of risk seeking versus risk avoidance, the broad principles of risk appetite frameworks and, critically, how risk appetite frameworks need to be linked to compensation and reward programmes. Risk appetite must be owned and driven by the board and senior management in order to be real, practical and pertinent to the business of taking managed threats and opportunities. Risk practitioners are responsible for implementing the process and enabling the decisions on risk appetite to be made by the board and senior management. Innovation cannot be successfully undertaken unless there is a clear understanding of risk appetite, and unless performance against the risk appetite metrics is measured.

Risk aversion versus risk hungry

Risk-hungry Australia spent much of the last few years building its industry and changing its landscape in order to respond to the huge demand for minerals and raw materials from China and Asia. Asia's extraordinary ascent has already dramatically changed the Australian economy, society and strategic environment. By 2020 it is said by some observers that Asia will not only be the world's largest producer of goods and services, it will also be the world's largest consumer of them. By 2013 Asia was already the most populous region in the world. In the future, it will also be home to the majority of the world's middle class.

For several decades, Australian businesses, exporters and the community have grown their footprint across the region. For Australia, the minerals and energy boom is the most visible, but not the only, aspect of Asia's rise. As the century unfolds, the growth in the region will impact on almost all of Australasia's economy and society.

This dependence by Australia on Asia's growth is both an opportunity and a threat. All the signals in 2013 were that Australia is hungry to maximize the opportunity and hungry to take the risks that are presented. Some would argue that Australia is too dependent on Asia and is looking at the short-term gain against the long-term threats and opportunities.

Chinese demand for Australian exports, especially raw materials, was one reason Australia didn't fall into recession after the 2008 financial crisis. Yet since then, the huge demand that China has had for minerals started to wane as Chinese authorities sought to rein in excessive credit growth, prompting a resulting impact on the Australian Dollar.

Less than 6 per cent of Australia is available to arable farming yet significant tracts of it are under threat from mineral and gas extraction. The massive requirement of water for mineral and gas extraction and the resultant environmental impact of contaminated effluent will provide an interesting challenge. Only time will tell if the risk-hungry drive for short-term wealth, or the risk-averse approach of some of the local populace who argue that this is 'madness', is correct.

Determining the risks to be hungry for and those to be averse to

When making a decision about the right risks to be hungry for and those to which one should be risk averse, the context of the goals of the decision makers is important. So how does one decide? Faced with the opportunity to invest or disinvest what are the defining factors one must take into account?

Earlier, we considered the expression 'capacity' with regard to the ability to take threats and opportunities and suggested that risk appetite is a combination of capacity to take threats and opportunities and the willingness or

FIGURE 5.1 Chart of performance against risk attitude

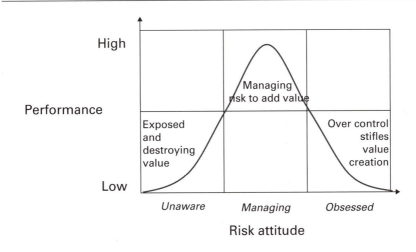

tolerance towards the taking of risks. An enterprise's tolerance for threats and opportunities will be determined by the weighting that it puts on each of those components of capacity.

Often, decisions in the boardroom are based not on the capacity of the enterprise to take opportunities and threats, but on the willingness of the rest of the board to go along with the decision: on the propensity to take risk. Figure 5.1 shows that we can draw a scale depicting attitude towards threats and opportunities, from unaware or ignorant of risk, to being obsessed about threats and opportunities. When placing risk attitude against a further scale showing performance, the best performance is obtained when the enterprise is neither ignorant about risk nor obsessed. It manages threats and opportunities to add value.

A risk appetite framework should clearly articulate those threats that need to be closely controlled and those where a more risk-taking approach can be taken; indeed some threats need to be accepted in greater quantities, in some instances, for the enterprise to thrive and grow. For example, an insurance company that refuses to accept 'insurance' threats will not survive – the business is about accepting insurance threats. A bank will need to take increasing amounts of credit risks to thrive and grow. However, these threats and opportunities are those that can be managed through good risk management. In the case of the insurance company, it uses underwriting to determine how much risk to take and what price to charge.

Applications of a risk appetite tool

Effectively developed, the risk appetite framework plays a pivotal role in four areas:

1 forward planning;
2 performance management;
3 encouraging managed risk taking;
4 threat minimization.

> As a tool for forward planning, risk appetite provisions can temper, or even provoke, an organization's strategic ambitions for extending its business portfolio, expanding into new territories and acquiring new companies. When incorporated within a risk-adjusted financial planning process, it can influence decisions on capital allocation and investment in threat mitigation. This ensures that companies undertake business where there is an appropriate relationship between threat and reward and focus on risk taking where a competitive advantage exists.

The risk appetite statement can bring a risk perspective to ongoing performance management by specifying the types of threats and opportunities and the levels of risk taking that are acceptable. This helps senior management to monitor the company performance on important ERM issues. The framework can also improve a company's enterprise risk management on several levels. First, the statement enhances a company's governance by securing senior-level engagement and by broadening ownership of the threat and opportunity agenda. Second, it sharpens enterprise risk management reporting by embedding company tolerances in the control/enhancer framework. Finally, the integration of ERM information with financial outcomes adds value to risk assessment exercises and guides companies in the direction of more effective threat-return management.

The key to developing a good risk appetite statement is to ensure that the team developing it is diverse. This might create discussion, even initial dissent, but this tension between people with different risk propensity is useful for creating a risk appetite statement that reflects the culture and intent of the organization.

Developing a robust risk appetite framework does not take an inordinate amount of time and effort. But ensuring that the framework is integrated into key decision-making processes can be challenging. Developing a management tool that is effective over the long term is dependent on four key factors:

1 Executive-level commitment to the exercise and investment in its content. The project needs a senior management sponsor and to be fully backed by the chief executive or equivalent.

2 A focused set of insightful metrics and targets linked to the company's performance. Senior management should focus on the most important metrics, even if more indicators are available.

3 Robust underpinning by appropriate analytics and a standardized tracking tool. Risk appetite tolerances need to be grounded in both historical and forecast data, peer company data and rating agency thresholds. The reporting tool must be easy to use, compatible with the company's financial model, and able to incorporate other sources of operational performance data.

4 Thorough embedding in key business processes. The risk appetite framework should be integrated with strategic planning and capital allocation processes. It should be used when preparing budgets, evaluating potential major acquisitions, divestures and capital investments.

Those organizations that make developing a risk appetite framework a high priority will quickly anticipate undesired business outcomes and optimize returns in rapidly shifting competitive landscapes. By doing so, they will develop a significant competitive advantage.

Risk capacity versus tolerance

Risk appetite is defined in many public documents as 'the types and amount of risk an organization is willing to take in pursuit of its objectives'. Thus many people confuse capacity and tolerance towards taking threats and opportunities, or even ignore capacity altogether, thinking that risk appetite is only about the 'willingness' to take threats, or its tolerance towards risk.

For example, consider a large worldwide hotel chain. There will be a statement that there will be zero tolerance for fraud risks. That is neither a realistic assessment of their risk appetite, or indeed their capacity for fraud risks. Their capacity with regards fraud is quite high in reality, and even multi-million dollar frauds are unlikely to cause huge financial distress to the organization. Yet they still have a stated tolerance towards fraud of zero. The reason they articulate it thus is that they can then set in place appropriate rewards and sanctions for being out-with the risk tolerance statement.

Capacity is a hard fact. It's about how much capital (and other assets) an organization needs to sustain a certain level of threat and opportunity. Tolerance is about willingness to take risk. Thus risk appetite is a deliberate discussion about the ability to be able to take threats and opportunities in order to achieve strategic objectives, taking into account the organization's capacity and its tolerance levels. In some these might be set differently for varying risk types.

The thematic review of risk governance by the Financial Stability Board[1] calls risk tolerance 'risk limits':

> A firm's risk appetite should be set below the risk capacity of the firm so that a buffer exists between risk capacity and risk appetite. The firm-wide risk profile (comprises individual business unit risks) should be measured, monitored and managed to ensure that the firm's overall risk stays within specified risk limits.

A firm generally sets risk limits that will constrain risk within its approved risk appetite. Some business units/lines may exceed the risk limits set and no longer operate within the approved risk appetite. Breaches in risk limits should be reported to the board or risk committee and management should propose actions to reduce the risk of the business unit/line to within the approved risk appetite.

Developing risk appetite frameworks

Maturity

In practice, for many organizations combining capacity with tolerance is a step too far, too complicated for a first time attempt at arriving at a risk appetite statement. Only the more mature organization (see Chapter 8 on risk maturity models) should embark upon combining risk capacity with risk tolerance as the next step along their journey. When we talk about risk-mature organizations, this might refer to the ERM management culture, the ERM framework and processes and or the frameworks and systems used (see Chapter 6 on risk culture).

The maturity of the business is also important to the way in which a risk appetite framework is developed. This is not only with respect to the age of the business as a whole, but also the market in which it operates, either geographically or in relation to the product or service provided. For example, if an organization is entering into a new market, the risk appetite metrics might show a small incremental desire to bear threats and take opportunities, which might be relaxed over time as the organization learns more about the environment for this new market.

Risk propensity and culture

A risk appetite statement also needs to take into account the propensity and awareness of the individuals who are determining the risk appetite statement. Take, for example, a young finance director who hasn't been through the mill of time, who has not been through two or three recession recycles. That finance director will have a different propensity and different behaviour to one who has been through two or three different events like economic downturns.

The culture of an organization is also a key factor. Consider an organization, for example, which has a great ERM process. It ticks all the boxes in terms of maturity; it has a great Chief Risk Officer (CRO) who is the organization's representative at all major ERM conferences and speaks publicly at those conferences. Yet what the board do is entirely different. One of the issues is that there often is a glass ceiling between the CRO and the board. Even if the CRO is on the board, it is rare that he or she is influential enough to be able to ensure that strategic decisions take threat and opportunity into account.

The collective decision making on the board is too often lacking good enterprise risk management, or good articulation of their risk appetite. For example, in the nuclear industry, operational risk management is absolutely paramount. They have to be very threat averse when considering operational threats. There must be 'fail-safe' controls over 'fail-safe' controls over 'fail-safe' controls. However, from the final report from TEPCO on the causes of the Fukushima disaster[2] the direct causes leading to the reactor core damage accident of Fukushima Daiichi include the fact that TEPCO's tsunami estimate was insufficient in the end, and the root cause of this accident was the inadequate preparedness for a tsunami. In other words, they had not taken a wide enough view of risk. Thus it could be argued that in the case of Fukushima, management didn't necessarily cater for the extraordinary events and there was a lack of transparency in the way in which the management of threat was portrayed to the board. Often, if the board's attitude is that they don't like to have that news, and there is an ERM report going up to them that contains bad news, the report is edited before it gets up to the top.

Risk propensity can be modelled as a function of two aspects: the propensity for risk taking and the desire for creativity. For example, if we are looking for a good blend for a team to develop a bridge, we have people who might score high on both scales of risk taking and creativity; these are architects. They have the bright ideas. They are driven by concepts, ideas and image as opposed to substance and cost. If we have a group of architects who are solely responsible for developing the risk appetite statements, their propensity to take threats and opportunities will be huge. Architect-led projects tend to be over budget, late, but beautiful.

Conversely, people who score low on risk taking and creativity could be considered to be the quantity surveyors. These are people who are responsible for counting the number of bricks, calculating the amount of capital we need, checking that the budget is met. These, in terms of risk propensity, are the antithesis of the architects. A risk appetite statement led by quantity surveyors will be conservative and will concentrate on mainly operational and financial metrics. Those that score in the median range of each of those scales of risk taking and creativity might be the engineers, project management, marketing department, HR department, audit and IT.

There is a theory that the more people we have, the more difficult it is to reach a consensus in terms of risk-based decision making. So the more people on the board, the more difficult it would be to reach same understanding and this might make the risk appetite quite low. However, it depends on how the board members organize themselves. Large boards often elect a smaller executive board. The key to good ERM at board level is to ensure that there is a good balance on the board between those with a 'cautious' approach (quantity surveyors) and those with a less cautious approach (architects).

Ability to control and enhance threat and opportunity

There are some threats and opportunities that are outside the control of the organization. The Institute of Risk Management (IRM) sets out a useful framework[3] that unpacks the complexity of control taking versus risk taking. This framework sets the propensity to concentrate on value creation as a paradigm that is opposed by the alternative need to concentrate on value protection, and we have adapted it to show the approach to risk from top down to bottom up; see Figure 5.2. The framework promotes the idea that the strategic level is proportionately more about risk taking than exercising control, while at the operational level the proportions are broadly reversed. Clearly the relative proportions will depend on the organization itself, the nature of the risks it faces and the regulatory environment within which it operates.

FIGURE 5.2 Approach to risk from top down to bottom up

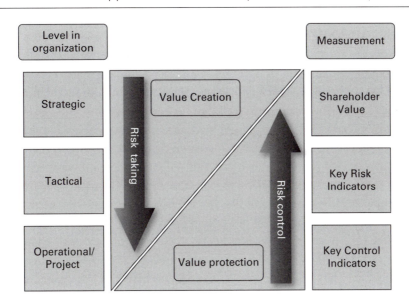

Adapted from IRM Risk Appetite and Tolerance Paper

Current performance

Risk propensity is also informed by the current performance of the enterprise. If the organization is highly leveraged with large amounts of debt and little free capital, then the aspects of risk appetite relating to risk taking might be different from those organizations that are cash rich. There is no real rule to this aspect of risk propensity driving risk appetite. Some organizations that are highly leveraged may only be comfortable with that amount of margin and will be cautious when setting their risk appetite metrics. Others, that are highly leveraged, may be more aggressive in their threat and opportunity taking attitude because they might consider that they are sweating their assets and that is more important to them. Much depends on the stakeholder requirement, and the perception of what the stakeholders expect.

The level of performance in relation to brand value can affect the propensity for risk. Brand value could be considered to be easy to reduce and hard to improve. If the brand is high a small drop in the value is less dangerous to the organization than if the brand is low. Thus an organization with a low brand value and to whom brand value is important would place this at the centre of the risk appetite framework and metrics (see Chapter 9 on corporate social responsibility).

The risk of not taking a risk

When establishing a risk appetite statement we also have to take into account the threat or opportunity of not taking the decision. Imagine we are standing at the side of a very fast and deep running river, 100 metres wide. Do we jump in? Our first inclination might be 'no'. In fact that might even be our second response as well. But the correct response is to ask, 'Why should I?' That is precisely the right answer. Consider that there is a massive herd of thousands of buffalos bearing down on us. We are certain that there is a 100 per cent probability we will be trampled to death if we don't jump in. There is no other alternative. However, if we jump into the river, there is an 80 per cent chance we will die, but there is 20 per cent chance that we will live. So what's the risk of not taking the risk?

Likewise, an organization faced with a ruinous situation with regard to, for example, product problems at the same time as experiencing competitive pressure, may have to be very inventive and perhaps risk taking, and set its risk appetite for breaking into new products or services.

CASE EXAMPLE   Coca-Cola[4]

In April 1985 Coca-Cola took the ultimate risk. It removed market-leading Coca-Cola from the US market and introduced New Coke. The decision was made after extensive marketing, including canvassing 190,000 consumer opinions and taste-tests of various Coke formulations. The launch was spectacular in that within 24 hours more Americans were aware of the birth of New Coke than had known about man's first steps on the moon in 1969. However, the market reaction did not match the research. Within days, several opinion polls showed that consumers overwhelmingly preferred the original Coca-Cola to the new Coke. There were floods of complaints across the United States.

In this case, blind testing did not tell the full story. Coca-Cola had minimized the 'product' risk, but completely underestimated the brand risk. Consumers told the company that they were going to buy the new Cola, but they were thinking more hypothetically. As a result, the company over-read the research.

Consumers wanted to remind the company that their favourite soft drink belonged to them. It was more than a drink, it was a brand that was an integral and inseparable part of their lives! Chairman CEO Roberto C Goizueta can laugh about it today; he might even make the same decision again based on the research that was used. But few executives would have taken the risk that he and his company took.

The Coca-Cola Company listened and then dared to replace its winning formula. It was now daring enough to admit it had been wrong to do so. It meant to change the dynamics of sugar colas in the United States, and it did exactly that albeit not in the way it had planned. In the end, the company learnt that in order to maintain the interest and the respect of its consumers, it would have to continually differentiate its brands in ways that offered highly relevant value.

The original Coca-Cola reappeared as Coca-Cola Classic to regain the top slot as the United States' leading soft drink, while the new formula, today known as Coke II, remained on the market, bringing in additional sales and gaining extra market share.

Stakeholder expectations

In determining the risk appetite metrics, selecting the metrics to use, and indeed the scales for those metrics, there is a need to take into account the expectations of all key stakeholders and balance the apparently con-flicting requirements between them. For example, an organization that has one major customer that accounts for a large proportion of sales and profit needs to set the risk appetite metrics to retain the good will of that customer.

Risk appetite and value drivers

While the risk appetite framework and statement need to be based on the goals and objectives of the organization, just as important are its value driv-ers. Sometimes business objectives are out of date, and at other times they are about goals and forward movement of the organization. This leaves out the current state of the organization and those aspects that give the enter-prise its raison d'être. Value drivers lend themselves to being the focus for the risk appetite framework and metrics because they actually articulate the key value of that organization. It could be their people or it could be their secret ingredients.

CASE EXAMPLE KFC

If we look at KFC, it is its secret formula that gives it its market differentiation and protects it from rivals. These are the four key business objectives from its 2012 report and accounts:[5]

1 Build leading brands in China in every significant category.

2 Drive aggressive, international expansion and build strong brands everywhere.

3 Dramatically improve US brand positions, consistency and returns.

4 Drive industry-leading, long-term shareholder and franchisee value.

None of these business goals talks overtly about the secret formula, but it underpins each of them. It is a core value driver.

Key risk indicators

Key risk indicators are vital to ensuring that ERM adds value to the organization, enables good threat and opportunity-taking behaviour and drives the response. However, often key risk indicators (KRIs) sound like some form of complicated science, and certainly some risk practitioners get hung up on complex and hugely involved lists and measurements of how the organization is performing against KRIs.

The main issue for senior management is that the KRIs are measuring the most important threats and opportunities, that is the threats and opportunities that fundamentally affect the performance of the organization as defined by the risk appetite. Senior management therefore must challenge the KRIs, understand them, and value the regular reports of KRI performance. There must be a close link between KRIs and performance management as well as risk appetite. If core aspects of performance for the organization are not matched with equivalent KRIs and or the KRIs bear no link to the risk appetite, something is wrong. Key performance aspects might be profitability, cash flow management, brand management, recruitment, retention of key skills, debt management, capital management, IT security and so on. These must be matched with KRI reports that reflect how well the organization is performing.

For example, take a shareholders' expectation of at least a 5 per cent return on their investment each year. If the earnings for shareholders dip below this level, they may sell, the share price will drop, and the cost of and possibly the amount of borrowings will increase. This could then send the company into a downward spiral and will fundamentally affect future plans. There will be a number of aspects that can affect the dividend, from earnings reducing to costs increasing. The key performance indicators in this respect will concentrate on the level of earnings both in terms of pricing and volume, as well as on maintaining reasonable cost levels. The largest cost is raw materials, followed by staff costs and then equipment, so the key performance indicators, key risk indicators and risk appetite statements might look like Table 5.1.

Key risk indicators need to be scalable for the whole organization so that when business units report performance against the KRIs the intelligence can be aggregated to provide a report for the board. Key risk indicators hang off the risk appetite and must be STAFFS:

Strategic – must address the core strategies.

Tested – tested to check they work.

Adjustable – as time progresses, they should be subject to a continuous improvement process.

Formal – should be formalized.

Framed – the context for them should be clear.

Scalable – should be able to be translated for performance at all levels of the organization.

Key control indicators

The main concern for senior management is that there is a process in place for articulating the performance indicators, risk appetite and key risk indicators. The controls/enhancers that operational management put in place to manage the threats and opportunities to an acceptable level should be reported in such a way as to provide high level assurance that the controls/enhancers are working and active. These are the key control indicators that senior management should demand. Further down the line, operational management will have their own key risk indicators that give them assurance that all is well for each area of responsibility. Some examples are shown in Table 5.2.

TABLE 5.1 Examples of key performance indicators, risk appetite metrics and matching key risk indicators

Area of concern	Key Performance Indicator	Risks	Risk Appetite	Key Risk Indicator
Sales	Market share must be above 40% for 100% of the time	Competition enters	Market share no more than 55%, no less than 45% for any three month period	Market share goes above 55% or drops below 45% for any one week.
		Product failure/ public recall	99.8% to 100% maximum quality	Target of 99.5% maximum quality missed
Costs	Gross margin of no less than 65% maintained month on month	Raw material cost increases	Maximum increase of 2% over one year period	Increase of 0.5% at any one time
		People costs increase	Maximum increase of 3% over one month	Increase of greater than 2% at any time in period

TABLE 5.2 Examples of key performance indicators, risk appetite metrics, key risk indicators and key control indicators

Area of concern	Key Performance Indicator	Risks	Risk Appetite	Key Risk Indicator	Key control indicator for Board	Key control indicators for operational management
Costs	Gross margin of no less than 65% maintained month on month	Raw material cost increases	Maximum increase of 2% over one-year period	Increase of 0.5% at any one time	Monthly reports on levels of raw material costs with forecasts for next three quarters	*Daily* statistics on • raw material costs • exchange rates *Monthly* • forecasts • trends for following 12 months • market intelligence on alternative suppliers • weather forecasts for key areas of production • other environmental information

Organization behind the setting of risk appetite

The risk appetite framework should contain a risk appetite statement, risk limits and an outline of the roles and responsibilities of those overseeing the implementation of the framework. The risk appetite framework must be an integral part of the organization's overall enterprise risk management suite of documents.

The risk appetite statement should reflect the aggregate level and type of threats and opportunities that an organization is willing to accept to achieve its business objectives. Key features of the risk appetite statement are:

- It should be linked to the organization's short- and long-term strategic, capital and financial plans, value drivers and compensation programmes.
- It should include qualitative and quantitative measures that can be aggregated and disaggregated.
- Qualitative measure may include:
  - significant risks the firm wants to take and why;
  - significant risks the firm wants to avoid and why;
  - attitude towards regulatory compliance; and
  - underlying assumptions and risks.
- Quantitative measures may include:
  - measures of loss or negative events (such as earnings, capital or liquidity, earnings per share at risk of volatility) that the organization is willing to accept;
  - it should be forward-looking;
  - it should consider normal and stressed scenarios; and
  - it should aim to be within the organization's risk capacity (ie, regulatory constraints).

Risk limits are the application of the organization's risk appetite statement to:

- specific risk categories (eg, credit, market, insurance, liquidity, operational);
- the business unit or platform level (eg, retail, capital markets);

- lines of business or product level (eg, concentration limits); and

- more granular levels, as appropriate.

Risk limits are often expressed in quantitative terms, and are specific, measurable, frequency based and reportable.

Once approved by the board, the risk appetite framework should be implemented by senior management throughout the organization as an integral part of the overall enterprise risk management programme of the organization. The Risk Appetite Framework should further align with the organization's corporate strategy, its value drivers, its financial and capital plans, its business unit strategies and day-to-day operations, as well as its enterprise risk management policies (eg, limits, selection/underwriting guidelines and criteria, etc) and compensation programs.

Where the risk appetite framework sets aggregate limits that will be shared among different units, the basis on which such limits will be shared should be clearly identified and communicated. It is useful therefore to set limits that are scalable for each part of the organization and expressed as, say, a percentage of various aspects of performance.

Effective control, monitoring and reporting systems and procedures should be developed to ensure ongoing operational compliance with the risk appetite framework, including the following:

- The CRO (or equivalent) should ensure that aggregate risk limits are consistent with the firm's risk appetite statement.

- The CRO (or equivalent) should include in regular reports to the board or risk committee, and senior management, an assessment against the risk appetite statement and risk limits.

- Internal audit should routinely assess compliance with the risk appetite framework on an enterprise-wide basis and in its review of units within an organization.

The board and senior management of an organization should receive regular reports on the effectiveness of, and compliance with, the risk appetite framework throughout the organization. These reports should include a comparison of actual results versus stated risk appetite framework measures. Where breaches are identified, action plans should exist and be communicated to the board. The risk appetite framework should be an integral part of the board's discussions and decision-making processes. This reporting should take place regularly – perhaps monthly in the form of dashboards and then annual performance reviews in an annual report.

Embedding risk appetite in the culture

While the board are responsible for setting the risk appetite framework including ensuring that monitoring and reporting systems are in place and working, operational management must be accountable for putting the framework into practice. In reality, this means that all business decisions that impact the performance of the organization must be monitored against the risk appetite.

The best working practices for making this happen are framed around key risk indicators and key control indicators. The board must insist on performance measurement against these risk and control indicators and a clear reporting of performance against the risk appetite.

Examples of risk appetite statements

The following represents a part of a health care organization's risk appetite statement. The organization has specific objectives related to quality of customer care, attracting and retaining high-quality physicians and health researchers, and building sustainable levels of profit to provide access to needed capital and to fund existing activities.

A healthcare organization's risk appetite statement

The Organization operates within a low overall risk range. The Organization's lowest risk appetite relates to safety and compliance objectives, including employee health and safety, with a marginally higher risk appetite towards its strategic, reporting and operations objectives. This means that reducing to reasonably practicable levels the risks originating from various medical systems, products, equipment and our work environment, and meeting our legal obligations, will take priority over other business objectives.

A global insurance company

The following risk appetite statement says that it 'separately consider(s) each of the regions in which we operate'. It goes on to state that:

This has confirmed that each region is sufficiently capitalized in its own right and that the distribution and allocation of capital to the relevant businesses in each region largely reflect the different risk profiles within those regions. This has also supported the decision and successful execution of our debt repayment programme. Even when applying significant economic stresses to our current capital, the Group remains sufficiently capitalized. We have also identified management actions that could be taken to remedy the Group's capital or liquidity position in a severe shock event where capital or liquidity levels significantly breach our risk appetite limits for a sustained period.

It further reveals that:

The Group's overall risk profile, reflected by our economic capital results, is stable and indicates that the Group is comfortably within appetite on all capital measures, despite the weakened global recovery.

This risk appetite statement does four things effectively; it:

1 Focuses the risk appetite statement on the key value drivers.

2 Communicates, with sufficient precision, that the organization wants to sustain its business over a long period of time.

3 Expresses a low risk appetite in pursuing all the organization's objectives.

4 Expresses a very low appetite for risks associated with employee safety and compliance.

Table 5.3, from that insurance company's 2012 report and accounts, sets out its risk appetite preferences for seven aspects of risk appetite as well as its performance for three years and expected return relative to target.

TABLE 5.3 Example of risk appetite statement

Risk category	Risk preference	2010 profile(%)	2011 profile (%)	2012 profile (%)	Expected return relative to target
Market (policyholder)	For	26	27	17	Excellent
Credit and counterparty	Against*	22	13	11	Neutral
Business	Neutral	24	24	29	Good
Market (shareholder)	Against	4	6	4	Poor
Liability	Strongly for**	8	13	15	Excellent
Operational	Strongly against	12	11	9	Very poor
Currency	NA***	4	5	15	NA***

* Unless taken in the form of well governed and managed banking-related credit risk.

** Assumes risk is correctly priced.

*** No risk preference is set for currency as this risk is essentially a balance sheet translation risk.

Questions for senior management and the board to ask

(Including model answers based on best practice – at a high maturity level.)

Does our ERM operating model and framework take into account different perceptions and expectations of risk?

Yes, we have looked at various stakeholder perceptions and expectations for risk and risk appetite and have factored them into our risk appetite statements.

Does the organization have an overarching risk appetite framework that is scalable for each part of the organization, understood in the context of each business unit's goals, and framed in a common language?

Yes, the risk appetite metrics are all translated into real metrics for each of our divisions, business units and individual product lines. These have taken some years to come to fruition, and we anticipate that they will continue to change as time progresses and we become more mature in our approach.

Does the organization encourage managed risk seeking versus risk avoidance, through implementing the broad principles of a risk appetite framework?

Yes, in our risk appetite approach we have a balanced approach to managed risk taking where we are talking about opportunities to grow and enhance our business versus risk minimization where the business is threatened.

Is our risk appetite framework linked to compensation and reward programmes?

Our risk appetite framework is linked to the remuneration programme only where this is appropriate; for example, in our (wholesale banking business) we do not encourage risk-taking behaviour unless it is within the set boundaries.

Do we ensure that risk appetite is owned and driven by the board and senior management in order to be real, practical and pertinent to the business of taking risk?

Yes. The board take a lead in the process and set the risk appetite themselves.

Are we certain that there is a clear understanding of risk appetite, and measurement of performance against the risk appetite metrics?	Yes, we have risk appetite metrics that mirror the performance metrics that drive the organization.
Are the risk appetite metrics translated into key risk indicators that challenge us to improve our performance over time?	Yes, the risk appetite metrics are all translated into key risk indicators for each of our divisions, business units and individual product lines. These are linked to our performance metrics to enable us to continuously improve our performance.
Are the key risk indicators linked to the most important corporate goals and value drivers?	Our risk appetite metrics are based on our most important goals and value drivers, and as our key risk indicators are based on those risk appetite metrics, there is a continuous link between KRIs and goals/value drivers.
Are the key risk indicators scalable for all parts of the organization?	Yes, but it has not been easy to establish a set of scalable key risk indicators; it took a lot of time and effort, but has enabled us to have assurance in the drive to continuously improve competitive advantage.
Is there a system for escalating problems with compliance with the KRIs to the board?	Not only is there a system for escalating areas of non-conformance with the KRIs but we have a complete system of audit and reporting conformance and progress, as well as regular review of the KRIs, their relevance and levels to ensure that we continually challenge performance.

Notes

1 http://www.financialstabilityboard.org/publications/r_130212.pdf

2 http://www.tepco.co.jp/en/press/corp-com/release/betu12_e/images/120620e0102.pdf

3 http://www.theirm.org/publications/risk_appetite.html

4 http://businesscasestudies.co.uk/coca-cola-great-britain/who-dares-wins-success-through-intelligent-risk/who-dares-wins.html#ixzz2eUYLd2T7

5 http://yum.com/annualreport/

ERM culture, blame, boundaries and elephants in the room

Outline

Enterprise risk management is a very useful tool for banishing a blame culture that is brought about by a lack of clear boundaries, and for encouraging people to innovate and take managed threats and opportunities within those boundaries. ERM cultures are developed over time by carefully encouraging people to step outside themselves and to share common goals for managed threat and opportunity taking and risk-based decision making. To articulate those boundaries the risk appetite needs to be established from the top downwards and then people should be encouraged to take more managed threats and opportunities within the risk appetite of the team or business unit.

People's behaviour in taking managed risk within the boundaries established by risk appetite is predicated on their own sense of safety or comfort zone. We explore the link between managed risk taking, risk-based decision making, attitudes towards managing change and the work of Maslow and Herzberg where they explore people's propensity to work more collaboratively when they have satisfied their own basic safety needs.

In developing a healthy, managed risk culture, people need to understand the boundaries and management must respond appropriately when people get it wrong within those boundaries. The risk manager's role in this is to put in place the key risk indicators that measure how much risk is acceptable.

ERM cultures and the blame culture

An ERM culture has been described as encompassing the values, beliefs, knowledge and understanding about threats and opportunities shared by a group of people with a common purpose. This applies, in particular, to the employees of an organization or of teams or groups within an organization. It also applies in every industry and on an international basis. The Institute of Risk Management[1] proposes a simple ABC approach as helpful in understanding how culture, and hence risk culture, works in practice. Attitude, Behaviour and Culture are the ABC referred to here.

The culture in an organization arises from the repeated behaviour of its members. These behaviours are shaped by the underlying values, beliefs and attitudes of individuals, which are partly inherent but are also themselves influenced by the prevailing culture in the organization. Culture is therefore subject to 'cycles' that can self-reinforce in either virtuous, or vicious, circles. Culture is more than a statement of values – it relates to how these translate into concrete actions. Everyone will have had direct experience of the different cultures in different places of work, even in organizations apparently working in similar circumstances. We would expect to find that the culture of, for example, a utility company would contrast significantly with that of a manufacturer. Equally there could be cultural differences between two different manufacturers and two different utility companies.

'Risk culture' refines the concept of organizational culture to focus particularly on the collective ability to take managed risk and to minimize threats, but the wider organizational culture itself is an active backdrop determining, and itself influenced by, risk culture. Blame cultures exist where there is a lack of understanding of the boundaries in which individuals or groups of individuals can operate. Those boundaries are established by a distinct and consistent tone from the top in respect of managed risk taking, risk-based decision making and threat avoidance.

Boundaries are informed by the wider stakeholder requirements and the timing of threats and opportunities. Ethics can help in determining the longer-term impact of boundary setting and consideration of the wider stakeholder requirements.

When setting boundaries for managed risk taking and risk-based decision making, there needs to be a common acceptance throughout the organization of the importance of the continuous management of enterprise threats and opportunities, including clear accountability for and ownership of

CASE EXAMPLE JP Morgan Chase

In May 2012 JP Morgan Chase disclosed a multi-billion-dollar trading loss on its 'synthetic trading portfolio'. By its own admission the events that led to the company's losses included inadequate understanding by the traders of the risks they were taking; ineffective challenge of the traders' judgement by risk control functions; weak risk governance and inadequate scrutiny. According to the *New York Times,* individuals amassing huge trading positions were not effectively challenged, there were regular shouting matches and difficult personality issues.

specific risks and risk areas. This allows transparent and timely information that flows up and down the organization with bad news rapidly communicated without fear of blame. Risk event reporting and whistleblowing encourages learning from mistakes and near misses.

The board should be aware that there is no process or activity too large, too complex or too obscure for the threats and opportunities to be readily understood. This applies equally to strategic planning as it does to everyday operational threats and opportunities.

In avoiding blame cultures, appropriate risk taking behaviours should be rewarded and encouraged and inappropriate behaviours should be addressed and sanctioned. There should also be sufficient diversity of perspectives, values and beliefs to ensure that the status quo is consistently and rigorously challenged and the alignment of culture management with employee engagement and people strategy must ensure that people are supportive socially but also strongly focused on the task in hand.

Using risk appetite as a tool to destroy the blame culture

Using risk appetite, risk events and near misses as part of a learning culture (see Chapter 5) are some of the tools that can help break down and banish a blame culture. People bring to work their own attitude, behaviour and culture towards managed risk taking and risk-based decision making. Those are determined by a number of factors:

- individual propensity and personality;
- past experience;
- fear of being punished;
- fear of failure;
- expectation of success and associated reward;
- understanding of the expectations of the organization.

The organization can affect some of these, but individual propensity, personality and past experience cannot be changed. This is why the setting of boundaries is so important; this will affect in particular the fear of being punished and expectation of success and associated reward. By setting out clear boundaries and a context for these boundaries, this will help to change attitudes and behaviours and thereby change the culture of the organization.

The crucial link in all of this is that the organization sets out its risk appetite and within that the boundaries within which each individual can take managed risks without fear of punishment. It goes without saying that this needs to be reinforced strongly through repeated behaviour throughout the organization.

CASE STUDY   A true story (names have been changed)

The young officer waited outside his commanding officer's office. He was too nervous to be seated, much to the annoyance of the secretary who was trying to concentrate on a tricky piece of work.

A loud voice from within the office called 'Enter', and the young officer entered, saluted, and stood, willing himself to be still, his cap in hand while the commanding officer sat, still looking down at the papers before him. The commanding officer looked up. He proceeded to give the officer his next assignment, and then dismissed him, attending once more to his papers.

The young man still stood still. He was rigid with shock. The commanding officer looked up. 'Still here, Smith?' he asked. 'Is there something more you need?'

'Sir, I thought I was here to be disciplined over the recent occurrence?' His voice rose slightly at the end of the sentence as if to ask a question.

'Smith, you have just destroyed a valuable aeroplane by failing to put down the landing gear in time when you came in this morning. I've just spent a huge amount of money training you. I should think that that is enough training for one day. It will not happen again.'

Years later, that same young officer was himself the commanding officer. He never forgot that training lesson and used the story to explain, in his words, the fact that taking managed risk within boundaries would not be punished, but step outside those boundaries and there would be severe sanctions.

Managing risk

Encouraging people to take managed risk

Once the risk appetite boundaries have been established, one would think that it would be easy to persuade people to take managed risk within those boundaries. However, some people find it difficult to believe that they will not be punished if something goes wrong, even if it is within the given boundaries. Others might be tempted to test the boundaries.

Meredith Vaughan, President of Vladimir Jones, Colorado Springs[2]

One of the first questions our agency asks new clients is about tolerance for risk, both the marketer's personal view and the corporate perspective. This helps us understand how far we can push the work and how likely our strategic approach will ever see the light of day.

But we don't often ask ourselves the same question. What is our own tolerance for risk? We need to know. There is nothing worse, as one CMO I know says, than an agency that 'borrows a client's watch and tells him what time it is'. And that's what happens when the agency doesn't celebrate its own risk takers. Our willingness to take chances impacts both our work product and our agency environment.

For me, taking risks is incredibly difficult. With risk comes the possibility of failure, and I hate to fail. Yet I know that a successful agency must be a place where risky thinking can thrive. We have a saying at our agency: 'Wisdom makes you successful. Failure makes you wise.' This is easy for me to say – but harder for me to put into daily practice.

It's scary to celebrate a team for bringing a great idea to life that may not be the right solution today but could pay off at some undefined point in the future. How do we find the courage to do it? The key is to identify which type of failure is ok and which risks the agency is never willing to take.

Here are two categories of unacceptable risk at our agency:

1   Risk that is executional only and not based in a core insight designed to achieve our client's business objective. The work must respect the client and be grounded in smart, strategic business thinking.

2   Risk that jeopardizes the internal trust that develops when we are all working on the same team and for a common goal. It's a matter of showing people that they can think creatively, but within a commonly understood set of boundaries. Our canvas is pretty wide open, but it's never infinite. Internally we have to be on the same page about the canvas itself, though not necessarily the colors (sic) we will paint with, or the design we will create.

As creative people, we are a bit like children who crave a little discipline in order to be at our best. And, like kids, we are most creative when we are free to be fearless.

Some people become technical experts within their comfort zone but those who rise to be CEOs are the ones who are prepared to break eggs to make omelettes. But CEOs need to get the most out of others in the organization, and that means encouraging people to work outside their comfort zones and to become entrepreneurs in their own areas of expertise.

People's fear of acting outside their comfort zone makes them look for someone to tell them what to do. We also call this not sticking their neck out, or keeping their head below the parapet. It causes the organization to stagnate, stall and even falter. Conversely, if there is clear and transparent encouragement for people to take the initiative and act by taking managed threats and opportunities, then innovation can take place and people can be stretched to achieve more and more. A really good analogy for this is the study of the behaviour of buffaloes and geese.

Leadership, buffaloes and geese

Buffaloes follow the herd. The leader is the strongest male and the rest of the herd blindly follows where he leads. Native Americans were able to catch huge herds of buffaloes simply by driving the leader towards a cliff. As the leader jumped over, the rest of the herd followed and crashed to their deaths. A tick box approach to ERM through mandates, rules and sanctions will develop buffaloes in the organization.

Conversely, when geese fly, they do so in a V formation, taking turns to be leader. When the lead goose gets tired, it rotates back into the formation and another goose flies at the point position. The geese practise being in the lead and can take that position as long as they are able. The stronger the goose, the longer it can stay in front. An organization that encourages its people to become managed risk takers is encouraging people to be like geese, where they will take the lead in certain situations, then fall back to let others take the lead.

CASE EXAMPLE from the author's experience

As the director responsible for operations in a financial services organization, I became a 'goose' when I had to disobey a direct instruction from the US chairman;

We had been implementing a multimillion dollar IT system in the organization. The business was a 24/7 operation supporting thousands of clients who were relying on the service, each second of each day.

The new system was to replace the main operating system and we had experienced the usual hiccups along the way, but were essentially on time and on budget. The switch-over time was coming up, and I realized that the project team were planning on implementing a straight switch-over from the old system to the new with no period of parallel running or testing. They explained that the contingency time had all been used up and the US chairman had threatened huge penalties if the project ran over.

So I picked up the phone and asked to be put through to the US chairman, whom I had only briefly met; I was sure he was not aware of me so far down the pecking order. He took my call. I explained briefly what the situation was and that my decision was to have three days of parallel running, which would mean that the project would be delayed by three days. I was prepared to argue with him if he proposed to countermand this decision, and I was also prepared to be fired for the decision because I felt strongly that I was not prepared to allow the business to be put on the line for the sake of three days. To my great surprise, he agreed that it was the best decision and he sanctioned the delay, but reset the boundaries with some other mutterings about the consequences of not incurring further delays!

A few weeks later I received a package at work. It was a book called *Flight of the Buffalo: Soaring to excellence, learning to let employees lead,* and there was a compliment slip from the US chairman's office. Alas there was no accompanying pay rise, but it did make me feel good to be recognized for being a goose.

The link between managed risk taking, mice, Maslow and Herzberg

The IRM model of culture change[3] sets out the theory that sociability and solidarity are the two keys to identifying what needs to change in the culture of the organization to develop a healthy risk culture; see Figure 6.1.

The IRM explains that the best position for an enterprise culture that encourages people to be entrepreneurs in their own field of expertise is in the top right-hand quadrant. People have a communal approach to what they do, valuing others as much as themselves and are highly motivated by the task, shared goals and mutual benefits.

These concepts of sociability and solidarity present echoes of Maslow's 'hierarchy of needs' and the subsequent Herzberg work which both present the theory that for an individual to start thinking about the greater good of fellow humans and working in a more networked, communal way, they need to feel safe; in other words, they should not feel threatened in terms of their job or home.[4]

If people feel that they are a part of the team, they do things for each other because they want to and there are common tasks, shared goals and mutual and fairly distributed benefits, then there will be a communal approach and acceptance of managed risk taking and risk-based decision making within the boundaries set by the risk appetite. Maslow and Herzberg put forward

FIGURE 6.1   IRM model of culture; sociability versus solidarity

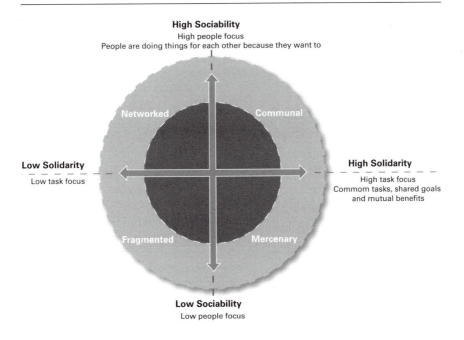

the idea that once people feel that they have a secure job, house, family and friends they are then ready to make the next leap and work for the good of others. So, to encourage a communal approach to managed risk taking, it's not good enough to set common tasks and shared goals; people have got to feel safe and secure. That means that if people take managed risks, within the given boundaries, and it doesn't work out, then they must not be punished, threatened or made to feel in any way unsafe.

This is tough in the brutal business world where the prevailing attitude is that if we screw up then we move towards the door, if not get pushed right out of it. This is not to say that there should be a group hug every time someone messes up within the rules (or indeed takes a managed risk within the boundaries set by risk appetite), but there does need to be a carefully managed conversation that draws out the lessons to be learnt, perhaps re-establishes or re-negotiates the boundaries, at the same time as makes the individual or group feel secure.

Developing a risk culture has to take cognizance of the art of managing change and the differing management styles that are needed. One of the themes of the book *Who Moved My Cheese?* by Spencer Johnson is 'what would you do if you were not afraid?' This book, the story of two mice and two little men, is about change management; people's ability to participate

> I knew that I'd cottoned onto a good thing when my new boss explained that he wasn't the kind of guy that was going to be there giving lots of guidance.
>
> 'I don't expect you to come to me for permission,' he said, 'just come and beg forgiveness.'
>
> I pondered this for some time before responding to him: 'At what point does forgiveness stop and become a foot behind my back?'
>
> 'When you lose more than one quarter's profit.' He answered right back at me; no hesitation and no flicker of the eye contact.
>
> This was a guy who said he didn't understand risk management, but in that instant I realized he knew exactly what risk management was and he had just explained the risk appetite for setting the boundaries within which I could take managed risk.

in change is based on their own propensity and approach to changes going on around them. It explains how to anticipate people's approaches towards culture change and how to respond to those who are resistant to change.

In encouraging a managed risk taking culture, it is useful to ask that question: 'What would you do if you were not afraid?' not only of ourselves, but to ask it constantly of others. Too often our response towards enterprise risk is based on the threat rather than the opportunity, and senior management need to ensure that they show by example that taking managed risk within boundaries is acceptable and to be celebrated, even if it goes wrong.

All of this talk about taking managed risk within boundaries becomes tricky when we look at the world of internal controls. Does your heart sink when you think about how your Sarbanes-Oxley controls (if you are subject to them) potentially destroy innovation and entrepreneurialism in the organization? Well if so, do something about it. Internal controls can be just as likely to respond to well managed risk taking within boundaries if they are designed with opportunity as well as threat in mind.

Links to remuneration

All corporate governance codes incorporate requirements regarding remuneration structures, because it is good practice to provide a link between risk and reward. It is a given fact that individuals can make bad decisions and affect the whole organization if their remuneration structure is inappropriate.

I was asked to do some work with a financial services organization some years ago where the sales team were remunerated purely based on volume. The risk management team were able to analyse the fact that all of the business sold in the previous five years was unprofitable.

Business was good, and growth was healthy, but profitability was dropping away alarmingly. So we came up with some solutions where the sales people's remuneration was based on the profitability of the product. We were able to produce a practical solution so they could conduct their pricing, in real time, based on the risk factors we analysed as being the key to profitability. We used pre-programmed hand-held computers and trained the sales people on their use. The business turned around and profitability increased by 100 per cent within six months of that decision.

Sometimes it is difficult to see a direct link between risk and remuneration, particularly if the threat or opportunity is 'long tail' – ie, it takes a long time to transpire or mature – or the control/enhancement of the risk is outside the control of the individual or even the organization. These are not valid reasons to avoid the subject; there are other mechanisms that can be put in place that focus an individual's attention on the risk aspects of their decisions.

A 2013 survey conducted by Towers Watson[5] reported that a third of insurance risk executives globally are unhappy with the links between executive compensation and risk management, but have no plans to change the current approach. The survey asked 539 senior insurance executives, including chief risk officers, CFOs and chief actuaries, about the progress and development of ERM activity within their companies.

Extract: *Insurance Networking News*, April 2013

'Insurers firmly believe that a stronger risk culture will add value to their organizations, but achieving full implementation requires a progressive approach over a sustained period,' said Mike Wilkinson, a director of the insurance management consultancy at Towers Watson. 'Aligning remuneration to risk can only be introduced once expectations have been established. Underpinning progress through performance management techniques and appropriate incentives is an important part of the process.'

'Responsibility for risk management lies squarely with boards and senior executives: communicating risk appetite and setting expectations on risk-taking. They need to live and breathe the risk culture, so we find it surprising that so many insurers appear to be shying away from taking the next step of linking pay to risk-related return metrics,' Wilkinson said. 'External stakeholder pressure to ensure employee incentives are better aligned with the long-term health of their companies will only intensify.'

There must be adequate systems of measurement to ensure that when boundaries are breached this is brought to the attention of senior management and boards. Establishing these systems of measurement and implementing them is firmly in the domain of the risk manager.

The elephant in the room and conduct risk

The expression 'the elephant in the room' refers to the great big item that everyone knows about, everyone can see, but no one talks about. It is a gaping hole that absorbs energy, holds up innovation and progress and, worse still, when it's owned up to it's going to show up a heap of problems, and the longer it goes on the more mess it's creating. Perhaps it is there because it's a favourite project of the CEO, or because there is some essential history attached to it, or perhaps we are making some great short-term gains from it.

On 12 February 2002 Donald Rumsfeld, at a press briefing where he addressed the absence of evidence linking the government of Iraq with the supply of weapons of mass destruction to terrorist groups said:

There are known knowns; there are things we know that we know. There are known unknowns; that is to say, there are things that we now know we don't know. But there are also unknown unknowns – there are things we do not know we don't know.

The expression can be set out in the form of a quadrant placing the verb – 'to know or not to know' against the nouns 'knowns and unknowns'.

FIGURE 6.2 Known knowns and known unknowns

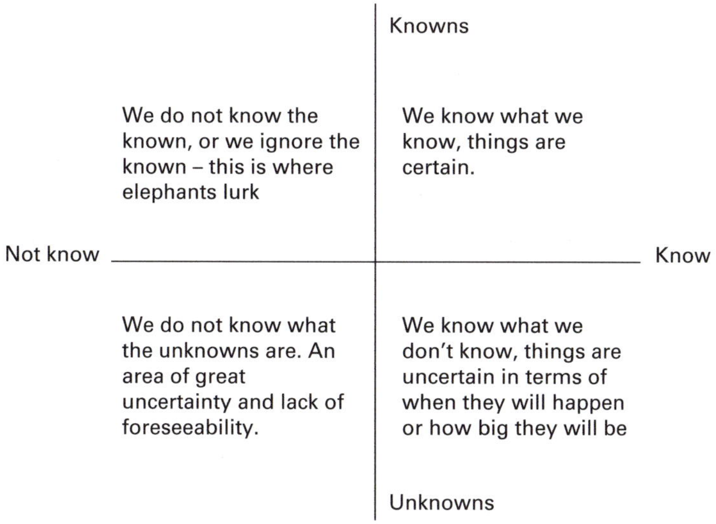

Rumsfeld talked about three of the parts of the quadrant: known knowns, known unknowns and unknown unknowns. There is a fourth quadrant – the 'not known knowns' – or in plain English the area where there is a common thing that is known but everyone ignores it – we do not know that we know it (see Figure 6.2).

This area of common knowledge that is ignored is sometimes the one thing that can bring the organization to its knees. For example, the UK payment protection insurance (PPI) scandal is one where many knew what was going on, but ignored it because they were delivering results for their employer.

CASE EXAMPLE PPI scandal in the UK

Initially when banks in the UK turned to expanding their product offering to their customers and in particular sold payment protection insurance (PPI) to huge swathes of unsuitable recipients of the product (such as the elderly, the unemployed and others who would never be able to claim the benefit), they concentrated too much on the short-term gain and ignored the longer-term effect on their business. Many people in the banks knew that the practice was going on, but they ignored it.

Publicly the banks were applauded for improving their margins, and risk analysis of the threats and opportunities would have found that in the short term, the opportunities outweighed the threats. This was a naive approach that failed to take into consideration the longer-term effect of selling a product that was not benefiting the majority of customers, many of whom were unable to make successful claims.

It has resulted since in the opprobrium of the regulators and a massive compensation programme for customers. This has been a huge cost to the banks in terms of fines from the regulator, the cost of the compensation, the administration and the loss of trust.

Conduct risk management is now very much in favour for preventing such things from happening and to avoid 'elephants in the room' from taking root in the culture of the organization. Businesses are forced to look through their books to identify products and sales practices that could come under the spotlight in the future. They need to go beyond how the product is sold to whether it meets customers' needs throughout the lifetime of the product, starting with product design and ending with post-sale service. We would call this 'managing the conduct risk throughout the product lifecycle'. The regulators have become very interested in this because the 'elephant in the room' can create a systemic risk for industry:

CASE EXAMPLE   FCA

As Martin Wheatley, now CEO of the Financial Conduct Authority (FCA), highlighted during his speech at the British Bankers Association Annual Banking Conference in October 2012, the FCA will also have a renewed focus on conduct in wholesale markets: 'This is because we realize there is a connection between what happens in retail and wholesale markets – and the risks caused by poor wholesale conduct can be passed between them.'

You only have to look at the impact that the banking scandal has had on the reputation of the entire banking industry to see that the conduct agenda extends far beyond simply ensuring that banks are transparent about the products that they sell.

Example of a conduct risk statement adapted from the ERM COSO Application Techniques

Illustrative overview from code of conduct

Our values

- The best solutions come from working together with colleagues and clients.

- Effective teamwork requires relationships, respect and sharing.

- Delivering what we promise and adding value beyond what is expected.

- Ensuring quality for the ultimate customer for the whole lifetime of the product.

- We achieve excellence through innovation, learning and agility.

- Leading with clients, leading with people and thought leadership.

- Leadership demands courage, vision and integrity.

Upholding the (firm) name

- Our clients and colleagues trust (firm) based on our professional competence and integrity – qualities that underpin our reputation. We uphold that reputation.

- We seek to serve only those clients whom we are competent to serve, who value our service and who meet appropriate standards of legitimacy and integrity.

- When speaking in a forum in which audiences would reasonably expect that we are speaking as a representative of (firm), we generally state only (firm) view and not our own.

- We use all assets belonging to (firm) and to our clients, including tangible, intellectual and electronic assets, in a manner both responsible and appropriate to the business and only for legal and authorized purposes.

Behaving professionally

- We deliver professional services in accordance with (firm) policies and relevant technical and professional standards.

- We uphold and comply with the standards of corporate governance set out in the organization.

- We offer only those services we can deliver and strive to deliver no less than our commitments.

- We compete vigorously, engaging only in practices that are legal and ethical.

- We meet our contractual obligations and report and charge honestly for our services.

- We respect the confidentiality and privacy of our clients, our people and others with whom we do business. Unless authorized, we do not use confidential information for personal use, (firm's) benefit or to benefit a third party. We disclose confidential information or personal data only when necessary, and when appropriate approval to do so has been obtained, and/or we are compelled to do so by legal, regulatory or professional requirements.

- We aim to avoid conflicts of interest. Where potential conflicts are identified and we believe that the respective parties' interests can be properly safeguarded by the implementation of appropriate procedures, we will implement such procedures.

- We treasure our independence of mind. We protect our clients' and other stakeholders' trust by adhering to our regulatory and professional standards, which are designed to enable us to achieve the objectivity necessary in our work. In doing so, we strive to ensure our independence is not compromised or perceived to be compromised. We address circumstances that impair or could appear to impair our objectivity.

- When faced with difficult issues or issues that place (firm) at risk, we consult appropriate (firm) individuals before taking action. We follow our applicable technical and administrative consultation requirements.

- It is unacceptable for us to receive or pay bribes.

Respecting others

- We treat our colleagues, clients and others with whom we do business with respect, dignity, fairness and courtesy.

- We take pride in the diversity of our workforce and view it as a competitive advantage to be nurtured and expanded.

- We are committed to maintaining a work environment that is free from discrimination or harassment.

- We try to balance work and private life and help others to do the same.

- We invest in the ongoing enhancement of our skills and abilities.

- We provide a safe working environment for our people.

Corporate citizenship

- We express support for fundamental human rights and avoid participating in business activities that abuse human rights.

- We act in a socially responsible manner, within the laws, customs and traditions of the countries in which we operate, and contribute in a responsible manner to the development of communities.

- We aspire to act in a manner that minimizes the detrimental environmental impacts of our business operations.

- We encourage the support of charitable, educational and community service activities.

- We are committed to supporting international and local efforts to eliminate corruption and financial crime.

This kind of statement would be different for each organization and each industry, with the financial services industry concentrating much more on financial conduct aspects than the cultural aspects shown here.

In the public interest

Most people will have heard of 'whistleblowing' from the high-profile cases reported in the media. Following the recent economic crisis there have been numerous examples of whistleblowing in the financial and banking sector and many examples within health care and social care. Whistleblowing is when an employee or worker provides certain types of information, usually to the employer or a regulator, which has come to his or her attention through work. The disclosure may be about the alleged wrongful conduct of the employer, or about the conduct of a fellow employee, client, or any third party. The whistleblower is usually not directly, personally affected by the danger or illegality, although he or she may be. Whistleblowing is therefore 'making a disclosure in the public interest' and occurs when a worker raises a concern about danger or illegality that affects others, for example members of the public.

However, although in many jurisdictions whistleblowers are protected under law from employer retaliation, there have been many cases where punishment for whistleblowing has occurred, such as termination, suspension, demotion, wage garnishment, and/or harsh mistreatment by other employees. For example, in the United States most whistleblower protection laws provide for limited 'make whole' remedies or damages for employment losses if whistleblower retaliation is proven. Many whistleblowers report that there exists a widespread 'shoot the messenger' mentality in corporations or government agencies accused of misconduct and in some cases whistleblowers have been subjected to criminal prosecution in reprisal for reporting wrongdoing, in spite of the legal protection.

To protect the public interest, and the long-term interest of customers, there must therefore be an overt programme in the ERM programme to encourage openness and frank whistleblowing with guarantees of protection for the messenger, as part of the risk culture. Similarly, other regulations that are in the public interest such as anti-money laundering and preventing the financing of terrorist activities should be included in the risk culture programme.

Questions for senior management and the board to ask

(Including model answers based on best practice – at a high maturity level.)

Do we know whether we have a blame culture?	We do regular cultural surveys both formal and informal to establish how comfortable people feel when taking managed risk.

How do we measure the risk culture in the organization?	We have a risk culture measurement tool that we run as an online questionnaire.
Do we establish clear managed risk-taking boundaries that are set by our risk appetite?	Yes, each division, business unit and team is given clear boundaries that they then translate into boundaries for individuals.
Do we ensure that we behave appropriately if people fail when they take managed risk within the set boundaries?	Yes, but this was difficult to achieve and we are still making adjustments to the culture; the balance between failing to take managed risk within the boundaries, taking too much risk (taking it outside the boundaries) and failures of judgement about how much risk is too much is a very tricky one to establish in practice. So we are implementing this slowly in the organization, tackling the most important areas first.
Do we manage culture change well?	Yes, we are good at managing culture change and recognize that it requires a different skills set than the one required when managing the status quo.
Do we understand the conduct risk inherent in the business model and future strategy, and can we explain how we manage it?	Yes, we have articulated the behaviours that are appropriate for ensuring that conduct within the organization is suitable for the lifetime of the product and we have carried out a complete audit of appropriate behaviours that are compatible with our code of conduct statement.
Can we demonstrate that we make 'good' rather than 'unsustainable' profits?	Yes. While we are driven on returns to our stakeholders, we have taken radical steps through our ERM programme to ensure that we do not

support short-term gains or profits that are at the expense of long-term sustainability of our relationships with our stakeholders.

Do we know if there are products or services in the portfolio that were compliant when sold but could be the focus of retrospective investigation in the future?

Yes and no. We regularly conduct a risk assessment of our past product portfolio and the level of sustainability of those products if they are still within their 'lifetime'. But we don't know what we don't know in terms of how our longer-term products will be regarded in the future as technology and attitudes change.

How will we bring customers into the product design process to make sure we understand their needs and can deliver a fair deal?

We already involve customers in the design process and indeed we encourage all our staff to be 'customers' through product discounting. By encouraging our staff to be 'customers' we get fast feedback about their needs and ideas for future enhancements and new products.

How do we determine whether customers understand what they're being sold and whether it meets their real needs on an ongoing basis?

While we include as much product knowledge and information in our packaging as we can, there is no substitute for the ongoing improvement of our sales staff. We have an active after-sales service that includes tracking the effectiveness of our products in meeting customers' needs and we involve sales staff in the knowledge and information-gathering process so that they learn continuously. We also have an active online support service from which we develop lists of FAQ (frequently asked questions) that are then fed back into the sales team's ongoing training.

Do we have a risk culture that encourages openness and supports people in speaking out in the interest of the business, the customers and the wider public?

We are not satisfied in just issuing a whistleblowing policy; we actively implement culture changes like the implementation of a whistleblowing policy as part of our ongoing culture shift project. We test the level of openness through top-down and bottom-up quarterly briefings as well as a host of other communication projects, including shadowing by senior management of operational staff for one compulsory week per year, and have even tested the level of openness by planting reportable incidents and testing to see how many reports come through. We go further than a static reporting system and we reward appropriate openness while discouraging 'fake openness' or the deliberate creation of reportable incidents by the person reporting them.

Notes

1 http://www.theirm.org/documents/Risk_Culture_A5_WEB15_Oct_2012.pdf

2 http://adage.com/article/small-agency-diary/risk-taking-key-creativity-boundaries/230241/

3 IRM Paper on Risk Culture; http://www.theirm.org/documents/Risk_Culture_A5_WEB15_Oct_2012.pdf

4 For more on this, see www.businessballs.com/leadership-management.htm

5 http://www.insurancenetworking.com/news/insurers-linking-exec-pay-risk-related-return-metrics-32149-1.html

Embedding and integrating ERM 07

Outline

Embedding risk management means that it is integrated with all other aspects of management, and that needs a culture change approach similar to any other culture change programme. To achieve this integration requires that it is led from the top and implemented in a structured way with ownership, clear deliverables and measurements. A clear road map and structure approach that is energized by a dedicated ERM team will help to ensure that the 'embedding' happens, and would clarify who measures and reports on successes and failures in a clear and transparent way.

ERM should be dynamic and responsive to change, tailored to the organization and to its business units, and given ownership in each of the three lines of play (otherwise called three lines of defence). The proof it is embedded is when it becomes a part of the way in which we do things round here – or an unconscious competence. In this chapter we set out a 16-point road map for embedding ERM on two scales: what we need to do, and how we do it.[1]

What does embedding mean?

There is a great deal of confusion as to what 'embedded enterprise risk management' means. Some think that it means that the standards are all met, and others maintain that when ERM is embedded, there are no failures or losses. In essence, embedding enterprise risk management means that ERM is integrated with every aspect of management activity – it is part of the psyche of the organization and eventually is practised with unconscious competence. Embedding ERM means that it happens without people having to think about it; in other words it needs to be integrated into all the business practices *and* the culture of the organization.

Integrating ERM into all the business practices and the culture will reduce uncertainty and enable better decision making, but it does not mean that uncertainties in the threats and opportunities will not arise. Only ceasing in business will guarantee no surprises. As with all other forms of good practice, ERM should be a fundamental part of good management and decision making at all levels of an organization. ERM that operates in a silo, where there is a tick-box mentality towards it and it only happens when someone checks the boxes, will not contribute to driving value and long-term resilience in the organization. Each aspect of risk management within the overarching ERM wheel might be seen as the sole repository for risk management expertise and too often pride and obstinacy prevent professionals from talking to each other. This means that silos of risk management build up within ERM and that's not good for business.

There is a fine balance between recognizing, respecting and valuing the difference between and the professionalism within these areas of risk management, and destroying them while trying to bring them all together under one ERM banner. It is true that they cannot continue as silos, entirely separate from each other, but it is also true that they cannot be subsumed into each other because the knowledge of the business, the techniques used and the measures of success are all so very different.

If you take an old and well established bank for example, its credit risk management team will be operating credit risk management techniques based on decades or even centuries of experience, data and skills. Conversely the operational risk management team might be less than five years old. An animal feed manufacturer will have a formulations and product design team that have decades of risk management expertise, but a brand new project risk management team. Embedding ERM does not mean that these teams need to stop what they are doing, but the best of what they do should be captured and shared to develop a consistent ERM language and approach, albeit the approach might look and feel different in each team.

To facilitate this consistency and cross-fertilization of tools, techniques and knowledge, some organizations use secondments from one team to another, shared learning, and getting them to audit each other for such aspects as compliance and risk management maturity. Having all the teams assist in putting together the one ERM operating model and then measuring the frameworks and policies against that model will give ownership and shared respect between the teams.

ERM should not operate in isolation but needs to be built into existing decision-making structures and processes so as to support planning, priority setting, programme management, financial reporting, audits and evaluations, the development of corporate business plans, business continuity, operations and performance assessment and other key functions throughout an organization. Embedding ERM in an organization's structures and programmes using a consistent risk management process creates a cohesive integrated risk-based decision making environment.

When considering embedding ERM, one could view it as any change management exercise: it needs top level support, there needs to be a good business case setting out the value of doing it (and the costs), there must be clear outcomes or goals for doing it, a well-defined action plan built around stakeholder requirements, with clear ownership and accountability, good communication and performance measurements for success, and a systematic approach for alignment with the culture. All of those elements need to be in place for a successful culture change. Table 7.1 summarizes the key components of embedding ERM.

Main aspects of embedding ERM

There are four main aspects of integrating ERM (see Table 7.2):

1 It is led from the top.
2 There is clear ownership in each of the three lines of play (see later in this chapter).
3 It is driven with energy.
4 There is continuous measurement.

Senior management will see from this list that this could apply to any management discipline such as cost reduction, project management, customer relations or diversity.

Figure 7.1 shows how the four aspects of embedding or integrating ERM can be expanded and the attributes that need to be demonstrated at each level.

1. Led from the top

This is about ensuring that there is executive and board-level support for the programme, maintained over time. Leaders should challenge and be demanding, rather than just saying the right things occasionally. Evidence

TABLE 7.1 Aspects of successful and unsuccessful efforts in embedding ERM

Successful Embedding of ERM	Unsuccessful Embedding of ERM
Embedding ERM is established when the following are in place:	*Consequence if they are not in place:*
Top management commitment and support	Lack of leadership or sponsorship
Compelling business case	Benefits not clarified
Clear shared vision for ERM	Direction or focus lacking
Realistic goals for embedding ERM	Unrealistic goals
Well-defined action plan for embedding ERM	Road map missing or unclear
Stakeholder involvement and support	Imposed on stakeholders without taking them into consideration, run as a tick-box exercise
Accountability for results	Lack of ownership
Managing the communications and culture	There is no endorsement for embedding ERM
Systematic approach to integrating ERM into the business activities	ERM remains in a silo or there is a chaotic approach towards integrating it
Aligning performance measurements	Outcomes not measured or inappropriately measured
Aligning the ERM programme and culture with overall organizational culture	No alignment

of embedding would include board and management committee minutes, staff magazines, websites and business plans. The sponsorship from the top should be consistent and visible, but also pertinent to the goals and value drivers of the business.

FIGURE 7.1 Main aspects of embedding enterprise risk management

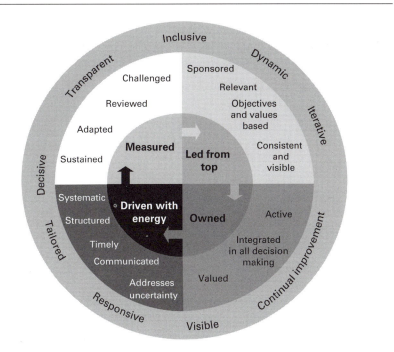

2. Owned

In all three lines of play there should be ownership, pride and commitment in driving continuous improvement. The board and senior management must own the leadership role for ERM. If someone is a 'risk owner' or a 'control (enhancer) owner', he or she should positively feel the accountabilities of ownership, and this should be linked to his or her performance management and reward. This could be evidenced through performance reviews, personal objectives and remuneration committee minutes. The ERM team own the framework for implementing, measuring and reporting on progress in ERM and should actively energize and track progress. Internal audit own and energize the assurance process.

For this ownership to be embedded, ERM needs to be integrated into the organization, not as a separate entity or function. It needs to be a core discipline integrated into day-to-day business processes and activities to gain any long-term traction. Is ERM considered to be part of the business planning, budgeting and strategy-setting cycle, and can this be evidenced? How is risk factored into new product launches or acquisition due diligence?

TABLE 7.2 Key attributes and principles of integrating ERM

Main aspect of ERM being integrated	Attributes that apply to *each* aspect of ERM being integrated	Attributes that apply to *all* aspects of ERM being integrated
Led from the top	• Leaders clearly sponsor activity • Leadership consistent and visible • It is relevant to the objectives and values of the business	
Owned	• Active • Valued • Integrated in all decision making	• Dynamic • Iterative • Supporting continual improvement
Driven with energy	• Systematic • Timely • Structured • Communicated • Clearly addressing uncertainty	• Visible • Responsive • Tailored • Transparent • Decisive
Measured	• Challenged • Adapted • Sustained • Reviewed	

Increasingly organizations are turning to risk-based decision making and management practices so that enterprise risk management becomes integrated with all other aspects of management.

Ownership is achieved by getting people to take on the new behaviour in the way they do things. There are extensive psychological explanations as to how you get people to change their behaviour for good, but when it becomes a part of the DNA of the culture and the behaviour exhibited, a part of the collective unconscious competence, then you will have a more innovative and enabled organization.

The outcomes of ERM also need to be valued. Do management value the outcomes such as risk information and business impact analysis reports? Do they take pride in the quality of the process and outcomes? Do they give feedback from their reviews? Do they request more information, or improvements in the reports? Are they impatient to drive improvement and make it even better, or do they want to get through that agenda item as quickly as possible? In some ways this is the 'golden test'. If this test is passed, it is likely the others have had to be addressed to some meaningful level. Evidence might include the extent to which management are constantly driving and demanding improvement in risk management information and support.

Enterprise risk management has to have the ownership of management and staff at every level. That requires making sure that there are both

---

CASE EXAMPLE from the author's experience

For three years I had diligently completed the board report on the performance of customer complaints and claims that fell into the business units' budgets. These reports were also required by our insurers, but seeing a positive downward trend in the frequency and cost of these complaints, the insurers suggested that they no longer required the intelligence.

I had never had any feedback from the board on these reports so I stopped compiling them. It took two years before the CEO said to me one day, 'What happened to those reports you used to do?' I smiled sweetly at him and replied, 'Were they ever of any use to you?' He shrugged and smiled wryly. We both knew that he'd never read them, so it didn't need any response. But he surprised me by asking, 'But how do we know that there are no underlying problems? When you compiled the reports I didn't read them, but I knew that you were tracking the situation and would have raised anything that we needed to be aware of or respond to.' I reassured him that I still tracked the situation and was happy with the risk management being conducted. He nodded and thanked me for the assurance but requested that I re-commenced sending a quarterly assurance statement, even it was just a short memo.

From this conversation grew a highly sophisticated ERM dashboard reporting process that was developed with the board, who had a real sense of ownership of the outputs and were constantly raising requests for more information.

incentives for taking ownership and sanctions for failing to take owner-ship, and therefore managed risk taking must be linked to the remuneration structure.

3. Driven with energy

There needs to be a systematic, timely and structured approach to creating the programme, gaining ownership and buy-in to the programme-related proc-esses as well as ensuring that it is communicated. This requires that outcomes are visible and actively discussed. We can't embed things if they are a closely guarded secret. People need to talk about risks as uncertainties and the out-comes of risk frameworks and processes. ERM needs to be on the agenda, and openly and transparently discussed. Clearly communication takes many forms, not all of which are open to evidence, but examples of evidence might include cascaded communication, intranet sites and meeting minutes.

We refer to the ERM team who would be expected to drive the enterprise risk management programme, but this is often successfully driven by other departments, such as internal audit. (See Chapter 11 on roles for leading and managing ERM.)

4. Measured

There must be some point to enterprise risk management, otherwise it's not worth doing. Measuring the successes and failures of the ERM programme, challenging and reviewing for the next stage of adapting ERM, are all part ensuring continuous improvement for managed risk taking.

Managed risk taking is a challenge, which, according to Charles Tscham-pion of General Motors,[2] 'is to first not take more risk than we need to generate the return that is offered'. The whole premise of managed risk tak-ing is in the word 'managed'. To know that the risk taking is managed there needs to be a form of measurement of the overall impact of risk that is being taken against the capacity of the organization to bear it. So we should not take more risk than we need to; conversely, we should take as much risk as we can bear. Measuring risk taking requires not only measuring the outputs of ERM, but also the value of risk up to and including the worst possible outcomes of threats and the best possible outcomes of opportunities (see Chapter 12 regarding valuing risk).

If there is a discipline and framework behind the production of the regu-lar risk dashboards, and the bases for measurement, forecasting and calcula-tions are set out clearly, there is the opportunity for challenge and audit of the programme, processes and outputs as well as the basis for refreshing the programme. This discipline and programme also provides sustainability in the ERM programme as there is not one area that is totally reliant on one person and can be replicated.

ERM might be the subject of the moment, but if it does not inform significant management decisions then it is largely window-dressing. We need to constantly ask ourselves, 'What was the last decision that was actively influenced by risk information?' The most obvious source of evidence would include risk dashboards, minutes of management decisions, and papers supporting business proposals.

Wider aspects of embedding ERM

The following list of attributes should be applied to all aspects of ERM:

- *Dynamic, responsive, tailored and iterative* – it should be responsive to internal and external change and to the climate that the organization is in.

- *Supporting continual improvement* – embedding ERM should support continuous improvement of all aspects of the organization's activities from strategic risk-based decision making to monitoring in the factory (see Chapter 14 on quality management systems).

- *Visible and transparent* – to succeed it should be overt and transparent to all in the organization and in today's business environment, that could mean using all possible methods, from online real-time reporting on the company intranet to using notice boards to post key ERM dashboards.

- *Decisive* – it should influence key decisions and strategies as well as providing a joined-up process by which senior management can see the aggregated effect of threats and opportunities on the capacity of the organization to sustain those risks.

Conscious and unconscious competence

The evidence that ERM is embedded is that it becomes a part of the way we do things around here; an unconscious competence.

The four stages of competence set out logical phases for how learning develops in our consciousness and how we develop skills that we exercise but don't have to think about. Embedding risk management into the culture means that it needs to be part of the unconscious competence range of skills for all in the organization. That requires a deliberate approach to getting ERM under the skin of everyone in the organization, into the DNA of the thought process and a part of every decision-making process.

None of that happens overnight; changing cultures takes time, effort and recognition that it's a journey rather than an end point. When ERM becomes part of the organizational culture, there will be fewer uncertainties and when they do arise the organization will be more resilient and able to respond to them.

A 16-step plan for embedding ERM

The following is an example of a road map for ensuring that enterprise risk management is improving in the organization based on asking 'Where are we?' 'Where do we want to be?' and 'How do we get there?'[3]

The following aspects form a programme of key success factors:

1 Issue: What's the issue?

2 Success: What does success look like?

3 Evidence: How will we know it when we see it?

4 Metrics: What precisely are we measuring?

5 Target: What's our target? By when, or in what timeframe?

6 Map: What are the enablers and route map?

7 Status: How are we doing against the plan?

8 Plan: What's the plan for getting to where we want to be?

There are eight aspects of ERM that might be included in the above plan:

9 Appetite: The capacity and appetite for taking managed risk.

10 Risk and capital: The opportunities and threats facing the organization and the capital to support that.

11 Stakeholders: Stakeholders' expectations.

12 Structure: Policy and framework.

13 People: Roles, accountabilities and reward/sanctions.

14 Controls/enhancers: Risk action plans for mitigating threats and enhancing opportunities.

15 Competencies: Risk competence and behaviours.

16 Maturity: Risk maturity.

These 16 aspects can be mapped against each other to form a plan of action for regular update and reporting, such as in Table 7.3. Some aspects have been completed as an illustration. We suggest that by using SMART[4] principles, success is more likely. (Go to www.koganpage.com/practicalerm to download an online tool to help you to do this in practice.)

To illustrate this, the following case study sets out a real example of how one aspect of ERM was embedded in the culture of an organization using a process of identifying key success factors.

The implementation of an embedded enterprise risk management culture is linked to the maturity of the risk approach in the organization (see Chapter 8 on maturity models) and the interaction between operational management, those in the ERM team and internal audit, or the three lines of play (see overleaf).

CASE EXAMPLE embedding ERM

The instruction to implement an environmental programme throughout the $3 billion organization presented quite a challenge. There were many issues to consider because of the diversity of businesses, geographical locations and cultures. This was a business that was highly decentralized; there were few edicts from the top and the businesses were expected to innovate and run themselves within the boundaries created, which were purely based on expected return on capital.

The main concern that I had was how to get buy-in from the businesses and local ownership to make this happen. The corporate vision had been established at the senior managers conference the previous year and was constructed with everyone's input. I knew this, because I too had been involved and had persuaded the collective audience to accept a statement on corporate social responsibility, making grand statements about how it would be good for business and setting out some key success factors for environmental risk management. Talk about having made a rod for my own back!

The 300 separate businesses in more than 45 different countries responded with enthusiasm during the long two years of work. We built a measuring tool for each business that calculated the environmental impact of every aspect of the business, from the indirect and direct sourcing, work on site, outputs and logistics. Each aspect was examined to build a profile of the expected or desired environmental performance against the actual performance.

Within a few weeks of starting the process, unit managers were reporting lower fuel costs and savings, just by engaging their people in measuring how much fuel and energy were being used. The ideas that people were coming up with for saving energy were hugely inventive, and the sheer number of ideas at the commencement of the programme was an indication that staff had been thinking of this ahead of management in this instance. One business was able to engage an especially active political group to help in the process of evaluation, which converted the group from negative campaigners to positive supporters.

At the senior managers conference two years later, the chairman himself presented the outputs of the programme, which we had measured using a number of key success factors, with pride and enthusiasm.

The three lines of play

We have previously referred to the concept of the three lines of play, often called the 'three lines of defence'. Intuitively, if we accept that risk is both positive and negative, calling them lines of 'defence' cannot be the best way to describe what needs to happen.

For example, if we took a football team and told them that the front line, midfield and defence were all three lines of defence, the front line might be a little deflated; their job is to go after goals, to attack the opposition. The expression 'defence' automatically puts the *whole* team into defensive mode, rather than attack and defence.

In the first line of play, operational management is the front line (see Figure 7.2). This is where nearly all of the moments of truth in taking managed risk occur; each decision, each action and each hesitation can bring about the opening up of an opportunity or the incurring of a threat. In the field of sport, this is like opening up an opportunity for attacking the opponent's goal or allowing the game to revert to one of defence by allowing the ball to slip behind the front line. Operational management need to lead their staff not only to support the scoring of goals, but also to avoid allowing the threat (of the opposition slipping past the front line) to occur.

The front line or first line of play has ownership, responsibility and accountability for assessing, controlling and enhancing opportunities or mitigating threats, together with maintaining effective internal controls/enhancers. Many organizations formalize a process of 'do-check-review' in the first line of play. This is particularly important where there is a function

TABLE 7.3 Key success factors for embedding ERM

Issue	Success	Evidence	Metrics	Target/time-scale	Map	Status	Plan
Appetite	Areas where risk tolerances have been breached reported and acted on	Each business unit reporting against their own set tolerance levels, evidence of adjustment based on performance	KRI performance versus tolerances set (percentage of risks within tolerance) Active response to excursions (close out of actions versus due date)	100% 100%	Appetite framework defined and approved. KRIs mapped to strategic goals and value drivers, Board approval and implantation at all levels in organization		
Risk and capital	Information is timely transparent and reported consistently	MI dashboards give enough information for management to make risk-based decisions	Senior management feedback on quality of information provided (scale 1–5)	4 by year end	Included in new risk system, al BUs using system for tracking and reporting		
Stake-holders	Regulators: use us as benchmark for others	'Licence to operate' secure. Strong relationships in all jurisdictions and credibility maintained and enhanced in terms of risk capability	'Silent running' as far as regulators are concerned. Senior management feedback (scale 1–5)	4 by next year end	Gap analysis against regulators expectations		

(continued)

TABLE 7.3 Key success factors for embedding ERM (*continued*)

Issue	Success	Evidence	Metrics	Target/ time-scale	Map	Status	Plan
	Rating agencies rating ERM	Consistent rating across all rating agencies for ERM at excellent level	Rating	S&P 'Strong' by next year end	Engagement with rating agencies. Presenting route map for ERM		
	Peer group: recognized by insurance industry peers as a leader on ERM and risk and capital management	Formal or informal benchmarking with similar organizations in terms of ERM including risk and capital management	Benchmarking indicates organization into top quartile against range of measures	top quartile performance by next year end	Baseline assessment and establishing benchmarking processes and groups		
	External; externally accredited as leader in ERM	External audit opinions and insurance/risk industry awards	Audit opinion/ Award win	1 major award in two years	Achieve all targets and submit at least three applications		

Structure	ERM Policies and frameworks clearly articulated and implemented within the ERM Operating Model	ERM Operating Model communicated, understood and adopted. OM being used by business	Percentage of staff read and understood OM. Operating model use in all key areas of risk for their own frameworks and policies	100% at all times	Operating Model approval, training and communication plans
People	Roles and accountabilities clearly defined and acted upon	Roles and accountabilities documented and agreed. Mapped to role descriptions. ERM included in all decision making ERM included in remuneration packages	% of relevant job descriptions. Employee survey results. ERM team included in commencement of projects. Dashboard use in remuneration recommendations	100% at all times	Governance standard approved. HR involvement in role descriptions. HR trained in use of dashboard and implications for remuneration agreed at all levels
Controls/ enhancers	Risk improvement plans delivered	Plans exist where risk levels are not within tolerances or controls/ enhancers do not represent best practice. Action plans are delivered to agreed timelines and resources made available	Percentage of action plans in place for risks outside tolerances. Percentage of action plans overdue	100% by year end. 0% by year end	Included in new risk system, al BUs using system for tracking and reporting

(continued)

TABLE 7.3 Key success factors for embedding ERM (*continued*)

Issue	Success	Evidence	Metrics	Target/time-scale	Map	Status	Plan
Compe-tencies	ERM becomes an unconscious competence	Evidence of risk-based decision making at all levels – zero negative occurrences, 100% success in taking opportunities	Percentage successful projects % successful strategic decisions % successful operational decisions	98% by year end 95% by end next year 99.95% continuously	Culture change programme implemented alongside Lean Six Sigma		
Maturity	Risk maturity is continuously improved	Internal and external benchmarking, external/independent audit opinions including rating agencies	Maturity level on 5 point scale. Employee survey	4 consistently across all aspects by end next year	Baseline assessment and establishing benchmarking processes and groups		

FIGURE 7.2 Model for three lines of play

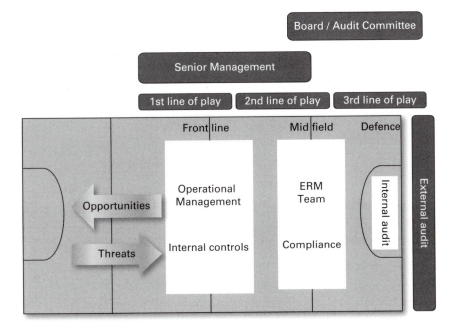

on which hinges a great deal of importance for the organization, such as getting the right formulation for food products, putting the right additive into drinking water, or giving the correct dosage of drugs to a sick patient.

In the second line of play the ERM team act as midfield, supporting the front line, enabling them to make goals happen, and helping fetch the ball back if it slips through. The second line of play are responsible for facilitating and monitoring the implementation of effective ERM practices by operational management and assisting the risk owners in defining the target risk exposure and reporting adequate risk-related information through the organization, whether it's about goals scored or goals conceded.

In the third line of play the internal audit function will, through a risk-based approach, provide assurance to the organization's board and senior management on how effectively the organization assesses and manages its threats and opportunities, including the manner in which the first and second lines of play operate. This assurance task covers all elements of an organization's ERM programme – governance, context, risk identification, assessment and response to communication of related information – throughout the organization and to senior management and the board.

Questions for senior management and the board to ask

(Including model answers based on best practice – at a high maturity level.)

How well is ERM embedded in the organization?	We think it is well embedded, and that is measured year-on-year when we conduct our risk maturity and risk culture reviews. We also involve stakeholders in these reviews and that gives us better assurance that we are being honest about our progress.
How do we define embedding and how far do we aspire to embed?	We define embedding ERM as being an unconscious competence where risk management techniques are used in everything that we do.
How can we tell?	We use a road map of key success factors to measure how we are progressing, where we regularly check how well we are doing. This road map sets eight key questions against eight areas of risk management. The responses are audited independently by our internal audit team who look for evidence of each assertion.
Is ERM integrated into all aspects of the way we do things?	We are well along the journey to being able to say 'yes', but there is still some way to go with some pockets of resistance where people still think it does not apply to them. However, each year, this group gets smaller and smaller, as shown in our continuous measurements of ERM maturity.
Does ERM operate in silos or pockets of different risk management practices?	No longer do those silos exist. All risk management personnel are recognized as being expert in their field, but they all work within the overarching ERM operating model, so the language is consistent, they all use an adapted version of the ERM methodology, and there is a great deal of cross-fertilization of ideas and culture between the various professionals with secondments and cross audits, shared learning and shared techniques and technology.

Do we lead the embedding process by setting the right tone at the top?	Yes, we hold regular events to include the board, particularly the non-executive directors and senior management in challenging and reviewing all strategic aspects of our approach to ERM, and we also can demonstrate that we use risk management techniques in the boardroom.
Do we have a deliberate and managed programme of planning and designing the approach and process of ERM?	Yes we do. There is a programme of planning and design for the implementation of ERM that is now several years old. This is run as an ongoing project and will be until we reach our next goal for attainment of maturity level X.
Is the ERM programme based on a fundamental understanding of the organization and its context?	Yes. This was our starting point; we have also reflected our culture and the way in which we implement change management.
Are there clear accountabilities, well managed resources, excellent communications and reporting mechanisms for establishing and articulating direction for integrating enterprise risk management?	Yes. Regarding resources, originally we set up an ERM team from secondees from the existing areas of risk management under a Chief Risk Officer, and now that we have several years of operating the ERM programme, some of these have permanently moved into the ERM team, but occasionally, in particularly busy times, they are seconded back to other areas of risk management. Accountabilities are demonstrated through the regular ERM 'star chamber' reviews where risk owners for corporate risks call in the control owners for their risk areas and there is a debate about the level of risk and control. Risk mapping is conducted for all strategic risks to enable us to understand the interrelationships between risks and to evaluate our capacity for bearing multiple risks simultaneously. This is all documented in our ERM annual report, which is then summarized for the organization's annual report for external scrutiny.

Notes

1 These are adapted from the 11 principles of risk management in ISO 31000.

2 *Against the Gods*, page 247.

3 Thanks to Alex Hindson of Amlin for the original material, which has been adapted.

4 SMART = specific, measurable, achievable, realistic and timebound.

Maturity in enterprise risk management

Outline

There are various levels of 'maturity' in the way in which ERM is embedded in the organization from ignorant, initiate, intermediate, integrated and influential. It is only at the integrated level that the organization can begin to leverage ERM to get maximum benefit and to truly optimize business strategies by taking managed risks.

Senior management and the board should engage with the decision as to the level of ERM maturity that is expected for the organization, and risk managers are responsible for implementing appropriate maturity measurement tools and tracking performance. There are distinct advantages to measuring progress against that expected level to ensure that the organization is able to optimize business strategies by taking managed risk. The risk maturity model is a tool for changing behaviours and enabling ERM to be embedded.

How risk maturity enables managed risk taking

The risk mature organization is one that is able to clearly articulate its risk appetite and to measure its performance against it. It is thereby able to respond positively to new challenges so as to seize the opportunity and maximize the returns while managing the threats and opportunities. It is more likely to be able to weather the storms of threats as they occur, and more likely to stay afloat when times get tough. Management are able to switch from a 'managing as usual' mode into a 'change management' mode and the capacity is there for staff to change up a gear and throw themselves into the new challenge in addition to their day job.

EY conducted a survey in 2011 that assessed the maturity level of risk management practices and then determined a positive relationship between risk management maturity and financial performance. Based on 576 interviews with companies and a review of more than 2,750 analyst and company reports[1] it identified the leading risk management practices that differentiated the various maturity levels and organized them into specific risk components. The findings suggest that:

- The top-performing companies (from a risk maturity perspective) implemented on average twice as many of the key risk capabilities as those in the lowest-performing group.

- Companies in the top 20 per cent of risk maturity generated three times the level of EBITDA (earnings before interest, taxes, depreciation, and amortization) as those in the bottom 20 per cent.

- Financial performance is highly correlated with the level of integration and coordination across risk, control and compliance functions.

The findings show clear business reasons for investing in improved risk management maturity and therefore it is in the interest of the board and senior management to be involved in ensuring that improvement in risk maturity is continuously monitored.

It is possible for an organization that is not risk mature to seize opportunities and to win through doing so, but be unable to articulate how the threat or opportunity was managed. This winning is more by luck than by planning. Sooner or later the organization that is not risk mature will encounter problems that will send it into crisis management mode, or worse. These organizations are often in constant 'fire-fighting' mode. It can be very exciting and there can be a great deal of fantastic decision making, but it can be exhausting for management and turnover of staff is often higher than normal because everyone is working in an environment of high tension and at maximum capacity. Such risk immature organizations are less likely to be able to respond to change, are slow in being able to seize opportunities when they arise and are less resilient in the longer term.

There are many examples of ERM maturity models that can be used, but it is important to adapt the language and style to fit the organization in question. A wrong reference to the internal structure, or a question posed to senior managers that should be aimed at operational management, can be infuriating.

Today's electronic world gives us the wonderful e-survey, which is by far the most efficient way of collecting the information about the level of ERM maturity in the organization, but care must be taken to word the survey in a way that ensures honesty in the answers. Some organizations will use a combination of e-surveys and interviews, the latter particularly for non-executive directors and possibly other stakeholders.

There is a spectrum for risk maturity from being completely unaware of threats and opportunities, to being influential with one's peers (see Figure 8.1):

- The *ignorant* organization is unaware of the need for managing risk, it has no structured approach to dealing with threats and opportunities, management is in crisis mode, always fire-fighting, and there is no learning from experience as the organization lurches from one crisis to another. It may attend to the most important aspects of compliance but tends to try to do the least that it can get away with. ERM is part of the unconscious incompetence (see Chapter 7).

- The *initiate* organization has started to implement some basic risk management, but this is centred on a small number of individuals who take ownership of the ERM programme and are seen internally as the people who manage risk. This stage is conscious incompetence; there are no formal or structured processes for managing threats

FIGURE 8.1 Example of matrix to show output of an ERM maturity assessment

	Enablers					Outputs	
	ERM Leadership	ERM Strategy & Policies	People	Partnerships & Resources	ERM Processes	ERM Handling	Outcomes
Level 5 Influential							
Level 4 Integrated							
Level 3 Intermediate							
Level 2 Initiate							
Level 1 Ignorant							

and/or opportunities apart from perhaps some policies and some risk registers. This organization is struggling to implement formalized risk management processes as these processes seem to be in addition to the day-to-day crisis management for all in the organization.

- The *intermediate* organization has streamlined and integrated some aspects of ERM into some of the business practices but not all – it is a semi-conscious competence. The organization is starting to see definite benefits coming from the ERM areas that are integrated, particularly in project management and other operational areas. Rarely does risk-based decision making actually take place in the boardroom although there is clear and mainly active support for ERM from the board. The board members talk the right words but are not yet leading by example.

- In the *integrated* organization, management of threats and opportunities is built into all routine business practices and is a conscious competence. Formal ERM programmes and processes are integrated into the way in which people manage the business and there is regular reporting of the performance of ERM against the risk appetite. An integrated multi-level programme is used to manage opportunities as well as threats. The organization uses risk information to actively improve business processes and gain competitive advantage.

- The *influential* organization is a leader in its field and its peers learn from it. ERM at this point becomes unconscious competence and risk management becomes a natural part of good management.

These aspects of risk maturity can be measured against seven aspects of ERM, which are based on the balanced scorecard approach of inputs versus outputs; see Table 8.1. Tables 8.2 to 8.8 provide a brief summary of some aspects of how the ERM maturity could be evidenced for each aspect of the inputs and outputs above. This is built from the experience of the author based on best practice, but the language and emphasis should be adapted for the individual organization.

Advantages and disadvantages of measuring risk maturity

There can be some cost involved in measuring the ERM maturity of the organization, particularly if the organization selects to conduct this at a granular level, such as comparing business unit by business unit, and also

TABLE 8.1 Seven aspects of risk maturity – inputs and outputs

Inputs	Outputs
ERM Leadership	ERM handling
ERM Strategy and Policies	Outcomes
People	
Partnerships and Resources	
ERM processes	

the perceptions of different sections of the organization such as by level of seniority or area of business. It is also important to communicate the reasons for doing this and the expected outputs, as the time needed for management, staff and stakeholders to complete the questionnaire or attend interviews is valuable. It is also really important to communicate the outcomes to all who participated.

The main advantage for senior management is that the output gives them a measure of how well ERM is embedded in the culture of the organization and, if conducted regularly, it also enables senior management to have assurance that progress towards the desired state is being made.

Action plan for measuring and tracking performance

Below is an action plan that risk managers could deploy for measuring risk maturity and tracking performance over a period of time:

Stage 1, set the target: the first stage for using a risk management maturity model is for senior management and the board to determine the level at which the organization needs to be. Assessing where the organization is now establishes a benchmark for future improvement. Just as important is to determine the desired level that adds most value for the organization. The board and senior management should make clear the level at which they expect ERM to be implemented

FIGURE 8.2 Example of completed maturity matrix

		Enablers					Outputs	
	ERM Leadership	ERM Strategy & Policies	People	Partnerships & Resources	ERM Processes	ERM Handling	Outcomes
Level 5 Influential								
Level 4 Integrated								
Level 3 Intermediate								
Level 2 Initiate								
Level 1 Ignorant								

· · · · · · · ·   Assessment year 1   — — ·   Assessment year 3   ——————   Target

TABLE 8.2 Risk maturity: leadership in risk management

Risk Leadership	
Level 5 Influential	There is eagerness in the boardroom to exploit new and existing opportunities, while managing the threats. The board and senior management use consideration of risk to drive excellence through the business, and are rewarded for well-managed risk taking within the risk appetite.
Level 4 Integrated	The board and senior management actively challenge risk information and demand improvements to support them in risk-based decision making. They hold risk owners to task and provide strong support and reward for well-managed risk taking within the boundaries set by the risk appetite.
Level 3 Intermediate	There is clear and mainly active support for ERM from the board but rarely does risk-based decision making actually take place in the board room. The board members talk the right words but are not yet leading by example. Middle management are encouraged to participate in ERM.
Level 2 Initiate	Senior managers begin to take the lead to ensure that approaches for addressing risk are being developed and implemented consistently and thoroughly across the organization.
Level 1 Ignorant	Top management are unaware of the need to manage uncertainty and risk and have not made resources available to improve.

and require that measurements are made and reported on periodically, perhaps annually, to ensure that progress towards the anticipated level is being made. It is for operational management to

TABLE 8.3 Risk maturity: programme for ERM

ERM Programme	
Level 5 Influential	Role model status where ERM capability in policy and strategy making is copied and shared with peers in industry.
Level 4 Integrated	The ERM programme is owned by the board (or a committee of the board) and is focused on delivering sustainable growth. There is a separation between the operating model for ERM and the frameworks and policies for individual ERM activities.
Level 3 Intermediate	The ERM programme has been through several iterations and reflects the organization's strategic direction establishing core responsibilities and roles. Risk management principles are being reflected in the organization's policies and strategies, communicated effectively and made to work through a framework of processes.
Level 2 Initiate	The first iteration of a risk framework is established and there is some negotiation of aspects with senior management, including roles and responsibilities. Some aspects of business policies and strategy include risk management; there is some evidence of ERM being operated in some business activities.
Level 1 Ignorant	There is no ERM or even a risk management framework.

set out the specific detail behind each of the elements and to develop the organization's own maturity model.

Stage 2, adapt the model: once the desired level to be achieved is established, a detailed model should be developed that reflects the style and culture of the organization. There should be a series of questions behind the model to be posed to senior and operational management and designed to reflect the language that is appropriate for that audience. It is tested with selected people to check that the language and approach are appropriate; for example, it's important to avoid leading questions that invite untruthful answers.

Stage 3, get inputs from a wide range of people: the organization may then run some form of self-assessment against the adopted model:

TABLE 8.4 Risk maturity: people aspects of ERM

People	
Level 5 Influential	ERM professionals are at the leading edge of their profession. Others in the organization are influential in their areas, winning prestige and external acclaim for their inclusion of ERM in their professions.
Level 4 Integrated	All key risk control and enhancer owners have been delegated the ownership of risk-based decision making in their areas and there is a drive from them for improvement of the reporting dashboards and other ERM programmes. All staff feel empowered to take well-managed threats and opportunities. Specialized ERM training is an integral part of ongoing personal development plans, and remuneration programmes are risk-based.
Level 3 Intermediate	People encouraged and supported to be more innovative. Regular training is available for people to enhance their ERM skills. Continuous professional development training in place for core group of people. ERM training takes place as part of induction training. Remuneration programmes include some aspects of risk management.
Level 2 Initiate	Some guidance is being made available and training programmes are being implemented to develop risk capability. Core group of people have skills and knowledge to manage threats and opportunities effectively.
Level 1 Ignorant	Key people are unaware of need to assess and manage threats and opportunities and to understand risk concepts and principles.

perhaps an online questionnaire. Senior management need to lead this part of the process, perhaps being the sponsor for the activity or having someone else send it out on their behalf. The language used in the invitation to participate in the questionnaire is important in encouraging participation and honesty in the responses.

TABLE 8.5 Risk maturity: partnerships and resources

Partnerships and Resources	
Level 5 Influential	Organization is regarded as a preferred partner and risk sharing takes place overtly in partnership contracts. Information integrity and asset security are assured. Financial and other resources are effectively managed.
Level 4 Integrated	Sound governance arrangements established; partners and suppliers are always selected on basis of risk capability and compatibility. Resources are well managed.
Level 3 Intermediate	Sound governance arrangements are mainly established; partners and suppliers are usually selected on basis of risk capability and compatibility but there are some areas where they are not. Resources are usually well managed.
Level 2 Initiate	Risk with partners is being managed for some key areas and across the organization. There are some boundaries for managing assets and financial and other resources.
Level 1 Ignorant	Key people are unaware of areas of potential risks with partnerships, suppliers and management of significant resources, and fail to understand the need to agree approaches to manage these risks.

Choosing and segmenting the participants is possibly the trickiest part of the exercise. This needs to be done with an eye to the output and what will happen to it. For example, it is really useful to be able to see the differing responses between the board and senior management, heads of business units, and team leaders. It's also useful to be able to see the difference between responses from those across different business units as well as different functions in those business units and in head office.

Stage 4, analyse the output: analysing the output should be relatively easy, if stages two and three have been done carefully. Care should be

TABLE 8.6 Risk maturity: processes for ERM

ERM Processes	
Level 5 Influential	Peers regard the ERM processes as leading edge and they are copied by others.
Level 4 Integrated	As well as all the attributes of level 3, there is a risk appetite process and a sound process for establishing the capacity of the organization to bear threats and take opportunities. Risk information to the board and senior management enables timely strategic decision making through a system of key risk indicators that address the strategic goals. Risk-based decision making is inherent feature of all policies and strategy-making processes.
Level 3 Intermediate	The ERM processes and all supporting tools have had several iterations and begin to address opportunity as well as threat. The system for recording risks is opened up to all those who 'own' risk, risk controls or risk enhancers. Internal audit participate in auditing compliance with the ERM programme as well as using the outputs of the risk system to inform the audit plan. Reports to the board and senior management are clear and focused on the corporate goals and value drivers.
Level 2 Initiate	ERM processes are established, evidenced by policies, guidance and toolkits. A system for recording threats and uncertainties is implemented but run for 'first line of play' by the risk team. There are some ad hoc reports to senior management, but these do not yet provide the right information for strategic decision making. Internal audit is not geenrally involved.
Level 1 Ignorant	There is no formal ERM framework and no stand-alone risk processes have been identified.

TABLE 8.7 Risk maturity: handling risks and outcomes of risk

Risk Handling	
Level 5 Influential	Selected as a benchmark by other organizations. If crises occur, they are well managed and the event becomes an opportunity for the organization.
Level 4 Integrated	Management of risk and uncertainty is well integrated with all business processes. Risk appetite drives the measurement of the amount of threat and opportunity to be taken and there is a conscious understanding of the amount of capacity at risk at all times. State-of-the-art tools and methods are used including a suite of key risk indicators that the board use for making decisions. ERM standards applied in all areas. Staff accept and practise ERM as standard requirement of good management.
Level 3 Intermediate	ERM is well on the way to being a part of most business processes, but not all. Risk appetite is being used in a rudimentary fashion but not in a comprehensive way.
Level 2 Initiate	Risk management processes are being implemented in some key areas. Risk capability self-assessment tools being used in some areas. There is general awareness of the need for risk management, but mainly for threat mitigation and compliance.
Level 1 Ignorant	No clear evidence that risk management is being effective apart from some compliance areas.

taken not to infer trends where there are small numbers of people in groupings, and those individual results that deliver very high or very low scores across all questions may need to be discounted from the exercise.

Stage 5, conduct gap analysis and plan: the output might determine that there is a large gap between the result and the desired outcome. This should be formulated into a plan of action for moving towards the desired goal with SMART[2] objectives.

TABLE 8.8 Risk maturity: outcomes from ERM

Outcomes	
Level 5 Influential	The capacity of the organization over and above the possible threats is such that rating agencies take note and rating improves. The organization is recognized as an employer of choice. Rating agencies and regulators send staff to the organization to learn.
Level 4 Integrated	Greater opportunities for taking over other businesses, faster and successful implementation of *all* new projects and new products.
Level 3 Intermediate	Fire-fighting rarely takes place, staff turnover levels are low, the organization's ability to respond to change is excellent. There is clear evidence of risk management contributing to significantly improved performance for all relevant outcomes, better value for money, positive and sustained improvement, potential for new opportunities, projects *normally* implemented successfully.
Level 2 Initiate	Some evidence of risk management contributing to improvement in outcome performance, demonstrated by measures including, where relevant, stakeholders' perceptions. ERM evidenced by being a 'box-ticking exercise'. Projects *sometimes* implemented successfully.
Level 1 Ignorant	No clear evidence of improved outcomes or any opportunities identified. Organization constantly in fire-fighting mode, projects *often* fail.

Stage 6, communicate the output and plan: communicating the analysis and the plan is the next logical phase, and all those who participated in the exercise as well as all other key stakeholders should be included in the communication process. It is good practice to have the member of senior management or board member who first sponsored the exercise to send out the communication and to invite feedback.

TABLE 8.9 Advantages and disadvantages of various levels of risk maturity

Level	Advantages	Disadvantages
Level 5 Influential	Being seen externally as at leading edge, influences peers, rating agencies and regulators	May expose confidential information, embarrassing to support if a threat event occurs publicly
Level 4 Integrated	Maximum value from ERM attained with balance between risk exposure and capacity well managed	May expose unwelcome information (elephant in the room; see Chapter 6)
Level 3 Intermediate	Value from ERM attained, areas where there is too much emphasis on risk can be relaxed	Investment in ERM is high, needs resources for training, measuring and supporting ERM
Level 2 Initiate	Some value from ERM attained, projects more likely to succeed, business more resilient	Investment in ERM is high, needs resources for training, measuring and supporting ERM
Level 1 Ignorant	Low investment in ERM	Destroying value, exposed, often in crisis mode, blame culture

Stage 7, implement action plan: the action plan for improvement in risk maturity might need some investment, particularly for training and supporting operational management, but most crucially in monitoring progress. This action plan might be combined with the development of the recognition, reward and remuneration process to provide even greater incentive throughout the organization.

Stage 8, run it again: some organizations run the exercise annually or every two years. Much depends on how much work is needed in the action plan and the timescale for improvement set out by management. Some regulators insist that risk maturity model assessments are run on an annual basis.

Stage 9, benchmark: many organizations, particularly in the public sector, like to benchmark their results with similar organizations. This is useful in establishing whether the organization can learn from others, or indeed teach others.

Questions for senior management and the board to ask

(Including model answers based on best practice – at a high maturity level.)

Does the board know the level of ERM maturity in the organization?	Yes, we've adapted an ERM maturity model for our own organization and have tested ourselves several times against this.
What level of assurance do you have regarding the level of maturity?	We use an online questionnaire that we send out annually to several hundred people in the organization and we stratify the responses based on the division, business unit and level of seniority of the individual. There are enough responses for us to be able to make statistically relevant assumptions on the responses and the change in responses over time.
Will that assurance stand up to external scrutiny by a customer or regulator, or indeed any other stakeholder?	When sending out the questionnaire we always include one group of individuals as a control group and select these from those who are furthest away from the ERM programme ie, not receiving any training and not control or risk owners.

Has the desired level of ERM maturity been articulated by the board?	Yes, the board have set out their own views on the level of ERM maturity that we should be at.
Does the board have a clear understanding of the benefits of improving ERM maturity?	Yes, they have already seen benefits in the outputs from the ERM and our level of sustainability. They support the concept of continuous improvement in ERM.
What is the business case for change and the added value of being at a different level?	The benefits in the outputs from the EMR programme have been quantified and we are able to predict the quantitative effects of further improvement.
Does the board wish to invest the time and money required to regularly measure ERM maturity?	Yes, the cost is quite low in terms of the running of the model now that it is established, and we can justify the 40 minutes or so of management and staff time in completing the annual ERM maturity assessment in terms of continuously raising awareness.
What reports does the board expect on ERM maturity and with what frequency?	Initially, the board required quarterly updates on progress, but now that we are several years down the road, we include the outputs from our ERM maturity and risk culture assessments in the ERM annual report.

Notes

1 http://www.ey.com/GL/en/Services/Advisory/Turning-risk-into-results-Managing-risk-for-better-performance

2 SMART = specific, measurable, achievable, realistic and timebound.

Resilience and sustainable habits

Outline

Risks are becoming more and more unpredictable and their impacts are getting larger[1] with global issues such as severe income disparity, chronic fiscal imbalances, rising greenhouse gas emissions, water supply crises, mismanagement of population ageing, major systemic financial failure, failure of climate change adaptation and distribution of weapons of mass destruction. All of these will affect each and every one of us.

The resilience of the organization to withstand the onslaught isn't just about short-term responses embodied in business continuity management (BCM) or crisis and disaster management; it's about longer-term responses that organizations should include in their corporate social responsibility (CSR) programmes. By planning ahead and predicting the short- and long-term effects of events, the organization can save money immediately and identify opportunities for streamlining and cost saving as well as help to turn the tide of increasing risks on a wider scale. We cannot afford to ignore issues of resilience either for the organization or on a global basis. We tend to forget that CSR is business continuity for the longer term, addressing the future wellbeing of all our stakeholders and our stakeholders' stakeholders. All CSR programmes must be consistent with the underlying culture of the organization, otherwise it can be shallow and false at best, and at worst can be a noose by which the organization can get hung.

Senior management need to be aware of their roles in BCM and particularly need to participate in exercises where their role and responses are tested and honed. There may need to be some senior management involvement in, first, mediating the expectations of the various business units within the organization to ensure that the BCM cost does not run away with itself; and secondly, ensuring that the opportunities for innovation and cost saving are secured. But the most critical role, in this hyper-connected digital era, for senior management and the board in the BCM process is communicating to the outside world and internally.

Business continuity management

Vital for the health of the business

The first thing that happens if there is a major crisis is that people go into shock. If the organization suffering the crisis allows this shock to develop into paralysis, this can lead to severe if not terminal problems.

CASE EXAMPLE   Business continuity in practice

The smoke from the smouldering factory was visible for several miles as I approached the scene after the four-hour journey through the night.

I stepped out of the car and prepared my mental checklist as I pulled on my high visibility jacket, safety boots and safety helmet. The fire officers pointed me in the direction of the temporary command headquarters for management and I walked into a small hut that had been the staff rest area. The factory manager sat with his head in his hands. The misery was palpable but what shocked me most was the inertia evident in the room. Several members of the management team just stood, propping themselves up against the walls of the hut. They looked at me, the newly appointed risk manager, expectantly.

Taking the cue from the factory manager who just nodded to me, I explained that I had about 10 minutes of questions, and then we would make a plan of immediate action to respond to the situation.

Having established that there had been no injuries, that there was no business continuity plan in place, and taking account the resources available, I explained that we were expected to act as if we were uninsured and to get on with what we need to do to remedy the impact on business. I also asked for one manager to act as scribe for everything we did, including the decisions made, the assumptions on which we made them and the actions taken. Another manager was detailed to act as visual recorder with a video and camera. This would provide the basis for the future business continuity plan as well as evidence for the insurers to assure them that we were acting in their best interest. They all expressed surprise, having expected to be told what to do by the insurers, but took my lead and marshalled the teams into various activities for immediate action.

When the loss adjusters arrived some six hours later, they saw a hive of activity in the various factory buildings, salvaging machinery and equipment, and people on the newly installed phones to customers, suppliers, staff and other stakeholders.

Those six hours were enough for us to establish communication with our customers and to ensure that the supply chain remained unbroken, having galvanized a sister factory into working extra shifts to fill our orders and receive our incoming stock. We lost no business and indeed were able to leverage the situation with some customers who increased their demand.

Several months later there was an interesting conversation with the insurers who were bemused by the huge claim for increase in cost of working[2] but every cent was paid as there was no business interruption claim.

Those six hours saved several millions of dollars for the insurers but, more important, established better and stronger relationships between the factory and its customers.

Crises can be caused not just by sudden and catastrophic events; they are just as likely to be caused by slow acting events that tip the organization beyond its ability to respond.

Consider the past world crises when oil prices skyrocketed; we have come to accept high-priced oil, and we will probably accept it until the next crisis causes prices to rise quickly upwards. As Nassim Nicholas Taleb, the former hedge fund manager, self-styled philosopher of risk, and author of *The Black Swan* tells us, the longer a system appears stable, the greater the disruption will be when stability breaks down. Global oil prices have been on average at their highest ever for the two years to August 2013, but they have also essentially been stable because the change in the average daily price has been slight. The problems will come if that stability evaporates.

BCM, a crucial part of ERM, is not about a complex plan that is so thick that the business continuity manager uses it as a step to stand on to make himself or herself better heard. Nor is it just about a set of protocols that need to be followed in the event of a crisis. It is about survival. The key is being prepared, and that means that every member of the senior management team needs to know what their role is and what is expected of them in advance of the worst happening. For that to happen, the senior management team and every non-executive director needs to have participated in a business continuity exercise that gets the heart pumping, adrenaline flowing and the imagination running riot. If, as senior managers, we have not participated in a business continuity scenario exercise, we need to ask some hard questions as to what is happening about it in the organization.

BCM in summary

There are three stages to the process of BCM:

1 before event planning – business continuity planning;

2 the event occurring – crisis management;

3 recovering after the event – disaster recovery.

Beware of the BCM process that is just called 'disaster recovery'. This is most likely driven by the IT team who will probably have a great plan to get our systems back up and running, but if we don't have a building to house the people, or indeed if we don't have people, there's not much point in recovering the system. BCM should cover all three phases of the event and should be wide ranging so as to cater for all the main processes and all the key risks.

Here are 10 absolute basics that a business continuity process should involve:

1 Develop and practise a contingency plan that includes a succession plan for the CEO and other key people.

2 Train backup employees to perform emergency tasks. The employees we count on to lead in an emergency will not always be available.

3 Determine offsite crisis meeting places for senior management and non-executive directors.

4 Make sure that all employees, as well as executives, are involved in the exercises so that they get practice in responding to an emergency.

5 Make exercises realistic enough to tap into employees' emotions so that we can see how they'll react when the situation gets stressful.

6 Practise crisis communication with employees, customers and the outside world – especially the press.

7 Invest in an alternate means of communication in case the phone networks go down.

8 Form partnerships with local emergency response groups such as fire, police and ambulance to establish a good working relationship. Let them become familiar with the organization and site.

9 Evaluate the organization's performance during each test, and work toward constant improvement. Continuity exercises should reveal weaknesses.

10 Exercise the continuity plan regularly to reveal and accommodate changes. Technology, personnel and facilities are in a constant state of change and this will drive the need to update the plan.

Mediating the business's expectations

Senior management may find that they will have to mediate and even dictate the expectations of the business.

One of the methods used in BCM is the business impact analysis (BIA). Each part of the business will make a return to the BCM team about what their important requirements for doing their work are and how long they can manage without those important requirements. These might include:

- key people;
- computing equipment;
- data;
- paper-based systems;
- IT: e-mail, operating programs and systems;
- buildings, equipment and other physical requirements.

Even with the best intentions, the people completing the business impact analyses will not reveal that there is any redundancy or additional capacity in their area, nor will they admit to not needing any of the equipment, people or other assets immediately after an occurrence.

Using BCM to innovate, streamline and save costs

Senior management should be aware that there are two aspects to the first stage of BCM – the planning phase that can create opportunities for innovation, streamlining and cost saving. To make the most of these opportunities, some strategic overview is needed of these aspects.

CASE EXAMPLE from the author's experience

I was conducting a business impact analysis with a client with a diverse business and turnover of over $3 billion. The core businesses had returned all the paperwork and we were collating the requirements on a spreadsheet so that we could compare these requirements with the availability of the systems and processes as well as assets and physical needs.

The first output from the spreadsheet showed that *all* the businesses needed *all* their systems and assets within two days of an event. We then overlaid a geographic analysis across the spreadsheet and the picture was no different. At that point the planning team had only catered for 10 per cent of the systems to be back on line within two days, 30 per cent of the systems being available within seven days and the remainder taking up to a month to reinstate.

A renegotiation with the business heads resulted in a drop of 20 per cent in their expectations but we were a long way adrift from being able to provide that, nor did we believe that it would be efficient to do so – the costs of providing what they wanted would have been so spectacular that it would have moved the business from profitability into loss.

With the help of the board, we turned the conversation around into one of asking the businesses what they would do if we could only provide 10 per cent of the systems to be back on line within two days, 30 per cent within seven days and the remainder taking up to a month to reinstate. Based on those responses we were able to facilitate some mutual assistance schemes across similar but geographically diverse parts of the organization. This then led to a fine tuning of the business continuity plan, which would respond to the most important needs of the most profitable businesses based on their contribution to the whole.

The first aspect is the risk identification process that goes on within BCM. Clearly it should be linked closely to the overarching ERM programme to avoid going over the same ground, but it also provides a new pair of eyes to view risk from the bottom upwards. By asking the question, 'What can we do to avoid this happening' new thoughts might occur about whether indeed the business unit needs to be doing what it is doing or if it can do it in a different way.

This is brought into greater focus when the second aspect of BCM addresses the BIA, and mediation is needed at a senior level of the combined expectations of the business units. A clever analysis of the BIA outputs might reveal serious deficits or surpluses in capacity, giving rise to an opportunity to rebalance the assets and people.

Testing the plan

There are several types of exercise or test for a business continuity plan that senior management should be aware of, support and participate in; see Table 9.1. Senior management should be aware of the role that they are expected to take in the event of an interruption to the business and should practise that role at least annually through one or a range of the exercises.

The role of senior management

Communication in the event of a crisis

The key role for senior management in the event of a major event (by which we mean an event that affects or could affect the whole organization) is to take the lead in dealing with the communication plans, particularly the media. In today's online, switched on world, our dirty washing will be out there in the public domain, sometimes before we see it. A well-managed communication process can turn a potential PR disaster into a marketing campaign that brings in new business and gets committed long-term loyalty from existing customers. Below is the sort of scenario that benefits from continuity management.[3]

Ten key steps for senior management in crisis response

The following steps are a summary of the key areas that senior management must address with regard to communication in the event of a crisis:

1 Select the key external spokesperson and two or three backups. They must be trained and must be able to speak with *empathy, authority, skill, sincerity and confidence;* de-select anyone who cannot do so, even if it's the CEO. The spokesperson must be appropriate for the audience, so consider the composition of the main audience.

TABLE 9.1 Five aspects of exercising a business continuity plan

Exercise	What it is	Benefits	Disadvantages
Checklist	Distribute plans for review	Ensures plan addresses all activities	Does not address effectiveness of plan
Structured walk through	Look through each step of the plan thoroughly	Ensures planned activities are accurately described in the plan	Low value in proving response capabilities
Scenario	Scenario to enact recovery activities	Practises roles and exercises the plan	Does not take into account all the variables that might occur
Parallel exercise	Full test but primary business activities do not stop	Ensures high level of reliability without interrupting normal operations	Expensive as all personnel are involved
Full interruption	Interruption event is replicated to the point of ceasing primary business activities	Most reliable test of the plan and exercising the roles	Can be a risk to business operations

2 Choose a social media management system. Download programs that allow one to follow Twitter accounts in real-time. Even better, use a service that allows tracking of everything said about the company online from Facebook, LinkedIn and Twitter posts to Blog mentions. Another option is to use Google Alerts, a free service that allows the spokesperson to receive e-mail notifications when chosen keywords are found on the web.

Imagine the scene when you wake up at 4 am to the sound of your phone ringing off the hook. Your subconscious knows before your body can fully register: something is seriously wrong with your business. You jump out of bed while calling your management staff and logging onto your computer at the same time.

If you own any kind of 24/7 business or one that is internet-based, your Twitter and Facebook feeds are probably already blowing up with complaints, the complaints team have gone into meltdown and your e-mail systems are being blocked by incoming messages. The media, and possibly TV crew, might even be taking up position outside your headquarters as you shake yourself awake. Your blood pressure is rising by the second.

So what are you going to do? It is up to senior management, or you as the business owner, to translate a crisis into an opportunity (even one that attracts new clients). Here's how to do it.

Establish a solid communication plan: every organization should have a minute-by-minute strategy for how it will deal with a service shut down or PR disaster. As part of your plan, make sure you can confidently answer the following questions:

Press: Who will handle the press in case of a crisis? Will that person be authorized to speak on TV and radio? Has he or she had the training to do so properly, with empathy, skill, sincerity and confidence? Will he or she need approval for every quote? Will the messaging be consistent with the social media communications? Will you have more than one person responding to queries? What messages will you proactively put out there?

Social media: Who will handle your social media accounts in case of a crisis? What will that person be authorized to write on social media? Will he or she need approval for every post? What will the messaging be across platforms? Will you have more than one person responding to posts? What posts will you proactively put out there?

3 Find out what's happening. Ensure that there is a good system for keeping management – or the lead person – updated on everything that is happening.

4 Be honest and don't speculate. Even if the organization doesn't have the full picture, it will need to make statements to the press. Stalling

the press will antagonize them. Holding statements are fine, but manage their expectations for the next update. Speculation and dishonesty are the worst sins and can get the organization into a lot of hot water with all manner of stakeholders. Just stick to what the organization is 100 per cent sure of.

5 Select a key internal spokesperson and two or three backups. Within minutes of identifying the crisis, go to the employees. Tell them what's wrong and what the team are doing – in detail – to fix it. Check back with them every 15–20 minutes.

6 Create a page on the organization's website (easily identifiable on the home page) dedicated to the crisis and update it as needed (read: several times per hour, depending on the severity of the crisis). Assign a person to proactively and publicly acknowledge the issue on social media channels and invite customers to visit a landing page on the website for more information.

7 Make an ally of the press. Give them an area to work in, with Wi-Fi and non-stop coffee. Make them comfortable and bring them into the team's innermost thoughts. If the team trusts them to differentiate between what's on the record and what's not, they will be worthy of that trust. Make it clear that if they breach that trust they will be excluded from briefings, or a replacement sought.

8 Drown out the lawyers. The lawyers will advise not to admit liability and will demand the right of veto over all statements. This could make a hash of the crisis and might even end up breaking the business. Discuss beforehand with the lawyers and insurers what kind of response may be necessary. Get a contractual agreement with the insurers that enshrines what needs to be said by whom, and establishes insurance liabilities for anything said beyond what would have been payable because of expressions of concern and regret. Then afterwards, in negotiations with the insurers, the organization needs to explain and prove that it protected their interests as much as its own; keep meticulous records.

9 Update, respond and repeat. Keep the press updated. It is crucial to continuously update clients during a crisis. It doesn't matter how many people are Tweeting or sending Facebook status updates, *respond to every single one of them.* This can take up serious amounts of personnel resources, but it is worth it. Respond personally (with a customer's @ Twitter handle each time); dedication to superior customer service will be appreciated. If a customer is

flying off the handle, ask them to message off-line and offer the response team's e-mail address. Shut off any automated marketing posts and e-mail campaigns during a crisis.

10 Catch up. The crisis is under control and the press and the Twitter/ Facebook feeds have finally calmed down. Does this mean it is time to relax? No. Instead of trying to forget the crisis ever happened, the organization needs to reach back out to each customer that sent a note by e-mail, phone or on social media to see how they are doing and if there is anything more the organization can do. This is the time to generate great goodwill and to make more business.

A crisis can strike a company when it least expects it. It's worth looking at the lessons learnt by BP, one of the most analysed crisis responses in recent times.

CASE EXAMPLE BP and the Deepwater Horizon event

In April 2010 there was an explosion on an oilrig that coated the Gulf of Mexico with at least 50,000 barrels of oil a day or in total over 780,000 m³, polluting and killing more than a thousand marine animals. Eleven people died in the explosion.

The press commented that it was obvious BP didn't have a plan for a crisis on this scale; it is noticeable in the way it fumbled its response to the media – it was not prepared at all. The top three mistakes BP made during the crisis are:

1 *Not owning up.* Under intense scrutiny from the public and the media on the leakage of the oil, BP did not admit guilt immediately. Instead, it blamed its contractors for a faulty pipe; it blamed the engineers for not informing them about that pipe; it pointed fingers at everyone but itself. In a crisis, it is important to take the blame instead of denying it. To the public it seemed that BP was irresponsible for not taking the blame immediately.

2 *Contradicting the truth.* When the media asked BP for updates on the leakage of the oil, it reported 1,000 barrels of oil per day leaked to the ocean but later this was revealed to be 5,000 barrels of oil per day. This angered the public and trust was broken. A company should always make sure it gets the media to report the truth instead of spinning the truth from the public because the latter can be worse if the stakeholders find out the truth.

3 *All talk, no action.* Lehane, a crisis PR expert commented: 'BP had a series of strategies to tackle the problem, however they did not implement the plan time after time.' This worsens the issue and slowly its words become less credible. BP should have ensured that it executed the strategies it mentioned to the public, and also provided a follow-up to the media stating the progress of the action being executed by the management.

The fourth point that needs to be made about the BP crisis was about sincerity and most critically *empathy:* former BP boss Tony Hayward defended his handling of the Gulf of Mexico oil disaster claiming he was right to take part in a yacht race during the height of the crisis. In an interview that would incur the wrath of Americans already infuriated by the world's worst oil-related environmental disaster, he insisted better PR would not have changed the outcome of the 20 April accident which killed 11 people. Speaking on a BBC documentary, he said that if he had a degree in acting from 'RADA rather than a degree in geology I may have done better' in handling the fallout.

And he spoke of his reaction to media criticism of his decision to take part in the Isle of Wight Round the Island Race in his yacht. He said: 'I was pretty angry. I hadn't seen my son for three months. I was on the boat between midnight and six in the morning US time. I'm not certain I'd do anything different. The only way I could see my son was to be with him on a race he was on.'

After pictures of 'America's most hated man' were published showing him on the yacht, senior Republican Senator Richard Shelby called his actions the 'height of arrogance'. It was not his only gaffe – during one tour of the polluted region, he told a reporter: 'I want my life back.'

Corporate social responsibility

There are three drivers for doing anything: survival, because we are told to do it, and/or because we think that it might be good for others.

CSR often starts off as being something that an organization has to do because everyone else expects it of them. Perhaps there is a requirement driven by competition in that all the others in the market have glossy CSR brochures or ambitious programmes announced in their annual reports. So the first driver – survival – kicks in.

CASE EXAMPLE   The Rana Plaza collapse

On 24 April 2013 the Rana Plaza in Savar, Bangladesh, collapsed. It was the worst ever industrial disaster in that region, but the nation's finance minister downplayed the incident saying that it was one of a series of 'accidents'.[4]

A total of 1,021 bodies had been recovered from the debris of the fallen factory building. The authorities said that about 2,500 people were injured in the accident and 2,437 people were rescued.

But the shock waves across the developed world stopped; there is no perceived lasting effect on the Bangladesh clothing industry apart from one manufacturer, Disney, having withdrawn business. As the *Financial Times* goes on to comment: 'Indeed, the signs are that the increase in demand from the low wage area of Bangladesh for low cost clothing is rampant.'[5]

So if you can buy cheap goods and sell them to a willing customer base at a profit, what is to stop you?

CSR is also closely connected with BCM, within the ERM wheel, in that CSR is business continuity management for the longer term. Effects may not be immediately apparent; for example, at some point the customers of those clothing companies whose goods were being made in the Rana Plaza will stop buying garments that are so low cost as to be unsustainable – if they have not already done so.

CSR is otherwise referred to as corporate conscience, corporate citizenship, social performance, sustainable responsible business/responsible business, or sustainable development. It is a form of corporate self-regulation that an organization takes on as one of its ERM components. There are other forms of regulation, both mandated and required by customers. Increasingly, organizations are expected to prove their CSR credentials when bidding for business or participating in pre-contract negotiations. This is the second driver for CSR – being told to do it.

Some go well beyond the perceived expectations of others, compliance or legal requirements, and implement it as a process with the aim of embracing responsibility for the company's actions and encouraging a positive impact through its activities on all its stakeholders. The third driver thus enters the frame – we think it may be good for others. Most frequently, however, CSR

Extract: PWC report on CSR trends[6]

Markets with low relative market share were found to have low spending; markets with medium relative market share show rather high spending and from there, generally speaking, the social spending declines with increasing market share. Hence, managers appear to invest more on CSR in areas with fierce rivalry, where they have medium market share.

Non-financial reporting is more than a component of being a responsible company. It has become an integral part of every company's relationship with employees, suppliers, customers, investors and communities. In fact, despite the warm and cozy sentiments that can be stirred by these reports, addressing issues that once took a back seat to financial results – if they had a seat at all – has become critical to a company's credibility, transparency and endurance.

is driven by the need to increase, improve on and sustain brand perception and goodwill.

A renewed European Union[7] strategy 2011–14 for corporate social responsibility was published on 25 October 2011 setting out a new definition of CSR as 'the responsibility of enterprises for their impacts on society'. The ISO 26000 Guidance Standard on Social Responsibility[8] sets out a schematic to explain how social responsibility contributes to sustainable development; see Figure 9.1.

The two fundamental practices for social responsibility are recognizing social responsibility, and stakeholder identification and engagement. Without those two practices as the starting point, the social responsibility process is empty and vacuous.

ISO 26000 sets out a useful framework for implementing social responsibility including:

- Scope – how wide and what to include in the social responsibility programme.
- Terms and definitions – the language to use.
- Understanding – the link between social responsibility and sustainable development.
- Principles of social responsibility.

FIGURE 9.1 Schematic overview of ISO 26000 – Corporate Social Responsibility

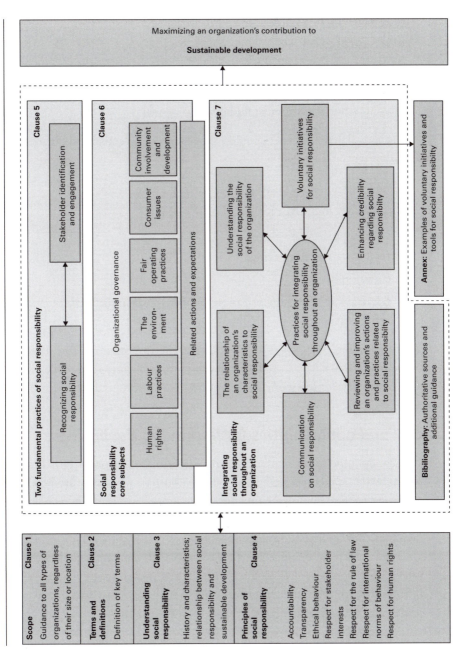

Maximizing an organization's contribution to

Sustainable development

Clause 5

Two fundamental practices of social responsibility

Recognizing social responsibility

Stakeholder identification and engagement

Clause 6

Organizational governance

Social responsibility core subjects

| Human rights | Labour practices | The environ-ment | Fair operating practices | Consumer issues | Community involvement and development |

Related actions and expectations

Clause 7

Integrating social responsibility throughout an organization

Understanding the social responsibility of the organization

Voluntary initiatives for social responsibility

The relationship of an organization's characteristics to social responsibility

Practices for integrating social responsibility throughout an organization

Enhancing credibility regarding social responsibility

Communication on social responsibility

Reviewing and improving an organization's actions and practices related to social responsibility

Annex: Examples of voluntary initiatives and tools for social responsibility

Bibliiography: Authoritative sources and additional guidance

Scope   Clause 1

Guidance to all types of organizations, regardless of their size or location

Terms and   Clause 2
definitions

Definition of key terms

Understanding   Clause 3
social
responsibility

History and characteristics; relationship between social responsibility and sustainable development

Principles of   Clause 4
social
responsibility

Accountability
Transparency
Ethical behaviour
Respect for stakeholder interests
Respect for the rule of law
Respect for international norms of behaviour
Respect for human rights

It then goes on to describe the core subjects within social responsibility

- human rights;
- labour practices;
- the environment;
- fair operating practices;
- consumer issues; and
- community involvement and development.

The practical activities that should take place to implement a social responsibility programme are:

- understanding social responsibility in the organization;
- voluntary initiatives for social responsibility;
- enhancing credibility;
- reviewing and improving;
- communication;
- relationship of the organization's culture and characteristics to social responsibility.

The underlying objective is to ensure that the organization and its stakeholders move towards sustainable development so as to protect the vulnerable in the developing world and to ensure better sustainability.

CSR and opportunities for improving the business

CSR can be good for business: by paying attention to the longer-term impacts on the wider stakeholders, we can build in buffers against future problems and even stop them from happening. But more important, it responds to the moment, the current attitude and concern for our world including the demands of our customers and consumers.

Often health and safety is wrapped into CSR and as with health and safety, CSR is increasingly, in the industrialized world, accepted as good for business. There is enough empirical evidence to show that if we have good health and safety practices, we will see business benefits:

- *Productivity and profits:* good health and safety measures mean that staff can do their work more easily and safely. This will boost morale, increase productivity, reduce costs and save insurance and legal costs.

Report on CSR in *Daily Finance*, 30 April 2012[9]

Corporate social responsibility has gone mainstream. From goliaths Apple, Walmart, and Procter & Gamble on down the line, you'd be hard-pressed to find a big company these days that doesn't have a program in place to address environmental issues and other socially minded matters.

You'd be equally hard-pressed to find a major corporation that doesn't go out of its way to tout these programs to you. But today, corporate social responsibility is about more than just good PR – it's also about good business and taking care of customers.

You've heard of vicious cycles, in which one negative action or event leads to another, and another, all of which feeds back into the first problem to make it more severe, pushing the cycle forward along a progressively worse course. What's happening with corporate social responsibility is just the opposite.

In this virtuous cycle, as consumers are becoming more environmentally and socially conscious they expect the goods and services they use to measure up, and therefore seek out the products and services that deliver. As consumer demand for these products and services increases, more and more companies are obliged to provide them to stay competitive. As more and more companies provide these products and services, consumers come more and more to expect them and consequently demand them more and more – and so on and so forth.

Different companies approach their parts in the virtuous cycle from different angles. Costco is known for taking care of its employees. It pays them well, better than industry peers. As such, Costco employees have a reputation for being friendly, motivated, and knowledgeable – thus making your shopping experience better and compelling you to return there the next time you need to go shopping.

- *Reputation:* good health and safety measures help build a positive reputation with clients and staff and their contacts, making the organization more likely to be an employer of choice.
- *Reduce absences and sick leave:* another benefit is that employees are less likely to take sick leave. This saves the business the direct and indirect costs of staff absence.

- *Retain staff:* reducing staff absence due to illness or accidents at work saves the time and costs of recruiting and training new members of staff as well as reducing the burden on those who cover for sick or injured colleagues during their absence.

Likewise, good environmental programmes can save costs such as power and fuel, reduce penalties and legal costs, and increase the organization's good reputation.

CSR and honesty

US energy giant Enron did little to help the cause of CSR. Enron was well-known for its CSR,[10] and published social and environmental reports on all the good work it was doing. But the trouble is, at the same time that it was espousing all the good stuff about its CSR programme, it was not telling the truth about its profits. When the truth emerged, it led to the company's collapse in 2001 and top executives were jailed for conspiracy and fraud.

Enron became a by-word for corporate *irresponsibility;* all of its community and environmental work was undermined by the fact that it was carried out by a company with dishonest business practices. The ethics demonstrated within the CSR programme must be pervasive throughout the organization in order to reap the benefits.

Questions for senior management and the board to ask

(Including model answers based on best practice – at a high maturity level.)

Are you aware of your role in the event of a crisis happening in the organization?	Yes, and I have two nominated alternates in the event that I am unavailable. We also have an 'on-call' system during times of heightened risk and I have periods when I am on that rota and have to be available 24/7.
Have you participated in any exercises regarding your role?	Yes, I participated in several desk-top scenario exercises and two parallel running exercises. The parallel running exercises were very useful for learning and we

reviewed the independent observers' reports as a board to ensure that we took up all the areas that needed improving. We plan to have a 'full interruption' exercise within two months and then to repeat a regular cycle of scenario (walk through, simulation or parallel) exercises each year.

Does someone from the senior management team mediate the expectations of the various business units within the organization to ensure that the BCM cost does not run away with itself and that the opportunities for innovation and cost saving are secured?

Yes, this was conducted by (for example, the finance director) in the first year of implementing BCM, and internal audit now ensure that there is a continuous check on the aggregated expectations of the organization compared to the resources we have invested for responding to an incident. We also check this in practice during the parallel exercises that are designed to check this out, amongst other objectives.

Who is the lead spokesperson for the outside world from the senior management team?

We have a communication structure where the primary lead spokesperson is any one of three executives, one of whom is the CEO. Other senior management have been nominated as spokespeople under certain circumstances and there is a structured approach for deciding who can and who cannot speak to the press under different conditions.

Are there nominated alternates in case that person is not available at the time?

There are two alternates for each of the key spokespeople at any one time.

Is there a tracking system to make sure that either the main spokesperson or the nominated alternates are always available?

We liaise continuously to ensure that one of the three nominated people is in the country at any one time.

Have all the potential spokespeople had appropriate training?

All of the nominated spokespeople are thoroughly trained for all forms of communication, including hostile radio and TV interviews, and they regularly take part in exercises.

Do they come over with empathy, sincerity and authority?	Yes, our PR company that does the training is under instructions to inform us if there is anyone who does not meet the criteria of being able to appropriately represent the organization in times of crisis.
Does the organization have a CSR programme?	Yes we have had a CSR programme for several years, initially concentrating on environment and more recently covering all social impacts of our organization from the supply chain to our neighbours and communities.
Does the organization recognize CSR as being good for long-term sustainability for the organization and its stakeholders?	We don't necessarily put it in those words, but we are aware of the advantages of being seen to care about our supply chain and the ethics of our organization for all aspects of CSR.
Is there evidence that the organization has engaged successfully with all stakeholders in developing the CSR programme?	Yes; not only have we published our stakeholder analysis and engagement programme in our annual report and accounts, but we also engage our communities and stakeholders in the design and content of our annual CSR review. We try to avoid 'fluffy' loose content and programmes, preferring to tackle real issues for and with our wider stakeholder group.
Is the CSR programme consistent with the underlying culture of the organization?	Our code of conduct, corporate vision and the CSR programme all follow three common themes of citizenship, corporate accountability and moral commitment.

Notes

1 http://www3.weforum.org/docs/WEF_GlobalRisks_Report_2013.pdf

2 'Increase in cost of working' is a term to describe the extra costs of responding to and remedying an insured situation to minimize the impact of the loss.

3 Adapted from http://www.huffingtonpost.com/yaniv-masjedi/social-media-crisis-advice_b_3624588.html

4 *The International Business Times* report by Palash Ghosh, 3 May 13, http://www.ibtimes.com/bangladesh-building-collapse-worst-garment-factory-disaster-ever-there-have-been-many-other-similar

5 http://www.ft.com/cms/s/0/24a9552c-f7ed-11e2-87ec-00144feabdc0.html#axzz2fEJkErmy

6 http://www.pwc.com/ca/en/sustainability/publications/csr-trends-3-en.pdf

7 http://eur-lex.europa.eu/LexUriServ/LexUriServ.do?uri=COM:2011:0681:FIN:EN:PDF

8 https://www.iso.org/obp/ui/#iso:std:iso:26000:ed-1:v1:en:en?utm:source=isoorg&utm:medium=isoorg&utm:term=isoorg&utm:campaign=26000link+from+isoorg

9 http://www.dailyfinance.com/2012/04/30/corporate-social-responsibility-good-for-business-good-for/

10 http://www.bbc.co.uk/news/business-19876138

Learning and communication

Outline

Positive and negative events can be incredibly useful in helping the organization learn and in encouraging better risk-based decision making leading, in turn, to the ability to take more managed risk. This requires encouragement at senior management level to ensure that the organization is open to learning; we can only learn from positive and negative events *if we want to learn*. But in order to learn and then use that learning to innovate, we need to be prepared to learn from failure. That takes some doing because it might require us to look deep into the soul of the organizational culture and tackle some things that we don't really want to.

Data alone cannot support learning. We need to use data and turn it into information and knowledge, in order for the decisions to be made and the learning to take place. The underlying data on risks that have happened can be used as a prism that we can look through so that we can predict the future. Thus the ERM programme needs to encourage the gathering of leading indicators such as near misses and things that might throw light on underlying trends that could present massive threats in the future. One can also use leading indicators that could encourage risk-based decisions on embracing opportunities in the future.

When handling huge quantities of data and seeking to gain information and knowledge from that data, ERM IT systems are very useful, but must be prepared for, selected and implemented in an ordered fashion so that the objective is achieved.

Organization-wide learning from risk information requires an internal communication process that should be constant, consistent, available, understandable and responsive to change. Putting all of these together presents a challenge, but it is one that some more risk mature organizations successfully address and, through the regular reporting of ERM information, the board are able to make good risk-based decisions.

At a Global 50 consumer product company, management has developed a governance structure that allows it to think about risk proactively, and has aligned its risk profile and exposures more closely with its strategy. Its governance leadership group and supporting management clarified the company's risk appetite, defined its risk universe, determined how to measure risk, and identified which technologies could best help the company manage its risks. Aligning risk to strategy, by identifying strategic risks and embedding risk management principles into business unit planning cycles, enabled the company to identify and document 80% of the risks that have an impact on performance. The payback on this effort has been multifaceted. Surveying risk so thoroughly gave the consumer products company the confidence to openly communicate its risk strategy to external stakeholders without worrying that the transparency would shake investor confidence. Most important, the alignment of risk awareness and management practices, from strategy to business operations, enabled the company to monitor risk developments more effectively. Managers could keep the organization within acceptable tolerance ranges, driving performance to plan. Mature risk management allowed this consumer products giant to improve its financial performance, strengthen stakeholder communication, and build greater trust in the market.

In setting risk strategy, top performers:

- Generate two-way open communications about risk with external stakeholders.

- Provide stakeholders with the relevant information that conveys the decisions and values of the organization.

- Have the board or management committee play a leading role in defining risk management objectives.

- Adopt and implement a common risk framework across the organization.

External communication should, of course, comply with the regulations that apply but, more important, it should address the stated objective for reporting externally, such as to give assurance to shareholders, customers and staff.

The learning habit

The trouble with risk management, whether it's enterprise wide or not, is that we mainly learn from negative events (hopefully, ones that have happened to other organizations rather than ours). After all, how do we know that enterprise risk management has worked? How do we know that the intervention that we put in place stopped something awful from happening or helped a particular opportunity to be realized? The learning habit is founded on knowledge and that requires information and data.

Turning data into knowledge and turning knowledge into learning

Senior management are often presented with reams and reams of ERM data. They are expected to learn the key messages from that data and then make decisions on that basis. Data is not knowledge or information. Learning and subsequent decisions can only be made when the right information is presented as knowledge and interpreted based on experience and the context of the knowledge. Commonly this is presented as a triangle inferring a linear movement from data, through information and knowledge; see Figure 10.1. A better interpretation of this is to regard both knowledge and information as being based on the data to produce opportunities for learning, as in Figure 10.2.

Information is different from data. It captures data at a point in time and to a certain extent it needs some knowledge to set the parameters for the snapshot. Many people confuse the two. When a CD with millions of pieces of data on it is lost, that data is not lost – it still resides back in the office on a database. What is lost is the information. If a hacker wipes the database and there are no backups, then we have lost the data. Whoops!

Data accuracy is not the only solution to having the right answer; it must be appropriately interpreted and reported through the information and knowledge processes.

FIGURE 10.1 Data, information, knowledge, learning triangle

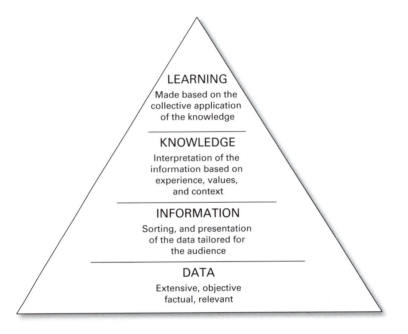

FIGURE 10.2 Schematic of learning relying on both information and knowledge

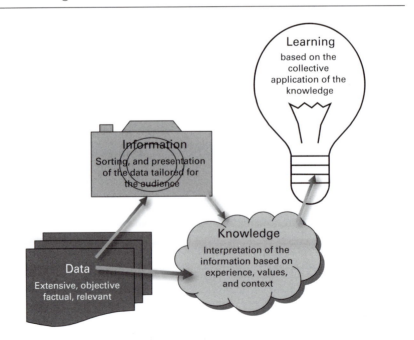

Extract from the Basel Committee on Banking Supervision, January 2013[2]

One of the most significant lessons learned from the global financial crisis that began in 2000 was that banks' information technology (IT) and data architectures were inadequate to support the broad management of financial risks. Many banks lacked the ability to aggregate risk exposures and identify concentrations quickly and accurately at the bank group level, across business lines and between legal entities. Some banks were unable to manage their risks properly because of weak risk data aggregation capabilities and risk reporting practices. This had severe consequences to the banks themselves and to the stability of the financial system as a whole.

An integrated approach in the organization to the treatment of data, information and knowledge to create learning opportunities will:

- Enhance the infrastructure for reporting key information, particularly that used by the board and senior management to identify, monitor and manage risks.
- Improve all decision-making processes throughout the organization.
- Enhance the management of information across business units, while facilitating a comprehensive assessment of risk exposures at the organization consolidated level.
- Reduce the probability and severity of losses resulting from risk management weaknesses.
- Improve the speed at which information is available and hence decisions can be made.
- Improve the organization's quality of strategic planning and the ability to manage the threats and opportunities of new products and services.

The American Red Cross is an example of an organization that suffered brand damage and incurred a huge fine by failing to monitor key risk intelligence, even though there was data from which it could have learnt.

Extract from *Forbes* commentary on the American Red Cross, 17 January 2012[3]

In January 2012, the American Red Cross, the largest supplier of donated blood in the US, was fined $9.6 million after federal inspectors found hundreds of blood safety violations at 16 of the organization's 36 blood collection centers nationwide.

In a 32-page letter to the Washington-based organization, Food and Drug Administration officials described an all-encompassing lack of controls to ensure the safety of the nation's blood supply. This followed an inspection report in 2010 which was not actioned.[4] The violations ranged from:

- understaffing,

- inadequate staff training,

- delayed logging of donations,

- ineffective screening of donors,

- failure to add new donors with infected blood to the national list of deferred donors,

- failure to share information on deferred donors between facilities,

- failure to quarantine and recall infected blood units,

- failing to notify health departments when donated blood was found to have been infected with HIV, Hepatitis C, or the West Nile virus,

- failing to promptly alert healthcare facilities when expired or infected blood had been distributed,

- failing to register adverse donor reactions as a result of giving blood,

- incorrect labeling of blood products, to

- poor quality assurance, including keeping blood products out of controlled storage for more than 30 minutes, a backlog of approximately 18,000 donor management cases, and insufficient record-keeping.

We only learn from risk events if we want to learn

Sometimes the lessons from the past, even if translated into clear and unequivocal messages, are not enough to change behaviour. In the investigation into the NASA Columbia disaster, some 17 years after Challenger, the review board began its investigation with two central questions about NASA decisions: why did NASA continue to fly with known foam debris problems in the years preceding the Columbia launch, and why did NASA managers conclude that the foam debris strike 81.9 seconds into Columbia's flight was not a threat to the safety of the mission, despite the concerns of their engineers?

Extract from Report of the Columbia Accident Investigation Board[5]

NASA culture allowed flying with flaws when problems were defined as normal and routine; the structure of NASA's Shuttle Program blocked the flow of critical information up the hierarchy, so definitions of risk continued unaltered. Finally, a perennially weakened safety system, unable to critically analyze and intervene, had no choice but to ratify the existing risk assessments on these two problems. The following comparison shows that these system effects persisted through time, and affected engineering decisions in the years leading up to both accidents

The Board found that dangerous aspects of NASA's 1986 culture, identified by the Rogers Commission, remained unchanged. The Space Shuttle Program had been built on compromises hammered out by the White House and NASA headquarters.

As a result, NASA was transformed from a research and development agency to more of a business, with schedules, production pressures, deadlines, and cost efficiency goals elevated to the level of technical innovation and safety goals. (The Rogers Commission dedicated an entire chapter of its report to production pressures.)

Prior to both accidents, NASA was scrambling to keep up. Not only were schedule pressures impacting the people who worked most closely with the technology – technicians, mission operators, flight crews, and vehicle processors – engineering decisions also were affected.

> Available resources – including time out of the schedule for research and hardware modifications – went to the problems that were designated as serious – those most likely to bring down a Shuttle. The NASA culture encouraged flying with flaws because the schedule could not be held up for routine problems that were not defined as a threat to mission safety.

The final sentence is telling: 'The NASA culture encouraged flying with flaws because the schedule could not be held up for routine problems that were not defined as a threat to mission safety.' Even though these very messages were identified by the Rogers Commission when reporting on the Challenger disaster, NASA failed to learn from the findings of the previous disaster.

The multiple causes of large failures are usually deeply embedded in the organizations where the failures occurred, have been ignored or taken for granted for years, and rarely are simple to correct because they are a part of the culture. An important reason that most organizations do not learn from failure may be their lack of attention to small, everyday organizational failures, especially as compared to the investigative commissions or formal 'after-action reviews' triggered by large catastrophic failures. Small failures are often the 'early warning signs' which, if detected and addressed, may be the key to avoiding catastrophic failure in the future.

To innovate, we need to learn from failure

The hallmark of innovative and successful organizations is not only the ability to learn from failure but also the ability to learn from 'near' failures – or near misses.

'Reverse stress testing' and business continuity exercises can be incredibly valuable. They are like non-destructive testing of the organization, almost like learning to fail in order to avoid failing. However, to learn from them, they must be documented in detail, which includes every decision, every piece of knowledge and assumption that informed that decision as well as the data supporting the knowledge and information. Another indicator for failure is those events that do not become failures.

Near-miss measurement needs to be operated so far down the organization that few senior managers even register it on their radar of important

In July 2010 in *Risk and Regulation*,[6] a 'near miss' was defined as follows:

> Although there is not a single, agreed-upon definition of a 'near-miss', for our discussions we will embrace the following broad definition: a near-miss is an event, observation, or situation that possesses the potential for improving a system's safety and/or operability by reducing the risk of upsets, some of which may eventually cause serious damage.

things to attend to, but the practice of measuring the near misses and the diligence in analysing them *must* be supported and led by senior management. For every so many near misses, one serious event will take place. For every so many serious events, one crisis will occur.[7]

Extract from the website 'Safety 101', 18 July 2012[8]

In 1969, a study of industrial accidents was undertaken by Frank E Bird, Jr, who was then the Director of Engineering Services for the Insurance Company of North America. He was interested in the accident ratio of one major injury to 29 minor injuries to 300 no-injury accidents first discussed in the 1931 book, *Industrial Accident Prevention* by H W Heinrich.

Since Mr Heinrich estimated this relationship and stated further that the ratio related to the occurrence of a unit group of 330 accidents of the same kind, Mr Bird wanted to determine what the actual reporting relationship of accidents was by the entire average population of workers. H W Heinrich's classic safety pyramid is now considered the foremost illustration of types of employee injuries.

There Bird analyzed 1,753,498 accidents reported by 297 cooperating companies. These companies represented 21 different industrial groups, employing 1,750,000 employees who worked over 3 billion hours during the exposure period analyzed. The study revealed the following ratios in the accidents reported: For every reported major injury (resulting in fatality, disability, lost time or medical treatment), there were 9.8 reported minor injuries (requiring only first aid). For the 95 companies that further analyzed major injuries in their reporting, the ratio was one lost time injury per 15 medical treatment injuries.

FIGURE 10.3 The classic safety pyramid showing the ratio of near misses or 'incidents' to more serious events

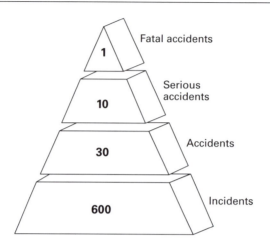

It has long been recognized in the health and safety world that near misses are 'leading indicators' for what is happening right now.[9] However, few organizations extend the practice of learning from near misses to other aspects of enterprise risk management. If the organization were to collate the data on such near misses, that could be used to create information to drive the knowledge that informs the learning process and leads to innovation.

Table 10.1 includes some examples for other aspects of ERM of near misses being leading indicators of opportunities for improvement (see leading and lagging indicators, below). Senior management should ask for a report on all aspects of ERM practised in the organization and for evidence that the leading indicators are being carefully measured and acted on.

Extract from *Risk and Regulation*, July 2010, on near misses[10]

On the one hand, risk managers must ensure that organizational mishaps can only happen far from the realm of near-disaster. But on the other, they seek to highlight risks and drive action by actively constructing near-misses: by convincing people that the organization came dangerously close to something it should desperately avoid. While near-miss events have come a long way, most risk managers wouldn't want their organizations to realize that.

TABLE 10.1 Examples of leading indicators that can be used for forecasting threat and change in threat

Area of ERM	Near misses as leading indicators for threat
Decision making	Decisions that are wrong
Planning	Plans not being followed
Budgeting	Budgets not being met
Treasury management	Inappropriate investments
Credit management	Aged debtors increasing
Actuarial	Mistakes being made
Legal	Law suits lost
Purchasing	Purchases being made outside the framework
Compliance	Number of compliance issues increasing
Brand management	Poor news reports
Change management	Change programmes over budget
Project management	Projects that fail to meet targets
HR management	Staff turnover and absenteeism
IT	IT outages
Logistics	Aged stock
Dispatching	Deliveries to the wrong place
Performance	Interventions needed to correct performance
Environment	Targets missed
Business continuity	Errors in information contained in plans

(continued)

TABLE 10.1 Examples of leading indicators that can be used for forecasting threat and change in threat (*continued*)

Area of ERM	Near misses as leading indicators for threat
Operations – product or service failures	Complaints
Operations – product flow	Times when operators intervened to enhance product flow
Operations – machinery breakdown	Changes in vibration or temperature

Leading and lagging indicators

Senior management should always challenge what they are being presented as risk information, and one of the questions is whether it is being informed by both lagging indicators – what's gone on in the past, and leading indicators – those things that will help us to understand the future.

Too many organizations are being driven purely on lagging indicators – which is like driving a car just using the rear and side-view mirrors. We get a great view of where we've been, but until you look through the windshield we can't know where we are going. Leading indicators are one of the tools that enable us to get a view of what's ahead for us.

The unique view of the organization in the boardroom also gives a clearer view forward than can be obtained further down the tree, so senior management need to use this unique view to question and challenge what they are being told about enterprise risks. The principle of using leading indicators for predicting threats can also be used for predicting opportunities; see Table 10.2.

ERM information systems

The amount of data gathered on risks and risk events can quite often turn into a huge nightmare and lead to misinformation and lack of knowledge. The answer is to harness the power of IT to marshal that data into usable information that will enable senior management to learn and make decisions.

TABLE 10.2 Examples of leading indicators for opportunities

Area of ERM	Examples of leading indicators for opportunities
Decision making	Increasing number of successful decisions
Planning	More plans being followed
Budgeting	Budgets being met more frequently
Treasury management	Investment delivering excellent results
Credit management	Aged debtors reducing
Actuarial	Ability to rely on outputs
Legal	Law suits won
Purchasing	Purchasing framework delivering savings
Compliance	Number of compliance issues reducing
Brand management	Good news reports
Change management	Change programmes delivered on budget
Project management	Projects meeting targets
HR management	Staff turnover and absenteeism reducing
IT	IT resilience
Logistics	No aged stock
Dispatching	Deliveries successful
Performance	No interventions needed to correct performance
Environment	Targets all achieved
Business continuity	Plans are robust and can be relied on
Operations – product or service failures	Fewer or no complaints

(continued)

TABLE 10.2 Examples of leading indicators for opportunities (*continued*)

Area of ERM	Examples of leading indicators for opportunities
Operations – product flow	No operator interventions needed to enhance product flow
Operations – machinery breakdown	Consistency in levels of vibration or temperature

Extract from *The Street*, July 2013 on Kodak[11]

(Kodak first invented the digital camera, and ended up in bankruptcy because of an inability to take account of leading indicators.)

In 1978 Steve Sasson, an employee of Kodak, made presentations to company representatives of his discovery of what he called filmless photography. These company representatives were in marketing, business development, organization and research and development. A business leader who worked with a company that processed microfiche imaging of checks attended one of the meetings and got excited about the camera, Sasson recalls.

'I remember this because I wasn't used to this: he got up, he took a check out of his wallet and slammed it down on there and said, "Take a picture of that." Which I did, and it went up on the screen. He looked at it and he said, "Boy, not enough resolution. If we had more resolution, we could really use this",' Sasson says.

It was one of the early problems with Kodak's electronic camera: Sasson's image didn't match the quality of Kodachrome prints.

Another problem was that the camera didn't fit into Kodak's vertically integrated business system. A more obvious problem was that the Kodak engineer was proposing a product that bypassed the need for film – the company's lifeblood, a lucrative business that produced 70% to 80% profit margins for a company that once controlled 90% of the rolled-film market. This was suicide.

Kodak fell into Chapter 11 bankruptcy on Jan 19, 2012, after a 30-year collapse of its dominant film business and a failure to identify a next big idea to replace it. The company has since sold many of its most recognized businesses and inventions. It has now been re-listed on the New York Stock Exchange but as a much smaller enterprise, no longer involved in consumer film.

However, senior management will often be approached for approval for budgets for ERM systems, and too many times a CRO will implement one ERM system, find it doesn't work and then choose another. It's not because they chose the wrong ERM system, it's normally a combination of the following:

- The organization is not ready for an ERM system.
- The data is not ready or accurate.
- There is no project plan in place.
- There are no resources to tailor it to the organization's needs.
- There is no clarity on how the organization will need to tailor it.
- Senior management do not state clearly their requirements for the risk information they need to make decisions.

CASE EXAMPLE from the author's own experience

I've implemented four ERM IT systems over the course of my career and have worked with many clients who have systems. There are six main points that I recommend to CROs:

1 Don't implement a system before there is an established ERM culture in the organization. Many people think that you use the system to implement ERM but that results in the organization thinking that ERM *is* the IT system. It then becomes a hindrance to embedding ERM. It must be positioned as one of the tools to enable all risk and control/enhancer owners to make their own changes to the records. It is a record of all the other work that goes on around identifying, evaluating and managing risks. Many people use cause and consequence analysis for risks to identify the many causes and consequences (this gives clarity to the cost benefit of controls/enhancers as well as the detail of the roles and responsibilities for risk and control ownership) and the system should be there to record the output of that analysis – not to drive it.

2 Get the data right first – remember rubbish in/rubbish out.

3 Make sure that you have a proper project plan in place for tailoring the system to *your* company's requirements.

4 Make sure you have the resources. It takes at least a year of one person's dedicated time to effectively gather the information needed to tailor it (coding

requirements, taxonomies, business unit structures, etc), to change the system, develop the reports, test and roll out – then add on the time to train the risk and control/enhancer owners.

5 Set out your specification for what you want out of the system *before* talking to vendors. Choose a system that will be able to record risks the way you want them recorded for now and into the future. Bear in mind that some risks present opportunities and the system should be able (in the future) to record risk appetite and desired future risk-state along various sliding scales.

6 Engage senior management in developing the outputs *first*. All the work in developing the system and structuring the information must be aimed at that output – *do not* just automate what you've got in place now.

Internal communication and dashboards

There are many drivers for internal reporting of risk information, such as the need to encourage accountability and ownership of risk and risk controls. But the starting point is to make the programme for ERM clear at the outset, setting out:

- Who takes ownership for the programme at board level.
- Where the mandate and commitment come from.
- How the programme is operated internally.
- How ERM is implemented.
- How it is monitored and reviewed in terms of its effectiveness and the outcomes.
- How it is updated and adapted.

Open encouragement for contributions for improvement of the programme should be plainly set out alongside a clear and well-designed consultation process based on the RASCI[12] principle:

Responsible: the role, person or entity that is designated 'responsible' is the one who performs the work. In other words he or she is the 'doer' of the task or activity.

Accountable: the person or role that has the final authority and accountability to a given task. For any given task, there is only one role/person accountable. This accountability can't be delegated to other roles, individuals or entities.

Supported: the roles/groups/departments that provide the resources and hence support that task.

Consulted: those people/roles who are consulted and whose advice is taken before and while performing the task.

Informed: the people/roles who are informed about the task.

The mechanisms for reporting the outputs from the ERM programme should include processes to consolidate risk information from a variety of sources, and may need to consider the sensitivity of the information. The internal risk reporting should also be constant, consistent, available, understandable and responsive to change.

Often in reporting the performance and outputs of the ERM process a dashboard approach is used where the key information is available to senior management on one page. We could give examples of risk dashboards at this point, but they would be meaningless unless we had defined the organizational objectives and the things that we need to measure against those objectives. Each organization has its own style for dashboard reporting; some prefer lots of charts on one page with graphs, barometers and/or words. Others prefer something simpler with one-page reports. However an organization reports risk information, it must be consistent with other means of reporting. The more risk mature organization would not need to report ERM outputs separately, as the outputs would be included in all the other areas of performance, such as operational outputs.

Extract from *Harvard Business Review*, August 2013[13]

(Summary of a survey of 217 companies in Europe by IIA.)

Systemic risk management tools and analytics that enable companies to track and analyze risk and then inform risk committee discussions are becoming more commonplace. More than half (56%) of survey respondents said their organization has increased its use of analytics for risk management in the past three years. Among the tools most often cited are risk 'heat maps' (41%), key risk indicator scorecards (36%), maps to identify risks inherent in the organization's strategy (30%), scenario analysis and war-gaming (25%), loss forecasting (25%), and loss simulation (24%).

External communication

External communication should, of course, comply with the regulations that apply but, more important, it should address the objectives for reporting externally, such as to give assurance to shareholders, customers and staff.

Many regulations require a risk statement in the annual report. Under Basel II and III and Solvency II the requirements for public reporting are onerous. Some organizations go much further than the requirements, but there is a fine balance between a total 'open kimono' approach to transparency and being careful in what we say in order to avoid frightening the shareholders. At the end of the day, the legal, regulatory and governance requirements must be complied with but the whole process of how we communicate risk information externally needs to be carefully planned and executed, depending on what we want to achieve.

The organization should develop and implement a plan as to how it will communicate with external stakeholders. This should involve a stakeholder analysis to enhance a two-way exchange of information and to provide feedback and reporting on communication and consultation.

External communication can be used to build confidence in the organization. More and more insurance companies are using the 'Own Risk and Solvency Assessment' (see Chapter 12) to inform and develop the external report, and this could be a good model for other industries.

It goes without saying that external communications *must* be clear and consistent and risk reporting will, where appropriate, include processes to consolidate information from a variety of sources. We should also consider the commercial sensitivity of the information when reporting externally.

Questions for senior management and the board to ask

(Including model answers based on best practice – at a high maturity level.)

Do we encourage a learning environment by using negative and positive events to learn from?	It's certainly easier to openly learn from positive events, but yes, we also use negative events to learn from. If these are internal events, we concentrate on how the system or process could have been improved rather than who did something wrong.

How does this learning enable us to make better risk based decisions?	The many examples of how we have improved systems and processes through the learning process is evidence of how we used the learning to make risk-based decisions; in other words, the very fact that we took steps to improve systems and processes is in itself a risk-based decision.
Do those risk-based decisions enable us to take more managed risk?	Yes, this is most easily evidenced in the product development area, where the pace of innovation is increasing due to the openness of our learning culture and the avoidance of repeating mistakes.
Do we get the right information and interpretation of that information as knowledge in order to support managed risk taking, or are we just presented with data?	We used to be presented with reams of data, but the management team are now much better at presenting knowledge to us that has the information and data behind it if we care to look. That knowledge does help us to make better risk-based decisions.
Do we understand the risk information provided; could it be better?	There is always room for improvement, but the quality of the knowledge and our decisions has improved vastly over the last few years.
Does the organization ensure that we use leading and lagging indicators when presenting risk information to senior management?	Yes, we have built up a good database of leading indicators for a number of areas of risk management where we would measure incidents and near misses, such as complaints in the operations risk area; slips, trips and reported hazards in the health and safety area; and corrections to the calculations in the actuarial team where they use a do, check review process in the first line of play. We track these leading indicators and use them to recognize changing trends and we design our response around the knowledge that the analysis provides.

Are we given appropriate assurance that the ERM IT systems have been properly and appropriately implemented?	We have a specific project for the design, selection and implementation of the ERM management information system and have resourced this appropriately.
Do we have clear objectives for our external risk communications?	Yes, we have worked with our marketing team to work on the objectives and the delivery mechanisms for external risk communications, which takes into account the expectations of various stakeholder groups.
Do our external risk communications deliver the objectives and are they clear and consistent?	Yes, in fact we have won awards for the clarity and objectivity of our risk communications.

Notes

1 *Harvard Business Review*: http://blogs.hbr.org/cs/2012/06/how_mature_is_your_risk_manage.html

2 http://www.bis.org/publ/bcbs239.pdf

3 http://www.forbes.com/sites/gerganakoleva/2012/01/17/american-red-cross-fined-9-6-million-for-unsafe-blood-collection/

4 http://www.citizen.org/documents/inspection-report-010312.pdf

5 http://anon.nasa-global.speedera.net/anon.nasa-global/CAIB/CAIB_lowres_chapter8.pdf

6 http://www.lse.ac.uk/researchAndExpertise/units/CARR/pdf/RiskRegulationCloseCalls.pdf

7 http://hbr.org/2011/04/how-to-avoid-catastrophe/ar/1

8 Safety 101; http://crsp-safety101.blogspot.co.uk/2012/07/the-safety-triangle-explained.html

9 http://www.safetyandhealthmagazine.com/articles/8896-the-measure-of-safety

10 http://www.lse.ac.uk/researchAndExpertise/units/CARR/pdf/RiskRegulationCloseCalls.pdf

11 http://www.thestreet.com/story/11991488/4/kodak-the-end-of-an-american-moment.html

12 Interpretation of RACI – http://sixsigmatutorial.com/what-is-raci-download-raci-rasci-matrix-templates-six-sigma/141/

13 http://www.ferma.eu/wp-content/uploads/2013/08/leadership-and-risk-management-executive-summary.pdf

Conformance, performance, roles, responsibilities and regulations

Outline

One of the main drivers for enterprise risk management is the increasing amount of legislation and codes of governance that determine that organizations should implement sound ERM programmes. This drive from regulation in some ways detracts from the fact that enterprise risk management, when implemented to improve performance, can release huge amounts of innovation and enable organizations to get to grips with the many uncertainties that might render it unsustainable.

In this chapter we explore best practice in the roles and responsibilities for leading and implementing ERM and the separation of duties between the 'three lines of play'. It is becoming more and more prevalent for legislation to provide requirements for the implementation of enterprise wide risk management. Most countries begin with some form of financial internal controls basis, but increasingly regulations widen the concept of internal controls to include, amongst other areas:

- ethics;
- conduct;
- risk appetite;
- efficiency;

- embedding ERM;
- operational risks;
- taking stakeholders expectations into account.

We bring together summaries of some of the ERM requirements and codes that might apply to various industries across the world. This does not take into account the numerous legislative requirements for other aspects of risk management that fall into the ERM programme, such as health and safety, product safety and so on.

Managing conformance versus performance

There is something wrong with corporate governance and ERM when based purely on compliance or conformance. It's a bit like expecting staff to do what they are told without helping them to understand why they are being required to behave in a certain way and encouraging them to innovate within the boundaries set out by the risk appetite.

While the board should have an understanding as to what the legal requirements are for managing risk in their organization, if we want to expand the concept into enabling a managed risk approach we not only have to comply with the requirement, but also move beyond 'internal controls' that are focused on threats, in order to embrace enhancements that are focused on opportunities. Further, as we have discussed elsewhere in this book, an organization that makes the leap into incorporating ERM in its culture (rather than just a conformance approach) can enjoy greater benefits from releasing innovation and from managing the uncertainties in the organization.

The role of boards in ERM

The main responsibilities for boards with regard to enterprise risk management can be summarized as things that must be done to comply with the various codes of conduct and regulations (conformance) and those things that should be done to maximize opportunities and minimize threats (performance); see Table 11.1. Directors, in most instances, are tasked with directing strategy. Operational managers, on the other hand, are responsible for implementing that strategy. Table 11.2 summarizes the roles of the board and senior management with regard to ERM.

TABLE 11.1 Conformance versus performance drivers for ERM

Conformance	Performance
• Determine the ERM objectives • Establish accountabilities for risk and internal controls • Define the organization's risk appetite • Monitor the risk management process at a high level • Monitor key performance indicators (KPIs) and key risk indicators (KRIs) at a high level • Steer and approve the ERM strategy • Manage the organization in a crisis	• Make risk-based strategic decisions based on KPIs and KRIs • Work with the CEO and the CRO in managing risk within and to the boundaries of the risk appetite • Challenge and review the risk appetite regularly to ensure that it enables delivery of the strategic objectives • Actively engage in scenarios to establish and learn the roles and differing behaviours required in a crisis

Effective monitoring on a continuous basis is an essential component of a sound system of risk management and internal controls/enhancers. The board cannot, however, rely solely on the embedded monitoring processes within the organization to discharge their responsibilities. The board should regularly receive and review reports on risks and internal controls/enhancers. Reviewing the adequacy and effectiveness of risk management and internal control/enhancer systems is an essential part of the board's responsibilities. The board will need to form their own view on effectiveness and adequacy after due and careful enquiry based on the information and assurances provided.

A risk management and internal controls/enhancers system is considered adequate and effective if it provides reasonable assurance for managing the organization's risks, safeguarding of its assets, reliability of financial information, and compliance with laws and regulations. 'Reasonable assurance' is a concept that acknowledges that the systems should be developed and implemented to provide management with the appropriate balance between risks of a certain business practice and the level of control/enhancer required to ensure business objectives are met. The cost of a control/enhancer should not exceed the benefit to be derived from it.

Management is accountable to the board for the design, implementation and monitoring of the organization's risk management and internal control/

TABLE 11.2 Summary of the roles of the board and senior management in maximizing performance

Strategic planning	<ul><li>Develop and approve the plan</li><li>Drive the plan</li><li>Provide direction and leadership for the strategic planning process</li><li>Use risk-based decision making to maximize opportunities and minimize threats</li><li>Use the KRIs and risk and capital information in making risk-based decisions</li></ul>
Risk appetite	<ul><li>Challenge and review the risk appetite regularly to ensure that it enables delivery of the strategic objectives</li><li>Consider the extent and types of risk that it is acceptable for the organization to bear</li></ul>
Managing the business	<ul><li>Steer and approve the ERM strategy</li><li>Monitor the risk management process at a high level</li><li>Monitor KPIs and KRIs at a high level</li><li>Hold management to account</li><li>Review with management how the strategic environment is changing</li><li>Work with the CEO and the CRO in managing risk within and to the boundaries of the risk appetite</li></ul>
Managing enterprise risks	<ul><li>Provide direction and leadership for the ERM process</li><li>Oversee the processes that management has in place to identify business opportunities and threats</li><li>Challenge the risk assessment for the risks *of* and the risks *to* the strategic plan</li><li>Monitor management's systems and processes for managing the business risks to the whole enterprise</li><li>Ensure the answers are appropriate and that the resources and structure are in place for properly identifying and managing risks</li><li>Test what they learnt against their own observations, experience, general knowledge and good sense</li></ul>
Dealing with crises	<ul><li>Actively engage in scenarios to establish and learn the roles and differing behaviours required in a crisis</li><li>Manage the organization in the event of a crisis, overseeing internal and external communication</li></ul>

enhancer systems and for providing assurance to the board that it has done so. The board should define the process to be adopted for the review of the effectiveness and adequacy of risk management and internal controls/enhancers. This should encompass both the scope and frequency of the reports they receive and review during the year, and also the process for their annual assessment, such that they will be provided with sound, appropriately documented support for the statement on risk management and internal controls/enhancers in the organization's annual report and accounts.

The reports from management to the board should provide a balanced assessment of the significant risks and the effectiveness and adequacy of the system of internal controls/enhancers in managing those risks. Any significant control/enhancer failings or weaknesses identified should be discussed in the reports, including the impact that they have had, could have had, or may have, on the organization and the actions being taken to rectify them. It is essential that there is openness of communication between management and the board on matters relating to risk and internal controls/enhancers.

When reviewing reports during the year, the board should consider what the significant risks are and assess how they have been identified, evaluated and managed. They should also assess the effectiveness of the related system of internal controls/enhancers in managing the significant risks, having regard, in particular, to any significant failings.

Governance for ERM

Good governance of ERM is essential for ensuring that the right risk-taking approaches are being taken.

Extract from the report of the Financial Stability Board, February 2013[1]

The recent global financial crisis exposed a number of governance weaknesses that resulted in firms' failure to understand the risks they were taking. In the wake of the crisis, numerous reports painted a fairly bleak picture of risk governance frameworks at financial institutions, which consist of the three key functions: the board, the firm-wide risk management function, and the independent assessment of risk governance.

The crisis highlighted that many boards had directors with little financial industry experience and limited understanding of the rapidly increasing complexity of the institutions they were leading. Too often, directors were unable to dedicate sufficient time to understand the firm's business model and too deferential to senior management. In addition, many boards did not pay sufficient attention to risk management or set up effective structures, such as a dedicated risk committee, to facilitate meaningful analysis of the firm's risk exposures and to constructively challenge management's proposals and decisions.

The risk committees that did exist were often staffed by directors short on both experience and independence from management.

The information provided to the board was voluminous and not easily understood, which hampered the ability of directors to fulfil their responsibilities. Moreover, most firms lacked a formal process to independently assess the propriety of their risk governance frameworks.

Without the appropriate checks and balances provided by the board, the risk management function, and independent assessment functions, a culture of excessive risk-taking and leverage was allowed to permeate in these weakly governed firms.

Further, with the risk management function lacking the authority, stature and independence to rein in the firm's risk-taking, the ability to address any weaknesses in risk governance identified by internal control assessment and testing processes was obstructed.

Figure 11.1 shows an example from the FSB report of an organization for ERM set out as an illustration of how risk governance can be implemented through the use of separate risk and audit committees.

As ultimate best practice, other aspects of ERM such as treasury, IT risk management, health and safety, project, environmental and BCM would also report risk issues into the risk committee or report via the CRO so that all possible threats and opportunities can be aggregated and compared to risk appetite and capacity of the organization. Some feel that all aspects of risk management, whether financial, operational, hazard or strategic, should report formally into the CRO rather than just for reporting risk issues.

FIGURE 11.1 Illustration of organization for ERM as laid out by FSB

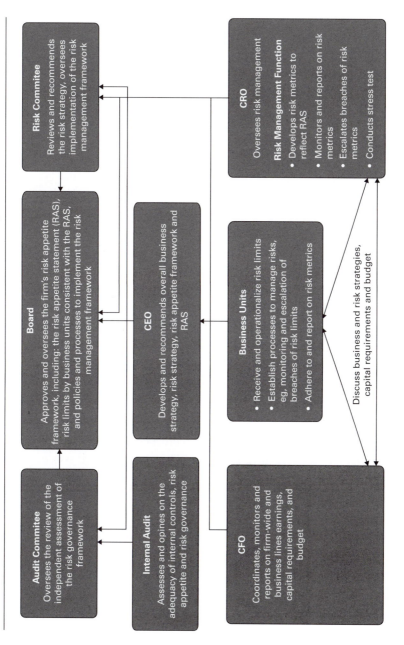

Risk Committee

Reviews and recommends the risk strategy, oversees implementation of the risk management framework

Board

Approves and oversees the firm's risk appetite framework, including: the risk appetite statement (RAS), risk limits by business units consistent with the RAS, and policies and processes to implement the risk management framework

Audit Committee

Oversees the review of the independent assessment of the risk governance framework

CEO

Develops and recommends overall business strategy, risk strategy, risk appetite framework and RAS

Internal Audit

Assesses and opines on the adequacy of internal controls, risk appetite and risk governance

CRO

Oversees risk management

Risk Management Function
- Develops risk metrics to reflect RAS
- Monitors and reports on risk metrics
- Escalates breaches of risk metrics
- Conducts stress test

Business Units
- Receive and operationalize risk limits
- Establish processes to manage risks, eg, monitoring and escalation of breaches of risk limits
- Adhere to and report on risk metrics

CFO

Coordinates, monitors and reports on firm-wide and business lines earnings, capital requirements, and budget

Discuss business and risk strategies, capital requirements and budget

Board risk committees versus audit committees

While the board itself has a responsibility to use risk management tools in risk-based decision making, it may wish to appoint a committee to discuss and review the outputs of risk management. Some might use an existing committee rather than set up a separate one, such as the executive committee, but if the board decides to set up a committee to assist it in its oversight of risk management, it is important that the board should have clearly documented terms of reference that set out the role and responsibilities of the respective committees (see Appendix 7 for an example of terms of reference for a board risk committee).

To help reduce some of the ambiguity that may arise, the board may wish to consider having common membership among the separate committees that are responsible for the oversight of different risks, or have the separate committees hold joint meetings at least once a year. In addition, it is important that the board considers the role of the remuneration committee in linking risk management with remuneration: the level and structure of remuneration should be aligned to the long-term interest and risk frameworks and policies of the company. (See Chapter 6 for more on ERM and remuneration.)

Having appointed a committee to carry out some tasks that are relevant to the board, it is vital that the results of the relevant committees' work should be reported to and considered by the board, otherwise the board risks missing key information and intelligence that may help it to leverage opportunities and mitigate threats.

Where the board decides to set up a separate risk committee to assist in its oversight of risk management, the independence of the committee from management and the diversity of background and skill sets of committee members should be considered. The board should balance expertise and objectivity in determining the composition of the board risk committee.

Key point

Regardless of the committee structure or other means the board employs, all directors must ensure the adequacy of their own director expertise with regard to risk awareness and management, and that means that they may need training.

Specialists who are non-board members could be invited to support the committee.

The roles and responsibilities of the risk committee should be made clear from the onset to avoid confusion, especially in relation to the audit committee. It is also important that communication be maintained between the board risk committee and the audit committee. Both committees should interact as often as possible to ensure timely information is exchanged and appropriate action taken where necessary. For example, results gleaned from workshops that assess the company's risks should feed into the audit plan.

In recent years risk management has been a part of the audit committee agenda, and because the audit committee already oversees risks related to the integrity of the financial statements, the audit committee was considered to be in a good position to have oversight of most of the company's threats – but alas, not opportunities. For this reason boards are increasingly appointing a separate risk management committee that takes a broader view but working alongside the audit committee, which challenges and provides assurance of the whole enterprise risk management programme and outputs.

Appointment of chief risk officer

While the board are responsible for strategy and oversight, management are responsible for implementing the strategy. Depending on the size, diversity and complexity of the organization, many appoint a risk manager or chief risk officer supported by appropriate resources. The CRO provides executive oversight and coordination of the company's risk management efforts. Smaller organizations may delegate that role to another member of management such as the head of finance, chief actuary, or even head of human resources. However, in appointing a CRO in whatever guise, organizations must be mindful that ownership of risks still resides with the relevant business units and not the CRO.

There are some very useful descriptions of the role and attributes of risk managers including a piece of work from AMRAE, l'Association pour le Management des Risques at des Assurances de l'Entreprise, which describes the role of a risk manager who is also responsible for risk financing.[2] This document is called a 'Professional reference tool'. A further example of the brief for the CRO and the ERM team can be found in Appendix 7.

The role of internal and external audit in ERM

This subject really deserves a whole chapter, indeed a whole book, as the 'third line of play' (see Chapter 7), internal and external audit, is vital in ensuring that managed risk taking is indeed *managed*.

Senior management often ask why it is that internal audit doesn't spot the big fraud or big loss event before it happens. There are many theories such as the lack of scepticism exercised by audit, or the lack of knowledge. The fact is that audit is in an invidious position for the following reasons:

- It is there to provide independent assurance on the internal controls, in other words just for the threats; the role of internal audit, according to the IIA's 1999 definition of internal audit[3] is to 'protect the assets, reputation, and sustainability of the organization'.

- Senior management are more interested in the balanced approach to risk; ie threats and opportunities so they don't always value internal audit, often leaving it under-resourced and under-skilled.

- Often the internal controls are focused on the minutiae of the business rather than the big hairy threats that might derail the business, because senior management don't regard themselves as being subject to internal controls.

- To be able to audit the internal controls and to assess the evidence provided that the controls are being adhered to, internal audit need in-depth knowledge of the business. It could therefore be argued that independence decreases proportionately with growing in-depth knowledge of the business.

The strongest of these disadvantages is the lack of transparency in the workings of the board and senior management. When has an internal auditor ever challenged management at the top level? Yet this is where the majority of the largest threats and opportunities occur. Figure 11.2 provides a description of the core roles for internal audit as opposed to the ERM team and operational management, which is adapted from the IIA model.[4]

The new code, 'Effective Internal Audit in the Financial Services Sector'[5] issued in July 2013 by the Institute of Internal Audit goes some way to addressing the lack of power and effectiveness in internal audit. The following is an extract.

FIGURE 11.2 Core roles in the 'Three lines of play'

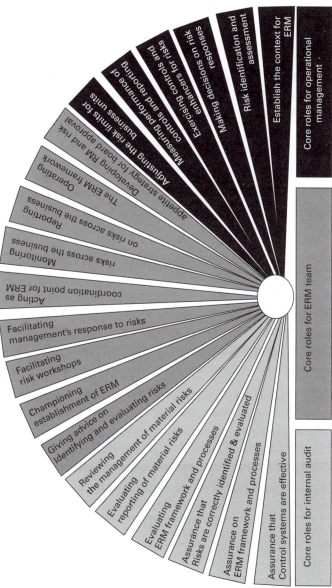

Establish the context for ERM

Risk identification and assessment

Making decisions on risk responses

Exercising controls for risks

Measuring performance of controls and reporting

Adjusting the risk limits for business units

Developing RM and risk appetite strategy for board approval

The ERM framework

Operating

Reporting on risks across the business

Monitoring risks across the business

Acting as coordination point for ERM

Facilitating management's response to risks

Facilitating risk workshops

Championing establishment of ERM

Giving advice on identifying and evaluating risks

Reviewing the management of material risks

Evaluating reporting of material risks

Evaluating ERM framework and processes

Assurance that Risks are correctly identified & evaluated

Assurance on ERM framework and processes

Assurance that Control systems are effective

Core roles for operational management

Core roles for ERM team

Core roles for internal audit

Role and mandate of Internal Audit

1 The primary role of Internal Audit should be to help the board and Executive Management to protect the assets, reputation and sustainability of the organization.

It does this by assessing whether all significant risks are identified and appropriately reported by management and the Risk function to the board and Executive Management; assessing whether they are adequately controlled; and by challenging Executive Management to improve the effectiveness of governance, risk management and internal controls.

The role of Internal Audit should be articulated in an Internal Audit Charter, which should be publicly available.

2 The board, its Committees and Executive Management should set the right 'tone at the top' to ensure support for, and acceptance of, Internal Audit at all levels of the organization.

Scope and priorities of Internal Audit

3 Internal Audit's scope should be unrestricted. There should be no aspect of the organization which Internal Audit should be restricted from looking at as it delivers on its mandate. While it is not the role of Internal Audit to second guess the decisions made by the board, its scope should include information presented to the board as discussed further below.

4 Risk assessments and prioritization of Internal Audit work. In setting its scope, Internal Audit should take into account business strategy and should form an independent view of whether the key risks to the organization have been identified, including emerging and systemic risks, and Recommendations of the Committee (The Guidance) assess how effectively these risks are being managed. Internal audit's independent view should be informed, but not determined, by the views of management or the Risk function. In setting its priorities and deciding where to carry out more detailed work, Internal Audit should focus on the areas where it considers risk to be higher.

Internal Audit should make a risk-based decision as to which areas within its scope should be included in the audit plan – it does not necessarily have to cover all of the potential scope areas every year.

(The guidance goes further in bolstering the role of IA with regard to senior management and the board.)

The Committee recommends that Internal Audit plays a stronger role in supporting the board of Directors to discharge its responsibility to protect the organization. The Committee recognized that Internal Audit must have sufficient standing and access to Executive Management, to perform its role.

While the guidance has recommended that Internal Audit should have the right to attend Executive Committee meetings and any other key decision making fora, in line with the IIA Standards on independence, the Committee does not support Internal Audit attending in a decision making capacity. This attendance is intended to help Internal Audit to gain an understanding of the business and its strategy, and to provide its perspectives on risk and control.

So the emphasis is still on managing threat, which is absolutely correct – the 'third line of play' is about preventing goals being scored by the bad guys, not to be up there in the front line scoring goals for the good team. (See Chapter 5 on exercising control versus risk taking.)

Compliance requirements for risk management: various countries and industries

While most ERM regulations are based on financial internal controls, more enlightened regulators understand that managing risk on the basis of financial internal controls alone is not adequate, as there are other threats that can render a system unstable. So they extend the requirement for internal controls to ethics, conduct, risk appetite, efficiency, embedding ERM, operational risks and taking stakeholders' expectations into account.

The following are extracts from some of the main regulatory requirements for ERM for different industries in various countries. It is by no means a complete list of all the regulations that apply, but it attempts to summarize the main regulations for overarching risk management requirements. ISO 31000 is a global standard; it is not a requirement by law nor is it set out as a conformance standard, being a framework and guidance. We therefore do not include a summary of it here, although we have referenced this code throughout this book.

The New York Stock Exchange Code

The NYSE Code[6] has three unique components:

1 Code of Business Conduct and Ethics: each company must develop and publish an appropriate Code of Business Conduct and Ethics.

2 Certification: Requires directors to certify that they are complying. Certification has an implication of a stronger requirement to comply with the provisions of Corporate Governance.

3 Public Reprimand Letter: The NYSE Code sets out the requirements for the use of reprimand letters.

The requirement is for the Audit Committee to 'Discuss policies with respect to risk assessment and risk management'. This is explained further in the commentary as follows:

> While it is the job of the CEO and senior management to assess and manage the listed company's exposure to risk, the audit committee must discuss guidelines and policies to govern the process by which this is handled. The audit committee should discuss the listed company's major financial risk exposures and the steps management has taken to monitor and control/enhance such exposures. The audit committee is not required to be the sole body responsible for risk assessment and management, but, as stated above, the committee must discuss guidelines and policies to govern the process by which risk assessment and management is undertaken. Many companies, particularly financial companies, manage and assess their risk through mechanisms other than the audit committee. The processes these companies have in place should be reviewed in a general manner by the audit committee, but they need not be replaced by the audit committee.

Dodd-Frank

Title XI – Federal Reserve System Provisions, Governance and oversight, applies to supervised non-banks and bank holding companies with total consolidated assets equal to or greater than $50 billion.

The Fed is required to establish prudent standards for the institutions they supervise that include:

- risk-based capital requirements and leverage limits;
- liquidity requirements;
- overall risk management requirements;

- resolution plan and credit exposure report requirements; and
- concentration limits.

The Fed may establish additional standards that include but are not limited to:

- a contingent capital requirement;
- enhanced public disclosure;
- short-term debt limits.

The Fed may require supervised companies to 'maintain a minimum amount of contingent capital that is convertible to equity in times of financial stress'. Title XI requires companies supervised by the Fed to periodically provide additional plans and reports, including a plan for a rapid and orderly liquidation of the company in the event of material financial distress or failure; and a credit exposure report describing the extent to which the company has exposure to other companies. Credit exposure cannot exceed 25 per cent of the capital stock and surplus of the company.

The title requires that in determining capital requirements for regulated organizations, off-balance-sheet activities shall be taken into consideration, being those things that create an accounting liability such as, but not limited to:

- Direct credit substitutes in which a bank substitutes its own credit for a third party, including standby letters of credit.
- Irrevocable letters of credit that guarantee repayment of commercial paper or tax-exempt securities.
- Risk participations in bankers' acceptances.
- Sale and repurchase agreements.
- Asset sales with recourse against the seller.
- Interest rate swaps.
- Credit swaps.
- Commodities contracts.
- Forward contracts.
- Securities contracts.

COSO

The Internal Control-Integrated Framework (COSO Framework) is published by the Committee of Sponsoring Organizations of the Treadway

FIGURE 11.3   COSO Cube as at January 2013

Commission (COSO). It provides a framework for undertaking enterprise risk management and has gained considerable influence because it is linked to the Sarbanes-Oxley requirements for companies listed on the United States Stock Exchange.

COSO Consultation as at January 2013[7]

COSO states that a direct relationship exists between *objectives*, which are what an organization strives to achieve; *components*, which represent what is required to achieve the objectives; and the *structure* of the organization (the operating units, legal entities and others). The relationship between these three components can be depicted in the form of a cube (see Figure 11.3):

- The three categories of objectives – operations, reporting and compliance – are represented by the columns.
- The five components are represented by the rows.
- An entity's organizational structure is represented by the third dimension.

There is more information on COSO in Appendix 2.

Sarbanes-Oxley – US listed companies

In Section 404 of Sarbanes-Oxley, there is a requirement that each annual report should contain an internal control report, which shall state the responsibility of management for establishing and maintaining an adequate internal control structure and procedures for financial reporting; and contain an assessment, as of the end of the most recent fiscal year of the issuer, of the effectiveness of the internal control structure and procedures of the issuer for financial reporting.

NAIC ORSA – US insurance companies

The NAIC Guidance on the Own Risk and Solvency Assessment[8] states that an effective ERM programme should, at a minimum, incorporate the following key principles:

Risk Culture and Governance: The structure that clearly defines and articulates roles, responsibilities and accountabilities; and a risk culture that supports accountability in risk-based decision making.

Risk Identification and Prioritization: This is a process that is key to the organization; responsibility for this activity is clear; the risk management function is responsible for ensuring that the process is appropriate and functioning properly at all organizational levels.

Risk Appetite, Tolerances and Limits: A formal risk appetite statement, and associated risk tolerances and limits are foundational elements of risk management for an insurer; understanding of the risk appetite statement ensures alignment with risk strategy by the board of directors.

Risk Management and Controls: Managing risk is an ongoing ERM activity, operating at many levels within the organization.

Risk Reporting and Communication: This is in order to provide key constituents with transparency into the risk-management processes and facilitate active, informed decisions on risk-taking and management.

CoCo

The CoCo (criteria of control) framework was first published by the Canadian Institute of Chartered Accountants in 1995. CoCo describes internal control as actions that foster the best result for an organization. These actions, which contribute to the achievement of the organization's objectives, focus on:

- effectiveness and efficiency of operations;
- reliability of internal and external reporting;
- compliance with applicable laws and regulations and internal policies.

CoCo indicates that control comprises: 'Those elements of an organization (including its resources, systems, processes, culture, structure, and tasks) that, taken together, support people in the achievement of the organization's objectives.'

It was introduced with the aim of improving organizational performance and decision making with better controls, risk management, and corporate governance. In 1995, the Guidance on Control was produced and described the CoCo framework and defining controls. The framework includes 20 criteria for effective control in four areas:

1 purpose (direction);
2 commitment (identity and values);
3 capability (competence); and
4 monitoring and learning (evolution).

EU Audit – for public interest entities

On 25 April 2006, the Council of the European Union adopted a new Directive, the 8th EU Company Law Directive on Statutory Audit, Directive 2006/43/EC, article 41-2b[9] on the audit of company accounts. It specifies the duties of statutory auditors, their independence and ethics, introducing requirements for external quality assurance by ensuring better public oversight of the audit profession and improved cooperation between oversight bodies in the EU. It describes 'public-interest entities' as entities governed by the law of a Member State whose transferable securities are admitted to trading on a regulated market of any Member State.

The main ERM requirements of the Directive require active interaction between the various actors in risk management and internal control. The board and the CEO are respectively responsible for providing oversight and monitoring risk management strategies and processes. To effectively assume these duties, they seek assurance from various sources within the organization:

> Without prejudice to the responsibility of the members of the administrative, management or supervisory bodies, or of other members who are appointed by the general meeting of shareholders of the audited entity, the audit committee shall, inter alia: monitor the financial reporting process; monitor the effectiveness of the company's internal control, internal audit where applicable, and risk management systems.

King III – all South African entities

In contrast to King I and King II, King III applies to all entities regardless of the manner and form of incorporation or establishment. Principles are drafted on the basis that, if they are adhered to, any entity would have practised good governance. Unlike most corporate governance codes such as Sarbanes-Oxley, the Code is non-legislative, and is based on principles and practices, on a 'comply or explain' approach[10] unique to the Netherlands until King and now also found in the 2010 Combined Code in the United Kingdom.

The Code covers the three key elements of leadership, sustainability and good corporate citizenship. It views good governance as essentially being effective, ethical leadership. King believes that leaders should direct the company to achieve sustainable economic, social and environmental performance. It views sustainability as the primary moral and economic imperative of this century; the Code's view on corporate citizenship flows from an organization's standing as a juristic person under the South African constitution and should operate in a sustainable manner.

The essential focus of the Code is that the board should 'exercise leadership to prevent risk management from becoming a series of activities that are detached from the realities of the company's business'. In this context, risk is positioned as a cornerstone of corporate governance and risk governance is substantially different to the requirement to implement risk management. Greater emphasis is placed on the board to ensure that it is satisfied with the management of risk.

While King III remains a 'comply or explain' code, there are some related requirements from the South African Companies Act, 2008 for the establishment of risk committees and the Municipal Finance Management Act, 2003, which set out responsibilities for internal audit to conduct audits of risk management.

Switzerland

SIX Exchange Directive

The SIX Exchange Directive requires disclosure of information and control instruments regarding the executive committee, the structure of the board of directors' information and control instruments applying to the issuer's executive committee, such as internal auditing, risk management systems and management information systems.

Swiss Code of Best Practice for Corporate Governance

The Swiss Code of Best Practice for Corporate Governance is one of many European codes of practice that set out the requirements for the internal control system dealing with risk and compliance in that the board of directors should provide for systems for internal control and risk management suitable for the company. In the Swiss code there are three main requirements:

1 The internal control system should be geared to the size, complexity and risk profile of the company.

2 The internal control system should also, depending on the specific nature of the company, cover risk management. The latter should apply to both financial and operational risks.

3 The company should set up an Internal Audit function which should report to the Audit Committee or, as the case may be, to the Chairman of the board.

The Singapore Corporate Governance Council[11]

This code states:

> A sound risk governance allows for the articulation of how, in the context of its risks, a company is able to:

- Achieve its business objectives.
- Formulate its value proposition.
- Assess its risk tolerance; and
- Design its processes with respect to the reasonable expectations of stakeholders.

UK Code of Corporate Governance – all companies on the London Stock Exchange

The UK Code applies to all companies with a premium listing of equity shares on the London Stock Exchange regardless of whether they are incorporated in the UK or elsewhere. It is a code of practice and is based on the 'comply or explain' principle. The main requirements with respect to ERM are as follows:

> The board is responsible for determining the nature and extent of the significant risks it is willing to take in achieving its strategic objectives. The board should maintain sound risk management and internal control systems.

The board should establish formal and transparent arrangements for considering how they should apply the corporate reporting, risk management and internal control principles and for maintaining an appropriate relationship with the company's auditors.

Basel II and III – all banks and investment entities

The objectives of Basel II and III are to:

- promote safety and soundness in the financial system;
- continue to enhance completive equality;
- constitute a more comprehensive approach to addressing risks;
- render capital adequacy more risk-sensitive;
- provide incentives for banks to enhance their risk measurement capabilities.

The Basel Accords are a set of rules on banking regulations in regards to capital. Basel III is a series of additions to the existing accords and is designed to limit the likelihood and impact of a future financial crisis. It requires banks to hold more higher-quality capital against more conservatively calculated risk-weighted assets. It also looks to ensure sufficient liquidity during times of stress and to reduce excess leverage.

Basel III requirements are being introduced from 2013 but some areas are still subject to change and total compliance is not expected until 2019. The long lead-in is designed to prevent sudden freezes in lending as banks improve their balance sheets.

Solvency II – all EU insurers and reinsurers from 1 January 2016[12]

Since the initial Solvency I Directive 73/239/EEC was introduced in 1973, more elaborate risk management systems have been developed. Solvency II reflects new risk management practices to define required capital and manage risk. While the Solvency I Directive was aimed at revising and updating the current EU Solvency regime, Solvency II has a much wider scope. A solvency capital requirement may have the following purposes:

- To reduce the risk that an insurer would be unable to meet claims.
- To reduce the losses suffered by policyholders in the event that a firm is unable to meet all claims fully.

- To provide early warning to supervisors so that they can intervene promptly if capital falls below the required level.
- To promote confidence in the financial stability of the insurance sector.

Solvency II is somewhat similar to the banking regulations of Basel II. For example, the proposed Solvency II framework has three main areas (or pillars):

1 Consists of the quantitative requirements (for example, the amount of capital an insurer should hold).

2 Sets out requirements for the governance and risk management of insurers including the 'own risk and solvency assessment', as well as for the effective supervision of insurers.

3 Focuses on disclosure and transparency requirements.

SII is not yet enshrined in EU law and the implementation date is estimated to be 1 January 2016. However, many countries such as the Netherlands and Ireland are moving towards adopting 'own risk and solvency assessment' or ORSA, as this provides good value to both the organization and to the regulator in determining the sustainability of the organization for the longer term. Further, in September 2013, in preparation for SII, EIOPA, the European Insurance and Occupational Pensions Authority, published four sets of guidance for supervising authorities including one on Governance and Risk Management (CP08), the ORSA (CP09), and Submission of Information (CP10). These guidance notes impose 'comply or explain' requirements for implementation of their content with effect from 1 January 2014. (An example of the provisions for an ORSA is in Appendix 5 and a discussion in Chapter 12.)

Questions for senior management and the board to ask

(Including model answers based on best practice – at a high maturity level.)

Do we implement ERM to conform to regulatory requirements or to improve performance?	We have proven to ourselves that good ERM helps us to improve performance, so while we keep an eye on our compliance issues, we concentrate on improving performance.

Does our approach to conformance or compliance inhibit our ability to innovate and respond to opportunities?

Sometimes there is a conflict where our compliance controls seem to constrain us, but this is normally in areas where the threat is greatest and it is appropriate for us to concentrate on controls rather than risk taking.

Are the roles and responsibilities for ERM clear within our organization?

Yes, we have clear responsibilities for various aspects of ERM set out in our ERM operating model as well as in the various frameworks and policies for risk management.

Do we, as directors, provide leadership for ERM and the right 'tone at the top'?

We try to, but it is not always clear what that means. We use risk management techniques in our decision making and we give clear and consistent messages when risks are not appropriately controlled or when opportunities for taking managed risk are missed.

Are we clear about the roles in the 'three lines of play' and do we, as directors, support the separation of those roles?

Yes, we understand this concept well and we do support it. We have a lot of debates at board level as to which line of play we are in because we switch all the time between those roles. We decided eventually that, as a board, we don't fit into the three lines of play model, but sit above them making sure that they operate effectively. However, when we are in our own roles, not in a board situation, we will take positions in the most appropriate line of play for our day-to-day jobs.

Do we understand the legislative requirements for ERM in every country in which we operate or are listed?

It is a constant battle keeping up with what legislation applies to us, and what is in the pipeline, but we do keep abreast of it through, a) dedicated compliance teams who monitor what it is that we need to be doing and whether we need to change anything and, b) project teams that prepare us for the changes that are to come.

Notes

1 http://www.financialstabilityboard.org/publications/r_130212.pdf

2 The document can be sourced from AMRAE: http://www.amrae.fr/sites/
default/files/fichiers_upload/RiskManagerFramework_AMRAE_2013_0.pdf

3 https://global.theiia.org/standards-guidance/mandatory-guidance/Pages/
Definition-of-Internal-Auditing.aspx

4 https://na.theiia.org/standards-guidance/Public%20Documents/PP%20
The%20Role%20of%20Internal%20Auditing%20in%20Enterprise%20
Risk%20Management.pdf

5 http://www.iia.org.uk/policy/media-centre/news/new-code-puts-internal-
audit-centre-stage-as-politicians-and-regulators-push-for-better-management-
of-risk-in-financial-services/

6 Source: *NYSE Listed Company Manual, Corporate Governance Standards*,
s303.A.07(D)

7 http://www.coso.org/documents/COSO%202013%20ICFR%20Executive_
Summary.pdf

8 http://www.naic.org/documents/committees_e_orsa_wg_related_docs_
guidance_manual_2013.pdf?goback=.gsm_3672682_1_*2_*2_*2_lna_
MANAGER_*2.gmp_3672682.gde_3672682_member_242319549.
gmp_3672682.gde_3672682_member_243533398.gmp_3672682.
gde_3672682_member_240088325

9 http://www.theiia.org/chapters/pubdocs/303/eciia_ferma_guidance_on_
the_8th_eu_company_law_directive_part_2.pdf

10 'Comply or explain' refers to a requirement to comply with the code or
explain why the organization does not comply with it. In many
instances it is easier to comply than to prove good reason why the
aspect of the code does not apply.

11 *Risk Governance Guidance for Listed Boards*, Corporate Governance
Council, Singapore, May 2012. http://www.mas.gov.sg/./media/resource/
fin_development/corporate_governance/RiskGovernanceGuidancefor-
Listedboards.ashx

12 Subject to ratification by implementation of the appropriate regulations
contained in Omnibus 2.

Deliverables from quantitative ERM approaches

Outline

Measuring risk – both threat and opportunity – can be essential when making strategic decisions as to whether to take a managed risk and in implementing risk control or enhancement programmes.

The simple approach to measuring risk is the evaluation of likelihood and threat, then multiplying the two together. This can be used to derive a value for risk. However, there are many financial industry models for valuing risk and capital that might be useful for non-financial organizations such as the 'own risk and solvency assessment' (ORSA), which could be adapted to breathe new life into an ailing organization. The basic assessment of this model is whether there is enough money to run the business if all the eggs break at the same time.

This chapter also explores stress testing and reverse stress testing as examples of how an organization can analyse how extremes of positive and negative events can impact its capacity. A half-way house between the simple 'likelihood and impact' approach and complex financial modelling could be a combined approach that enables an organization to evaluate the likelihood of various impacts along a range of impacts.

Measuring and valuing

Measuring risk

Life would be much more certain if we could place a value on all risks, whether opportunities or threats. There are some risks that lend themselves nicely to being valued and others that do not. If we could place an absolute value on a threat and an opportunity, then taking managed risks would become less of an art and more of a science. Measuring and valuing risk enables us to determine the payback for threat mitigation or opportunity enhancement actions. How else do we know whether to put in that risk control or enhancer?

Using some form of risk valuation is important in all enterprises because we cannot look at the potential payoff of any part of the enterprise and simply rank them from highest to lowest in terms of profitability at any given time. The reason is that it's possible to temporarily improve profits by doing stupid things, such as taking on risky ventures that aren't likely to succeed in the long term, or using substantial leverage such as borrowing large sums of money or trading in assets based on market movements as opposed to underlying intrinsic value.

Valuing threat

When we look at using the valuation of risk to take managed risks, insurance companies are great examples of how to do it well. They have made (and lost) much money from placing a value on risks and offering products, in return for a premium, that help to smooth the financial impact of those risks over time. The kind of risks that an insurance company can provide indemnity against are what they call 'fortuitous risks' – those that can only be an uncertainty ie they have to be random in nature. Insurable risks also have to be able to be quantified so that the insurance company can charge an appropriate premium. Threats that are 'certain' are not considered insurable, but there are other products that can be purchased from banks and other financial institutions that can provide some financial smoothing for certain threats, such as hedging and forward swaps. Table 12.1 lists some insurable and uninsurable risks.

For organizations, there are other losses that cannot be insured, such loss of brand and reputation after a major product failure, loss of a market through entry by a competitor, a competitor stealing a formula or intellectual property, major political upheaval, new regulations coming in, and so on. If these threats could be valued, it would make budgeting and decision making much easier, as well as making compensation programmes easier to manage and to be used to incentivize the staff in the organization.

There are obvious difficulties in calculating a hard financial value for all types of threat, but once there is a formula internally, and it is used consistently across business units and over time, it creates a benchmark that can be

TABLE 12.1 List of insurable and uninsurable threats

Example of threat	Insurable (with caveats)
Reputation loss	No
Damage or loss caused by fire, explosion, aircraft, lightning, storm, tempest, flood, crop failure, animal disease, breakdown of machinery, riot, civil commotion, theft, arson (by others)	Yes
Injury or death though accident	Yes
Ill health caused by others	Yes
Money loss	Yes
Loss of life	Yes
Ill health through natural causes	Yes
Business interruption from an insurable risk	Yes
Gradual wear and tear	No
Mildew and mould damage	No
Pest infestation	No (ish)
Failing to pay debts through redundancy	Yes
Capping losses for an insurance company	Yes
Damage or injury caused to others	Yes
Motor vehicles	Yes
Damage caused by deliberate acts such as arson by the owner	No
Asset liability matching	No
Loss of a key employee	Yes

improved upon. Arguably this can then be developed into a benchmark for other similar organizations.

One ERM management approach, where there is not enough data to provide a statistical analysis, is the 'matrix'. This is used predominantly to prioritize threats and provide an easy visual to represent threats. The normal approach to placing an estimate of likelihood and impact is to have a group of people individually assess the likelihood and impact of the threat, and then to moderate a discussion as to where the placement of the threat should be on the matrix. Some also use this to enable a value to be placed on threats.

The matrix for threats in Figure 12.1 shows an illustrative set of scales for likelihood and impact. In this matrix we have calculated the 'cost' of the threat, taking the (approximate[1]) midpoint of each of the elements and multiplying them by each other. We have also assumed a maximum possible loss of $40 million. The smallest threat (the bottom left-hand side), has a likelihood of 0–5 per cent and an impact of <$100,000. The midpoint of 0–5 per cent is 2.5 per cent. The midpoint of $0 to $100,000 is $50,000, and $50,000 multiplied by 2.5 per cent is $1,250. Thus the figures in each box represent a notional dollar value for risks that are placed in that box. It's worth noting that we've set out a timescale for the threat to occur – in the next three years.

Care should be taken not to take this method too literally. For example, if we have a list of 16 threats shown on this matrix, we wouldn't just add them

FIGURE 12.1 Example of matrix for valuing threats, (assuming maximum loss of $40 million)

cost $'000	0–5%	5–10%	10–25%	25–50%	>50%
> 5000	562,500	1,687,500	3,937,500	8,437,500	16,875,000
1000–5000	75,000	225,000	525,000	1,125,000	2,250,000
500–1000	18,750	56,250	131,250	281,250	562,500
100–500	7,500	22,500	52,500	112,500	225,000
<100	1,250	3,750	8,750	18,750	37,500

Likelihood of occurrence in three year period

up and say that's the potential cost of all of these threats. We would have to compare the types of risk to each other and apply a correlation deduction to them. This is because some of the threats might be mutually exclusive; for example it is unlikely that we would have a failure of the Eurozone at the same time as an EU competitor entering our market, causing a catastrophic impact on our business (because all other EU companies will suffer – perhaps not equally – from a failure of the Eurozone). For larger organizations with multiple product lines and spread across a wide geographical area, there can be further deductions made in the calculation of risk based on the diversity of the organization.

Care should also be taken over how the scales are developed. Senior management will be presented with these completed matrices, but should study them carefully to see if they make sense and challenge the figures when weighing up the size and wealth of the organization. Here are the kind of questions senior management should ask.

Looking at the impact scale:

- Is a maximum possible loss of $40 million realistic in this business?
- Is the scale set at the right level, ie is the top scale at >$5 million the level we think should be highest, or should it be higher or lower?
- Are the intervals sensible?

Looking at the likelihood scale:

- Is there a time period set?
- Taking into account the time period, does it match with our instincts for what constitutes a really likely threat or a really unlikely one?
- Is there consistency in the use of these matrices across the organization?

Consistency in the use of matrices across the organization is an interesting one. Solvency II and Basel III promote the concept that risks should be calculated to a confidence level of 1 in 200 years for SII (99.5 per cent) and 1 in 100 years for Basel III (99 per cent). The rating agencies insist that confidence levels need to be higher than that, such as 7 in 10,000 years to achieve an AA rating; that is 0.07 per cent or a 99.93 per cent level of confidence. That begs the question as to whether the first two measures on the likelihood scale should read:

a (three times 0.07 per cent – for three years) 0 to 0.21 per cent

b (three times 0.5 per cent – for three years) 0.211 to 1.5 per cent

This would change the matrix drastically and could result in adding complexity by extending the number of elements on each scale.

Project managers often use risk valuing methodology to calculate the cost of threat to projects as this helps them compare the cost of the mitigation against the possible cost of the threat and may use different versions of the matrix for different aspects and different timings of the project. More sophisticated project managers and risk managers apply models and calculations to the data such as Monte Carlo[2] simulations. Where there is more data, a statistical model would be more likely to be used, but again the senior manager should take care to check the outputs (and inputs if warranted) on a common sense basis, asking: 'Does that result look and feel right?'

We talked earlier about the velocity or proximity of risk being a third dimension that should be taken into consideration. The simple way is to show those threats on the matrix as either going up or going down; see Figure 12.2. We could propose several different formats for depicting velocity or proximity of threat, but then start to get into territory that is more correctly in the statistical arena, such as the model in Figure 12.3.

In the last section we explored how threat can be calculated. Increasingly organizations are using the same models to value opportunities. There are also many models that can be adapted to calculate opportunities, such as those used in the financial services and investment world, which we explore below.

FIGURE 12.2   Example of matrix for showing relative change in threats, indicating velocity or proximity

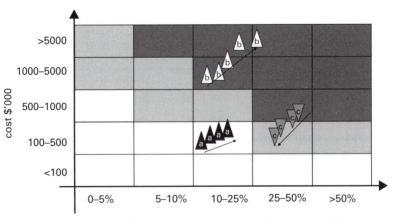

FIGURE 12.3 Three dimensional matrix to show likelihood, impact and time

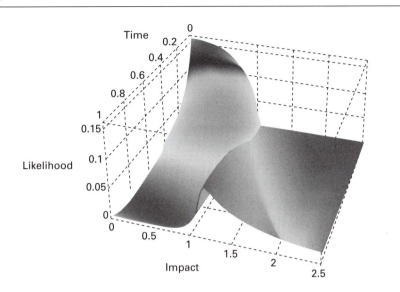

Models for valuing risk and capital

The financial sector

In financial mathematics, a risk measure is used to determine the amount of an asset or set of assets (traditionally currency) to be kept in reserve. The purpose of this reserve is to make the risks taken by financial institutions, such as banks and insurance companies, acceptable to the regulator.

Solvency II (for EU insurers and reinsurers, to be enacted some time in 2016) and Basel III (for banks and other financial institutions) require risks to have a value placed against them and the total to be compared to the capital held. This has created a model that can be adapted (if simplified) for other industries.

Both SII and Basel III have the concept of three pillars. Here is the summary of the SII three pillars:

- Pillar 1 is the quantitative pillar in which we calculate the possible cost of threats, the stressed cost (see more below), and the capital requirements.

- Pillar 2 is the advanced risk management assessment, documentation and assumption review, validation process, use test and ORSA, with involvement of the regulators.

● Pillar 3 is the external (and ongoing internal) reporting and disclosure process.

The aim of SII and Basel III is to ensure that insurance companies and banks remain solvent even if the worst risks come about. That means that the amount of assets in the business must always be greater than the amount of threat.

The calculations required for Solvency II to establish the possible cost of threats are complicated. The capital requirements as created by the liabilities or risks are determined by the nature of the products sold and the additional risks in the business. So if an insurer has sold 100 policies for motorcycle insurance, it knows that there will be a number of claims against those policies and, based on its data, it would calculate what it thinks those claims will cost. This forms the 'best estimate'.

We can apply this approach to all product lines. The underlying calculation of the best estimate is at the core of the calculation and relies on different statistical and actuarial models based on data, trends and comparative data tables. A risk margin is then added to the best estimate, which is calculated using a risk-free rate to reflect the need to hold more capital to pay for the claims if inflation increases – this is calculated as if the organization were to be sold as a going concern. Together, the risk margin and the best estimate make up the 'technical provisions'; see Figure 12.4.

Above the technical provisions the business would calculate the additional capital requirement needed if the product risks were to be worse than anticipated, adding in non-product risks such as operational risk, group risk, liquidity risk, credit risk, premium matching and so on, to a level of confidence of 1 in 200. This level is called the 'solvency capital requirement' or SCR. The MCR is the minimum capital requirement, calculated as a proportion of the SCR, at which the regulator has additional powers of sanction.

There is a method called the 'standard formula' which many insurance companies opt to use to calculate their SCR, but if it does not suit the business for some reason, they can opt for an 'internal model' to calculate their SCR, but this means more hoops and hurdles (use test, validation, etc) to be overcome to prove that the calculations, correlations and diversification discounts are correct.

While the arguments are still going on as to when SII is to come into force, more and more insurance companies are recognizing the value of the ORSA from Pillar 2 for helping them run their businesses and for making strategic decisions.

FIGURE 12.4 Illustration of risk and capital calculations for Solvency II

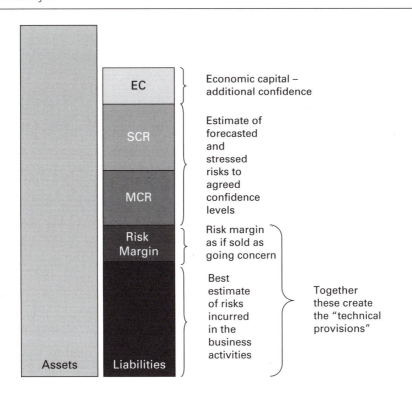

Working capital in non-financial services organizations

Outside the financial sector, working capital represents the operating liquidity available to an organization. Along with fixed assets such as plant and equipment, working capital is considered a part of operating capital. Net working capital is calculated as current assets minus current liabilities. It is a derivation of working capital that is commonly used in valuation techniques such as DCFs (discounted cash flows). If current assets are less than current liabilities, an organization has a working capital deficiency, also called a 'working capital deficit'.

Each industry will have its own ways of calculating its capital requirements (albeit named differently) for such areas as:

- changing cost of raw materials;
- increase in cost of energy;

- fluctuations in exchange rates;
- pay inflation;
- project overruns;
- bad debts;
- product failures;
- increasing cost of borrowing;
- fall in revenue;
- increased cost of IT;
- change in regulatory environment;
- operational risks, such as loss of key employees, non-insured costs of insurance risks.

A company may be endowed with assets and profitability but short of liquidity if its assets cannot readily be converted into cash. Positive working capital is required to ensure that a firm is able to continue its operations and that it has sufficient funds to satisfy both maturing short-term debt and upcoming operational expenses. The management of working capital involves managing inventories, accounts receivable and payable, and cash.

If the organization's operating expenses increase beyond the expected level, and the accounts receivable go into default, there may be a problem with liquidity. This is where some contingent capital might be useful to counter the resultant peaks and troughs and the ERM disciplines laid out in the SII summary above; operating a form of ORSA may save an organization from bankruptcy.

Own risk and solvency assessments – a useful model

Non-financial companies could do well to develop a simplified version of the ORSA: it makes sense to know there is enough capital to help weather the worst storms, or if all the eggs in the basket break at the same time.

While the concept of the ORSA has been brought about for EU insurance companies through Solvency II and separately for insurers in the United States and Bermuda, this is a useful model for other organizations to consider adopting if they struggle with balancing capital and risk. The ORSA under SII involves:

1 Assessing the overall solvency needs of the organization. This involves taking into account the risk profile, risk tolerance and risk appetite levels and the business strategy for the coming planning period.

2 Maintaining compliance, during the whole of the future planning period, with the capital requirements against the solvency needs in point 1 above, and with the requirements on technical provisions. Technical provisions are those reserves that are needed to match the insurance liabilities taken under the whole range of insurance products sold by the insurer.

3 Taking into account the significance with which the risk profile deviates from the assumptions underlying the SCR.

4 Justifying the approach for the assessment of the overall solvency needs, and ensuring that it is both quantitative and qualitative. It must also include a sufficient number of stress tests and scenarios and must include a prospective dimension.

5 Incorporating the information provided by the actuarial function on the validation of technical provisions.

6 Integrating the results of the ORSA in all strategic management processes.

7 Running the ORSA at least annually, and adapting it to the volatility of the risk profile of the insurer.

Stressing the risks for the capital requirements involves recalculating the risks to a degree of confidence that is set by the regulator. For the SCR, the level of confidence is 1 in 200 or 99.5 per cent. As mentioned earlier in this chapter, rating agencies expect the level of confidence to be higher, such as 7 in 10,000 or 99.93 per cent. Arguably much of this happens already in a well-run organization with a risk-aware finance team. However, what is different is the combining of all the risks that might happen, stressing of the risks to a higher level of confidence, and projecting this forward for the business planning period.

Risk-adjusted return on capital

Risk-adjusted return on capital or RAROC first came into being in the late 1970s when it was developed in the United States by Bankers Trust of New York. It is a risk-based measurement for analysing profitability across businesses, having taken into account risk in those businesses.

In its time it was ground-breaking and hugely interesting to traditional risk managers who were struggling to get risk management into the consciousness of the board and senior management. The logic behind it was sound: if the risks a business unit was building up were calculated, and then counted against the profitability of that unit, there would be a great incentive for getting the unit to do something about reducing the risk.

It is now becoming more and more popular in the new guise of return on risk-adjusted capital (RORAC), which is where the risk adjustment of capital is based on the capital adequacy guidelines as outlined by the Basel Committee, currently Basel III. It is calculated by taking the expected risk-adjusted return and dividing by the economic capital or value at risk.

Calculating a risk-adjusted return

In the investment world there are several methods for calculating a risk-based return, but it's important for comparison of two or more investments that the investor uses the same method for each investment to get relative performance results.

The Sharpe ratio is the most widely used risk measuring tool. Through this method one can calculate the expected return by potential impact of return volatility, the total earned amount of return per unit of risk. An increase in Sharpe ratio of a fund means that its historic adjusted performance is better. An increase in number will bring an increase in return per unit of risk. The Sharpe ratio formula is:

(portfolio return - risk-free return)/standard deviation of portfolio return

The 'risk-free return' is calculated assuming that the investment is without risk at all. This might be represented, for example, by the rate from a secure government bond.

Risk-adjusted return varies, depending on several factors like risk tolerance, financial resources, willingness to hold a position for a long time for market recovery in the event the investor made a mistake, investors' opportunity cost and tax condition.

There are other methods such as the alpha and beta calculations:

Subtract from the rate of return on an asset a rate of return from another asset that has similar risk.

This gives a different rate of return that shows how the asset performed over and above a benchmark asset with the same risk.

We can also use the beta of the asset multiplied by the benchmark return
to create a hypothetical asset that has the same risk characteristics.

The difference between the asset return and the beta times the
benchmark is the risk-adjusted return, also known as the alpha.

In all industries, the key is to find relevant data and to get as much of it as
possible. Perfection would be lots of years of data and trends that give us
the ability to forecast different impacts of risk on the model. This is where
statistical actuaries come into their own. Their experience and access to data
enables them to turn the data into real forecasts. The only caveat is that their
conclusions need to be carefully checked with a degree of common sense.

In reality, however, we do not live in a perfect world and are unlikely to
have all the data we need that would perfectly match the current situation.
We therefore have to rely on statistical models that explore different options
and scenarios for testing the attributes of data sets and the relationship of
one data set to another.

Stress testing and reverse stress testing

Once we've got some sort of idea of the size of the threat, in terms of likelihood and impact, and of the timing, there needs to be some sort of check as
to whether we've got it right or not. The financial services sector uses stress
testing and reverse stress testing.

Stress testing is where we apply stresses to the model. This isn't as complicated as it sounds, as most of us naturally stress test things, like checking
that the baby seat in the back of the car is secure by rocking it one way and
another once it's been fastened, or gently trying to pull open the freezer door
once it's been closed to check that a good seal has been created.

The first thing to do is to think about the elements of the model for risk.
If we've used data over time to arrive at a prediction for the future behaviour of a risk, then we set out some basic questions to test. For the baby
seat, our elements are, a) that the seat belt might not be looped through the
right parts of the baby seat; and b) the seat belt tongue might not have been
locked into its buckle. By adding a little push to the right and to the left, we
are adding additional stress to the connections to ensure that they are ok.

Imagine that you've got 25 years of data on how a particular product
has performed in terms of reliability. You need to make a prediction of how
reliable the product will be for the future based on a number of aspects. The

first step is to look at the data over time and pull out the outlying or extreme events if they were not typical of the overall performance. You can then interrogate the data with some questions based on the two key elements – the data might be wrong, or you might be taking the wrong period to establish trends:

- What if the data errs by 10, 30, 50 or 100 per cent?
- How does the data perform for the last two, five, 10 and 25 years?
- If the above test showed differences in the trends, why do those differences exist, can they be explained, are they indicative of what is likely to happen in the future?
- How does the data perform for a snapshot in time (look back at the trend for two to five years ago) and how does that change the forecast?
- What happens to the trend if we put back in the extreme events and reforecast the data?
- What does the trend look like if, say, we combine the worst performing trend of the last two years and the data is incorrect by 200 per cent (select realistic combinations of the factors)?
- What is the effect of risk controls or enhancers on the trend? Can we see the effect of those controls/enhancers in the data when they are enabled?

In summary, stress testing is about taking sensitivity to an extreme value.

Sensitivity testing works in one variable only and only works when the relationship between loss and increase in value remains valid. We start with understanding the risks and the risk controls/enhancers that exist within the business and then decide on the key variable we are seeking to stress. Then we decide which stress tests we intend to address and the level of stress testing that is appropriate.

Sensitivity testing is about applying small changes to determine the effect on the data and looking for the areas where a gradual, predictable trend changes into a step change, which allows us to understand the key areas to track in our ERM process. Imagine driving a car that has a turbo charger; there comes a point in the acceleration where the turbo kicks in and the car moves forward quicker than before. Therefore, when you are coming to a halt outside your garage and need to pull forwards a bit more, you don't put your foot down hard on the accelerator if you want to keep the car and garage door intact. You find that point by testing, in a safe environment, how much you can put your foot down before the turbo kicks in. This is sensitivity testing.

Reverse stress testing is about working backwards from a scenario of complete failure and analysing the combinations of elements that might conspire together to cause that failure, reviewing them with and without the risk controls/enhancers. This is similar to conducting scenario workshops in BCM where we take an extreme scenario and work out not only how to rectify the situation, but also what might have caused that scenario to occur and then conduct an analysis of the risk controls/enhancers breakdowns.

If we continue with the car driving analogy, the reverse stress test is to imagine that there has been an accident, perhaps causing fatalities. What are the elements that could conspire to bring that situation about?

- Driving too fast combined with lack of alertness for the road conditions.

- Someone else causes the accident by their own negligence (such as driving the wrong way down the carriage-way or pulling out when he or she did not have right of way) combined with driving too fast and lack of alertness for the road conditions.

- The car suffers some sort of catastrophic breakdown (such as loss of a wheel, or brake failure) combined with driving too fast.

The purpose of going through this scenario testing is to ensure that you have been realistic in your risk valuation and to review the risk controls/enhancers that are in place. The common element in each of the scenarios above is driving too fast, so ask yourself: what are your risk controls/enhancers for that?

Both stress testing and reverse stress testing are useful, not only for financial services organizations but also for all other enterprises, including government agencies and not-for-profit.

A combined approach

- Measuring risk using the matrix approach would be considered in the financial world as simplistic and downright dangerous. Conversely, for non-financial organizations the financial measurement approach may be too complex. Perhaps there is a half-way house that might work for non-financial organizations that are interested in ensuring that they are prepared for the worst.

The chart in Table 12.2 from COSO[3] follows on from the suggestion that the two methodologies can sit side by side as a two-stage process starting with the qualitative approach and then diving into the quantitative

TABLE 12.2 List of advantages and disadvantages of qualitative and quantitative aspects of risk management

Technique	Advantages	Disadvantages
Qualitative	• Is relatively quick and easy • Provides rich information beyond financial impact and likelihood such as vulnerability, speed of onset, health and safety and reputation • Is easily understood by a large number of employees who may not be trained in sophisticated quantification techniques	• Gives limited differentiation between levels of risk (ie very high, high, medium, and low) • Is imprecise: risk events that plot within the same risk level can represent substantially different amounts of risk • Cannot numerically aggregate or address risk interactions and correlations • Provides limited ability to perform cost-benefit analysis
Quantitative	• Allows numerical aggregation taking into account risk interactions when using an 'at risk measure such as 'cash flow at risk' • Permits cost-benefit analysis of risk response options • Enables risk-based capital allocation to business activities with optimal risk-return • Helps compute capital requirements to maintain solvency under extreme conditions	• Can be time-consuming and costly, especially during model development • Must choose units of measure such as dollars and annual frequency, which may result in qualitative impacts being overlooked • Use of numbers may imply greater precision than the uncertainty of inputs warrants • Assumptions may not be apparent

approach for the most important threats and opportunities (if the risk can be meaningfully quantified).

Risks that cannot be valued

Some people would argue that we can place a value on all risks, whether threats and or opportunities. Others would argue the converse, that all threats and opportunities are uncertainties and therefore to put some value on them is a stab in the dark.

> What is certain is that the more we are able to measure performance, the better the performance will become; in other words, 'what gets measured gets managed'.

The simple act of paying attention to something will cause us to make connections we never did before, and we'll improve those areas – almost without any extra effort.

Can tricky areas such as reputation be measured? We've already talked about brand being measured, in Chapter 3. Public bodies, in order to measure their reputation, track news column inches and the pages that the stories are reported on, as well as whether the articles are positive or negative. This can be developed into a score card to measure qualitatively how well the reputation is holding up, but few would venture into the realms of putting a quantifiable amount against it. We don't have to use currency to measure risk and performance for qualitative risk areas, but it has to be in there somewhere, even if as an implied or a secondary measure.

The following case example shows that the Kingdom of Bhutan has recognized that currency or hard value needs to be behind measuring performance.

Gross National Happiness and Gross National Product[4]

New Bhutanese PM Tshering Tobgay has cast doubt on the country's pursuit of Gross National Happiness (GNH). The concept is overused and masks problems with corruption and low standards of living, Mr Tobgay told AFP news agency.

GNH aims to measure quality of life in more complete terms than gross national product (GNP), striking a balance between the spiritual and material.

The term was coined in 1972 by Bhutan's former King, Jigme Singye Wangchuck. It has been at the heart of government policy since then, although recently some critics have taken to referring to GNH as 'Government Needs Help'.

Mr Tobgay said that while he supported the notion that 'economic growth is not the be-all and end-all of development', GNH should not distract from tackling Bhutan's pressing problems, including chronic unemployment, poverty and corruption.

'If the government of the day were to spend a disproportionate amount of time talking about GNH rather than delivering basic services, then it is a distraction,' he said. 'There are four issues that can compound to make matters extremely bleak: our ballooning debt that if we're not careful will not be sustainable; the big rupee shortage; unemployment, in particular youth unemployment; and a perception of growing corruption. These four combined can make a lethal combination.'

Because today's world operates on money as the basic economic driver, even the Kingdom of Bhutan is now learning to accept that the country cannot be run on happiness alone – there are other factors that must be taken into account, including economic ones.

Questions for senior management and the board to ask

(Including model answers based on best practice – at a high maturity level.)

Do we measure and put a value against threats and opportunities in order to make strategic decisions?	In so far as we can, we do. There are some areas that are easier to quantify than others, and where we have a qualitative risk (whether it's a threat or opportunity) we use qualitative measurements that fit in with our performance management framework for those areas.

Do we measure and put a value against threats and opportunities in order to evaluate the investment needed to control threats and enhance opportunities?	The risk/reward conundrum is always one that we take seriously and there are some instances where doing something about the threat is so prohibitive that we might even pull out of the business altogether if it is outside our zone of tolerance. At other times, we invest heavily to enhance major opportunities and minimize major threats and in doing so we take deliberate and detailed steps to cost the risk/reward ratio.
Do we use a simple model or a complex one?	Both. There are some areas of our enterprise that lend themselves to a complex model where quantification of the threat and opportunity is a science, and there are other areas of the business where we use simpler models, where quantification of the threat or opportunity is more an art.
Is there any merit in conducting an ORSA exercise?	We do it informally through the review process of the risk dashboards and the calculations behind the aggregated risk compared to our capital, but this is something that might be worth applying a little more rigour to as the risks are becoming ever more inconsistent.
Do we stress test our assumptions on risks to make sure that we've got our assumptions right?	There are a few areas where we do, but many areas where we don't. We conduct stress tests related to our business risk areas, where we do a lot of 'what-if' forecasts and consider the effect of various elements that can change the picture. It is something that we will take a look at for the other risks to see if the uncertainty is so great that we should do more of this.

Are there any risks that don't lend themselves to being valued? Do we have other ways of measuring them even we cannot place a value against them?

There are some areas of risk that are difficult to quantify, but that doesn't mean that we don't measure them. Take for example our reputation. We have detailed and sophisticated qualitative measurements that are continuously used to track various facets of our reputation, and they drive responses and investments in resources for the responses.

Notes

1 Statisticians would at this point be having apoplexy because we've not been really precise about the cut-off point between each of the bands and should have used $0.99 in between the impact bands so that, for example, an exact loss of $100,000 doesn't fall into two boxes. We have simplified this to make it easier to understand.

2 A Monte Carlo simulation involves running a number of algorithms across sets of data.

3 COSO *ERM Risk Assessment in Practice Thought Paper*, October 2012.

4 From http://www.bbc.co.uk/news/world-asia-23545641 2 August 2013.

Simple, elegant ERM tools for senior management

Outline

It is useful for senior management and the board to have some basic risk management tools and expertise in order to effectively make strategic decisions. There are often three main elements that need to be in place for a threat to exist: the environment, the trigger and strength (for opportunities) or weakness (for threats). Further, if one can differentiate between a cause and a consequence one can use that cause and consequence thought process to make clear decisions. The board should be sufficiently comfortable and adept at using those tools and should maintain an independent overview of risk management issues rather than try to dive into the detail too quickly.

While the day-to-day management of risk is not within the remit of the board, there are some useful risk management tools that the board and senior management can use in risk-based decision making, planning and forecasting. They can also be used to challenge the ERM programme and when reviewing ERM reports. The following tools are not all-encompassing, and the board may wish to use others, but these are the main ones that we have found have most resonance with senior management and prove the most useful.

The triangle of risk – trigger, environment, strength or weakness

Many opportunities and threats have three aspects to their existence or nature. The reason it is important for directors and senior management to appreciate this is that often they are confronted with situations where they might over-engineer their response to threats and under-engineer their response to opportunities.

It is easier to start with thinking about threats and to consider what it is that makes them exist. For a fire, for example, we need three things: oxygen, fuel and ignition; see Figure 13.1. The oxygen represents exposure or environment, the source of ignition the hazard or trigger and the fuel the vulnerability. Take one of those away and there is zero threat of fire, and if we take away two of them then the likelihood is no more reduced than if we take away one. Examples of these elements and sources/causes are shown in Table 13.1.

However, the element that we have removed might creep back into the area of the risk. Thus if the impact of a fire is important to the success of the organization, then a better precaution, to take into account the event of the control being broken (the control in this case is that we remove one corner of the triangle), we might remove a second corner, or even all three if we need to ensure a failsafe protection environment.

For a fraud to take place there must be motive, means and opportunity. Motive is created when someone wants to commit a fraud either because of circumstances causing a need, or because he or she wants to take revenge on

FIGURE 13.1 The three elements of risk as applied to a fire

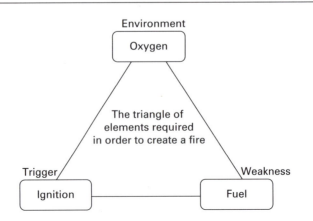

TABLE 13.1 The three elements of risk for a fire

Element	Example	Possible Source or Cause
Environment: Oxygen	Open air Wind	Ventilation Breath
Weakness: Fuel	Waste Packaging Combustible stock Combustible building materials and lagging Curtains	Poor design Poor housekeeping Poor maintenance
Trigger: Ignition	Open flames Sparks Spontaneous combustion	Poor design Smoking Lack of maintenance programmes Lack of knowledge

the organization. Means are in place when that person has the tools, knowledge, position and skills to commit and hide the fraud, and opportunity is when he or she is faced with a clear path for committing the fraud. People in certain strategic positions often have both means and opportunity, but not the motive. However, if something changes, such as a desire to wreak revenge on an ungrateful management team, he or she might become motivated to take the opportunity and use their means.

It is worth considering the elements that might go towards creating an internal fraud; see Table 13.2. The reason motive fits in as a trigger is that often the means and opportunity exist, and can exist for years. Senior management are often in unique positions to defraud the organization, but do not do so because they have no motive, but that can change.

For senior management, this environment/trigger/strength or weakness method can translate into a useful checklist for making strategic decisions. Take, for example, this *opportunity analysis* for entering a new market:

The *trigger* or motive might be the need to diversify and increase profitability; the *environment* or opportunity could be created if there is a gap in the market and/or lack of competition, and the *strength* or means might be there if it is

(*continues on page 247*)

TABLE 13.2 The three elements of risk for fraud

Element	Example	Possible Source or Cause
Environment: Opportunity	A clear pathway to committing the act	Breakdown of controls Ability to make system changes undetected
Trigger: Motive:	Desire to defraud the organization	Poor morale Lack of loyalty Threats from others against the employee or family Debts Inability to pay bills
Weakness/ strength: Means	Ability and knowledge about the systems	Level of seniority Good friends or influence with other people in positions to collude with Ability to change the elements within the system

REAL LIFE EXAMPLE

For some years I had been sending invoices to our Australian region for internal services from the Group, which included allocation of the main insurance premiums. One late evening, I was surprised to receive a phone call from the finance director of the Australian operation. He was even more surprised to find me at my desk, thinking that he was going to leave a message on my voice-mail.

His financial controller was on holiday and he was looking to tie up the half-year accounts but there was an outstanding mid-year invoice from me. I was puzzled. It had been three years since I had sent mid-year invoices, since we'd cut the internal costs for the services by 50 per cent due to much higher deductible levels for insurances.

We agreed to both do a reconciliation of what had been invoiced over the last three years and to resume the telephone conversation the next evening. The next morning I was just arriving in the office when the phone rang: it was the

Australian finance director. He didn't sound like the same person. His voice was ragged and breathing was hoarse. He explained that he had called the financial controller to ask for the codes for the computer so he could reconcile the three years of Group allocations of Group services and insurances. The financial controller had said that he'd get back to him. Two hours passed and then the FD received a call from the police to say that the financial controller had handed himself in at the police station, saying that he'd been defrauding the company for three years.

The story developed further to reveal that the financial controller, a close friend of the FD and godfather to his oldest daughter, had lent some money three years previously to his own son whose aviation business was having severe problems. These loans continued not only to keep the ailing business going, but to keep the pattern going – these were the amounts that would have been paid over to Group if we had continued with the old insurance arrangements. He had made out fake invoices purporting to be on behalf of the Group from a fictitious insurance broker, but with his own bank details as the payee.

The outcome was that the organization was able to take over the aviation business and sell it to cover the fraud of several millions of dollars. However, the relationships between senior management never recovered from the shock of the long-term betrayal by the financial controller.

Subsequent analysis of the situation revealed that the man had been in a position to defraud the company persistently over decades, but it was not until he had the pressure to help his son that he had any motive or a trigger to commit a fraud.

(continued from page 245)

possible to purchase existing expertise, skills, knowledge and facilities that can be used in the new market and there is adequate capital to support the investment required.

If we remove one of these, the positive opportunity no longer exists, or is severely weakened; see Figure 13.2.

The threat: there might be no desire in the business to enter into new markets *(lack of trigger)*, there is significant competition in that market place *(lack of environment)*, and there are no internal skills, or lack of capital to support the move *(lack of strength or existence of weakness)*; see Figure 13.3.

If any one of these elements exists, then it considerably reduces the opportunity to enter into the market, if not completely scuppering it.

FIGURE 13.2 The three elements of risk as applied to an opportunity

FIGURE 13.3 The three elements of risk as applied to a threat

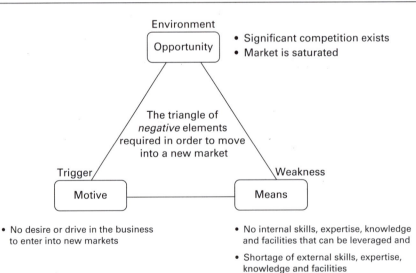

Using cause and consequence analysis to transform risk approach

Another popular risk management tool for senior management is a simplified cause and consequence analysis. This is sometimes called a 'Bow Tie' analysis because it can grow exponentially from the centre.

Having established the context, or goal that we want to achieve, we start with placing the 'risk' (in this instance we will concentrate on the threat side of the risk) in the middle; see Figure 13.4. Now we enter into an area of frequent debate as to what the threat is, and how to articulate it, but that's actually not important at this stage... it will be later.

To the left of the risk, we start to list the causes of the risk. This is the point when we can re-enter the debate about how to articulate the risk. The risk professionals would have us think of an event, but for corporate risks there sometimes is no event as such. It could be a situation that slowly develops, so there is no definable event such as running out of cash or the market drying up. There may be a temptation to start with the phrase 'failure to', but the advice is to try to avoid such phrases as it ends up as being the converse of the corporate goals or performance targets.

So let us consider the threat of the market drying up. What would be the causes? Figure 13.5 is an attempt at considering some of the controls/enhancers for the causes. We've also begun to link some of the controls/enhancers to the causes that they control. This helps us to work out which are the more important controls/enhancers. Then we would consider the consequences of the market drying up and look at what might be the controls/enhancers for those consequences; see Figure 13.6. These Bow Tie analyses can be used for working out the causes and consequences of opportunities as well as threats.

I promote the 'Bow Tie' for senior management as too often I have found big hairy risks sitting on the risk register for long periods with no discernable movement or understanding of the control environment.

No one wants to take ownership of these risks, because there is no one person who has the full stretch of authority to put all the controls in place – apart from the CEO – and then he or she ends up owning all the big hairy risks.

The Bow Tie helps to break down the risk into its component parts and provides transparency on who should do what.

FIGURE 13.4 The Bow Tie for analysing causes and consequences (1)

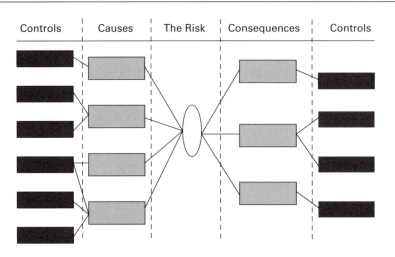

FIGURE 13.5 The Bow Tie for analysing causes and consequences (2)

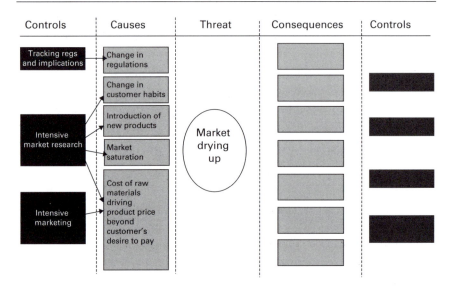

Related to the Bow Tie analysis is the Fish-bone or Ishikawa analysis, where there is a more structured approach to considering the causes of the risk, and it is possible to illustrate vectors (the strength and direction of flow) for each of the causes and sub-causes;[1] see Figure 13.7.

FIGURE 13.6 The Bow Tie for analysing causes and consequences (3)

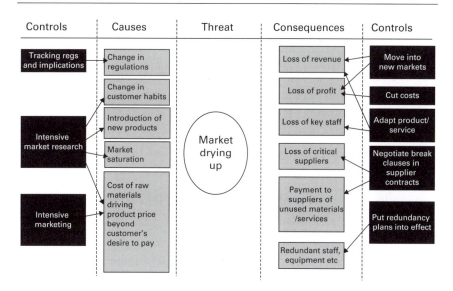

FIGURE 13.7 Fish-bone or Ishikawa analysis for risk

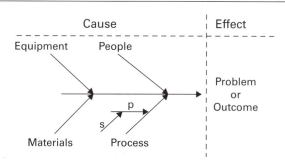

The reference to 'P' against the process is the primary cause, and the 'S' is the secondary cause. There are many versions of the Fish-bone analysis developed, in each case, for the particular business requirement where the key is to find the main headings or 'buckets' for the causes.

Advantages of using cause and consequence analysis

The beauty of these kinds of analysis is that we don't need much expertise to do it, nor do we need any equipment or materials, just paper and pen and input from a number of people. We can apply them to any situation

> Many of my clients use the Bow Tie to report risk to the board. In this way each risk owner gets a one-page report and can see instantly how well the risk is being controlled and if there are areas for improvement. They also know exactly who is responsible for that area, and can call for a full report.
>
> Behind each one-page report is a full database with audit trails, but the board don't need to be bothered with that so long as they get assurance from internal audit that the process is working well and the framework is being followed.

without having to call in the risk experts, and they help us to work out who is responsible for what in terms of the controls/enhancers as well as the importance of each cause. We can add to the analysis by indicating each control or enhancer owner and show how effective the control/enhancer is, in colours from red to green.

As the organization gets used to using this way of analysing risks and the process becomes ingrained, it can be extended to the analysis of opportunities. Using the Bow-tie or Ishikawa analysis by senior management is a powerful aid to enabling better risk-based decision making, thereby ensuring better managed risk taking.

Macro and micro risk management

When we refer to 'micro' risk management as opposed to 'macro', we refer to the risk management of a series of similar events, such as the management of product quality complaints. Senior management and the board become irritated when faced with lots of detail on micro risk management issues. Conversely, some board members can only relate to micro risk management issues and dive willingly into the detail as it keeps them within their comfort zone.

Take the example of managing product quality complaints. There does not need to be a detailed risk assessment of each of many similar complaints provided that one complaint has been examined in detail and that there is a well-rehearsed process for assessing the severity of the impact of the defect and responding appropriately to each of them. The macro risk management process is the operation of that well-rehearsed process and response, and all that needs to be reported to the board is where the process and response are breached, or where there are outliers in the expected frequency and/or impact of those complaints. This means that the board have to rise above the micro issues and challenge the process and data on a macro basis. In this way, the organization is much more likely to be operating a risk management process that will spot and respond to large-impact issues.

Questions for senior management and the board to ask

(Including model answers based on best practice – at a high maturity level.)

Do we, in our role of senior management, have the risk management tools to be able to effectively make strategic decisions?	We are able in many instances to use risk management tools on the level of unconscious competence – we do it without thinking about it, but there are other times when we have to remind ourselves, particularly if there is a hot and heavy debate about something and we have difficulty in reaching agreement.
Can we spot the three main elements that need to be in place for a threat to exist?	We take time out to consider if there are three clear themes that can relate to the triangle of risk, particularly if there is an area that we are worried about or where there are differences of opinion.
Can we differentiate between a cause and a consequence?	We consider this to be a core skill for senior management and directors.
Do we use that cause and consequence thought process to make clear decisions?	We think that this should take place each time there is a decision to be made.
Are we sufficiently comfortable and adept at using basic risk management tools?	We can always do better and are constantly trying to update our skills.

Do we maintain an independent high-level overview of risk management issues or do we tend to dive into the detail too quickly?

We know that the board and senior management should remain at the strategic level, even if the temptation is to delve into the detail, but sometimes it is irresistible!

Note

1 Thanks to Alan Chapman, www.businessballs.com

ERM and performance management synergies

14

Outline

We've already talked about opportunities and threats being categorized into four areas: strategic, financial, hazard and operational. The most practical way to align or to embed ERM for financial, operational and hazard risks is with the performance management and quality systems within the organization. It could be argued that strategic risk management could also be aligned in this way, but rarely do you find strategic performance management being subjected to the same rigour and structure that is applied to other risk areas. The answer is to apply risk-adjusted performance metrics to the organization to ensure continuous improvement and encourage innovation.

Performance management in the sense of total organizational performance management can sometimes be mistaken for individual performance management, which is a subset and a key component of organizational performance management. Most organizations now include a framework for operating key performance indicators (KPIs) to track that the business units are meeting their objectives, which in turn count towards the achievement of the organizational goals. These KPIs are made much richer and more likely to count towards success and innovation if they are matched with appropriate key risk indicators (KRIs) producing risk-adjusted performance metrics.

Lean practices and Six Sigma are increasingly being operated together as Lean Six Sigma. Together they are a powerful force behind driving continuous improvement, and when enterprise risk management is aligned and embedded with them, they are more likely to address the most critical opportunities and threats. Many quality management tools are the same as those used in risk assessment processes, so risk management alignment with quality processes makes complete sense and reduces waste.

Risk management alignment within the organization

There are close parallels between risk management and other drivers for quality in the organization. Depending on the culture of the organization, risk management could be seen as an integral component of any of these, or these quality drivers could be a component of ERM; it matters not which way round the organization plays it. What matters most is that the organization moves towards innovation, value creation and value protection in the most efficient manner, embracing risk-based decision making in every corner of the organization and taking a structured approach to improvement.

Performance management

We can debate the origins of the most recent financial crisis for some time, but all analyses of the fallout carry one clear message: there were inadequate risk assessment practices. Too many organizations took on too much risk with too little regard for reasonable, realistic long-term performance expectations.

The economic crisis of recent years is focusing senior minds on more robust approaches to risk management, with a new drive to keep pace with financial innovation, performance incentives and business goals. Reforms, both in the boardroom and from regulators, will stretch risk management across the organization and involve systematically linking risk and corporate performance management, leading to an informed view of reward.

Extreme volatility, even financial crises, isn't new. Organizations that keep their eyes on the ball – on improving performance, both financially and operationally – will emerge from these trying times better positioned to take advantage of opportunities. We can no longer regard compliance-driven approaches to managing risk as sufficient in an increasingly volatile, interconnected enterprise environment. Approaches to risk management need to provide business leaders and their boards of directors with an integrated view of risk and performance that defines how rapidly emerging events will impact operations, quality and, ultimately, shareholder value.

Recent research (see the box below) shows that many companies fail to connect risk and performance in the course of basic performance management. Just 37 per cent of nearly 100 senior executives at US-based multinationals surveyed by PricewaterhouseCoopers in 2008 said their companies link KRIs to corporate performance indicators:

Extract: Research from PwC[1]

External stakeholders are already motivating companies to take a fresh approach to aligning their risk appetites and performance objectives in a smarter, more systematic way. Company directors, credit rating agencies, and institutional investors alike are scrutinizing the risk/reward relationship and formalizing their own linkages between risk and performance, creating new expectations and market demands for businesses. A further inducement is being crafted by the Obama Administration, which has telegraphed its clear intent to more closely tether compensation in financial services to long-term performance, through either regulatory or legislative action. The bonus culture has been a hallmark of Wall Street, but it's not entirely unique to the big banks. The reforms to compensation and incentives that emerge on Wall Street will likely have an influence on the wider American business community.

There is no handbook for integrating risk and performance management, but it should be understood at the start that this is not merely a defensive response to greater uncertainty in the business environment and, for some, to pending regulation. Companies are recognizing that the same drivers of increased volatility – capital mobility, rapid innovation, and the development of new business models—also offer opportunities that they must exploit to increase revenue, improve shareholder value, and satisfy evolving customer demands.

With an integrated, principled approach to managing risk and business performance, companies can seize with greater confidence the opportunities that an interconnected economy presents.

> The process of connecting risk and reward starts at strategy setting. When company leaders understand the greatest sources of value creation and destruction across their organizations, when they assign clear accountability for risk management and performance management, and when they systematically quantify the rewards associated with the risks, they change the decision-making game for their managers.

It is rare to find organizations that have integrated their ERM and performance management processes so that KPIs are supported by matching KRIs. Both disciplines are designed to support organizations' efforts in making decisions and meeting their goals – ERM through the identification and management of those risks that could affect business objectives, and performance management through the identification and measurement of the drivers needed to achieve results.

Risk-adjusted performance metrics offer senior management tools that strike the appropriate balance between meeting performance goals and achieving appropriate returns for the risks being taken. The application of risk-based performance management will also lead to incentives that are more aligned with an organization's long-term success.

Performance management methods

Six Sigma

Six Sigma is a method intended to reduce variations in operational processes, from manufacturing to handling of paperwork. It is based on the statistical analysis of defects or variances from expected quality. It began in 1986 in Motorola in the United States. Today, Six Sigma is used as a holistic business performance methodology, on a global basis, in organizations as diverse as hospitals, local government departments, prisons, industrial companies, banks, insurance companies and multinational corporations.

In the organization, Six Sigma is led by practitioners who are graded on their knowledge and expertise and awarded 'belts' such as the Master Black Belt who trains and coaches Black Belts and others, and the Black Belt who leads problem-solving projects and trains and coaches project teams. Some organizations and certification companies promote other layers, such as green, yellow and white belts.

General Electric[2] description of Six Sigma

Globalization and instant access to information, products and services continue to change the way our customers conduct business.

Today's competitive environment leaves no room for error. We must delight our customers and relentlessly look for new ways to exceed their expectations. This is why Six Sigma Quality has become a part of our culture.

First, what is Six Sigma?

It is not a secret society, a slogan or a cliché. Six Sigma is a highly disciplined process that helps us focus on developing and delivering near-perfect products and services.

Why 'Sigma'? The word is a statistical term that measures how far a given process deviates from perfection. The central idea behind Six Sigma is that if you can measure how many 'defects' you have in a process, you can systematically figure out how to eliminate them and get as close to 'zero defects' as possible. To achieve Six Sigma Quality, a process must produce no more than 3.4 defects per million opportunities. An 'opportunity' is defined as a chance for non-conformance, or not meeting the required specifications. This means we need to be nearly flawless in executing our key processes.

Key concepts of Six Sigma

At its core, Six Sigma revolves around a few key concepts.

Critical to Quality:	Attributes most important to the customer.
Defect:	Failing to deliver what the customer wants.
Process Capability:	What your process can deliver.
Variation:	What the customer sees and feels.
Stable Operations:	Ensuring consistent, predictable processes to improve what the customer sees and feels.
Design for Six Sigma:	Designing to meet customer needs and process capability.

ERM, performance management and Six Sigma all share the same goal: that the organization meets its objectives or even, as GE puts it, 'delight our customers and relentlessly look for new ways to exceed their expectations'.

The Six Sigma process includes a requirement to conduct a risk assessment, and the implementation of an ERM programme could be conducted in a Six Sigma environment. Central to the core of Six Sigma is root cause analysis. This is a powerful tool for all levels of decision making. Yet rarely do ERM and Six Sigma become integrated at all levels in the organization, because Six Sigma requires repetitive activities and data to function well. It is therefore more often integrated into operational risk management rather than at the enterprise level for strategic risk-based decision making (see Chapter 2 on risk types).

There is a synergistic relationship between ERM and Six Sigma: the continuous improvement methodology in Six Sigma assists leadership in managing both the operations of the organization and the inherent risk associated with it. Six Sigma, rather than being 'something else to do' can therefore become a robust framework in which an organization can manage its risks in many areas of the enterprise.

Lean processes

Closely connected with Six Sigma, and based on Kaizen principles, Kaizen is often practised as Lean Six Sigma[3]. Kaizen has the following principles:

- Long-term success requires daily improvements.
- Leaders must go to the *gemba* (actual workplace) to find facts.
- Leaders must demonstrate respect for their people.
- Effective metrics must show the condition of flow, synchronization and levelling across the enterprise.
- Kaizen efforts must lead to Lean, and Lean must lead to 'green' – delivering wider ecological and social benefits.

Lean has a five-step process for guiding the implementation of Lean techniques:

1 Specify value from the standpoint of the end customer by product family or activity.
2 Identify all the steps in the value stream for each product family activity, eliminating whenever possible those steps that do not create value.
3 Make the value-creating steps occur in tight sequence so the product or activity will flow smoothly toward the customer.

4 As flow is introduced, let customers pull value from the next upstream activity.

5 As value is specified, value streams are identified, wasted steps are removed, and flow and pull are introduced, begin the process again and continue it until a state of perfection is reached in which perfect value is created with no waste.

Combining this with Six Sigma for eliminating variance creates a very powerful process improvement tool. These can be used in conjunction with operational, hazard and financial risk management to improve value, eliminate waste and reduce uncertainty from other risk areas.

In theory, combining Lean Six Sigma with strategic risk management has merits. However, in practice, the most valuable part of the process, root cause analysis, is probably the closest that one could get senior management to practising Lean Six Sigma in risk-based decision making.

Total Quality Management

Total Quality Management (TQM) has for some years been increasingly superseded by Lean Six Sigma. In principle it has the same aims, but Lean Six Sigma is a more structured (and better packaged) framework and process. Based mainly on statistical and manufacturing processes, TQM is used at all levels of an organization – typically through 'quality circles' or Kaizen work teams to analyse and review activities and uncover inefficiencies.

The tools used in TQM in support of quality improvement or quality management programmes, including Kaizen and other and philosophies, are very similar to those used in ERM circles.[4] The main quality tools that are also known as risk assessment tools are:

- The 'Five whys' – asking 'Why?' at least five times to uncover the root cause of a problem.
- Flowcharts – a boxes and arrows method of examining activities, potentially used in brainstorming, also found in business process modelling.
- Fish-bone/Ishikawa diagrams – fish-bone-structured diagrams for identifying cause/effect patterns, in which primary categories are generally predetermined according to context.
- Timeline analysis – tracking the key quality and risk issues along the lifetime of a product or activity.
- Run chart – a graph that plots data/change along a timeline.

- Pareto chart – a line and bar graph displaying cause/effect ratios, especially the biggest relative cause, based on Pareto theory.

- Histogram – a bar graph displaying data in simple categories that together account for a total.

- Checklist – pre-formatted list for noting incidence, frequency, etc, according to known useful criteria.

- Control/Shewhart chart – a standard pattern of performance/time for a given process, often in run chart format, which acts as a template to check conformance and deviation.

- Scatter diagram/scatterplot – a graph that plots points (typically very many individual instances) according to two variables, which produces a useful visual indication of the relationship between the two variables.

- Questionnaire and checklist – use of structured questionnaires and checklists to collect information to assist with the recognition of the significant risks and quality issues.

- Workshop and brainstorming – collection and sharing of ideas and discussion of the events that could impact the objectives, stakeholder expectations or key dependencies.

- Inspection and audit – physical inspections of premises and activities and audits of compliance with established systems and procedures.

- HAZOP and FMEA approach – Hazard and Operability studies and Failure Modes Effects Analysis are quantitative technical failure analysis techniques.

- SWOT and PESTLE analysis – Strengths, Weaknesses, Opportunities and Threats, and Political, Economic, Social, Technological, Legal and Environmental analyses offer structured approaches to quality and risk recognition.

The argument for promoting continuous quality improvement is irrefutable and has been proven time and again to deliver competitive advantage. By combining it with a range of risk management techniques under an ERM programme ensures that it can be appropriately resourced where it will add greatest value. For example, using leading risk indicators to show where areas are deteriorating in quality will enable a greater focus for quality management in those deteriorating areas. So in this case we use quality management as one of our risk responses. It could be argued that this is a 'reactive' position and that quality management should be a 'proactive' activity. And so it should be, but in reality all management systems can become stale and out of fashion. Combining quality systems with risk management provides a new energy for the drive for continuous improvement. In practice, most organizations would concentrate on aligning mostly hazard, operational and perhaps financial risk management areas with quality systems as opposed to the whole gamut of ERM practices; these are the areas with considerable amounts of data and repetition of activity that can be mapped, tracked and quality and risk improved over time.

Questions for senior management and the board to ask

(Including model answers based on best practice – at a high maturity level.)

Is strategic planning and decision making subjected to the rigour of tracking performance that you would expect from other areas of the organization?

We track the number of decisions we take at board level and we review the success of those decisions over a period of time. Our tracking system enables us to review the quality of risk management tools that we engage overtly, but not those that we engage instinctively. Strategic planning is subjected to a rigorous and detailed risk management review which is conducted by an independent risk management expert alongside the senior manager preparing that divisional strategic plan that goes towards the overarching strategic planning process. This has been an exceptionally useful exercise in developing a joined-up strategic planning risk evaluation that looks at the threats and opportunities coming out of the strategic plan and the actions and investments that we need to make to ensure that we maximize the opportunities and minimize the threats. We expect this level of rigour for all business planning areas as well as for budgeting.

Does each of the key performance indicators have relevant and appropriate matching key risk indicators?	Yes, but some KRIs cross-over several KPIs. We did a mapping exercise looking at matching KRIs to KPIs and while there were no 'un-paired' ones, there was lots of cross-over.
Do you use risk-adjusted performance metrics to drive better performance and management of risk?	Yes we do. We make adjustments based on risk outputs to performance of the divisions, business units and expect them to do the same for their teams and individuals.
If you operate quality systems in the organization, is ERM aligned and integrated with them?	Individual risk management aspects are aligned with quality systems, but not all. We think that the main hazard, operational and financial risk management areas are the ones that should be aligned to provide greatest value.

Notes

1 http://www.pwc.com/en_US/us/risk-performance/assets/pwc-risk-performance-2009.pdf

2 http://www.ge.com/en/company/companyinfo/quality/whatis.htm

3 http://www.lean.org/whatslean/principles.cfm

4 Thanks to Alan Chapman at businessballs.com: http://www.businessballs.com/qualitymanagement.htm

The key strategic questions for senior management and boards to ask themselves

Outline

At the end of each chapter in this book is a set of questions for the board to ask themselves, with some model answers; they total more than 90. In this chapter we summarize those questions into just 21 key strategic questions that can be used as a way for boards or directors to ask themselves about risk and how it is implemented in their organizations, to ensure that the organization is open to the idea of taking managed risk and to make sense of the complicated world of enterprise risk management.

Directors' roles include asking management tough questions to assure themselves that risk has been fully considered in the strategic and business planning processes. This chapter poses suggested questions for boards to ask the chief executive, senior management and itself. For each question we have included some explanation and recommendations.

Recognizing the risks *of* versus the risks *to* the strategic plan

Top management, however structured, through boards, committees and/or cabinets, are recognized as being responsible for driving the strategic direction for the enterprise. Through the organizational structure there needs to be clearly delegated processes to ensure that the strategic plan is approved, and that there are monitoring and management processes in place to ensure that the business risks coming out of the strategy are identified, evaluated and responded to.

In addition, the risks affecting the strategic plan need to be identified, evaluated and responded to. For example, there may be a plan to move into a new product area. This plan would require an evaluation of the risks this brings about in all areas of the business, not least other product areas, the implications of diverting resources and capital, and the effect on other areas of the business strategy and value drivers. These are the risks *of* the strategic plan. Then consideration needs to be given to the risks that might affect the strategy for entering into a new product area. These are the risks *to* the strategic plan.

These questions are a guide that can be adopted for each organization to focus appropriate discussions about the ERM programmes, concentrating on whether the processes and frameworks achieve the right ERM objectives, rather than whether the processes and frameworks are being followed. The questions are set out below, then each is answered in the rest of the chapter, with recommended practices provided.

A. Strategic planning and ERM

Identifying, analysing and assessing business risks and opportunities:

1 How do we integrate ERM with the organization's strategic direction and plan?
2 What are the principal business risks both coming from the strategic plan and those that threaten (enhance) that plan?
3 Are we taking the right amount of risk?
4 Do we know which risks, if managed well, will increase or decrease the value of and results for our organization?

B. Risk management processes

Designing and implementing strategies for managing business risks:

5 How effective is our process for identifying, assessing and managing business threats and opportunities?

6 How do we ensure that risk management is an integral part of the planning and day-to-day operations of individual business units?

7 How do we ensure that the board's expectations for risk management are communicated to and followed by the employees in the organization?

8 How do we ensure that our executives and employees act in the best long-term interests of the organization and its stakeholders?

9 How is risk management coordinated across the organization?

10 How do we know that we are getting the most from our ERM strategy?

C. Risk monitoring and reporting

Implementing processes to monitor and communicate business risks:

11 How do we ensure that the organization is performing according to the business plan and within appropriate risk tolerance limits?

12 How do we monitor and evaluate changes in the external environment and their impact on the organization's strategy and risk management practices?

13 What information about the risks facing the organization does the board get to help it fulfil its stewardship and governance responsibilities?

14 How do we know that the information the board gets on ERM performance is accurate and reliable?

15 How do we decide what information on risks we should publish?

16 How do we take advantage of the organizational learning that results from the risk management programme and activities?

17 How does the board ensure that at least some of its members have the requisite knowledge and experience in risk?

D. Questions directed at the board itself

Questions appropriate for discussion among the directors:

18 How do we, as a board, help establish the 'tone at the top' that promotes a 'risk aware' culture?

19 What are our priorities as a board in the oversight of risk management?

20 How does the board handle its responsibility for the oversight of opportunities and threats?

21 How satisfied are we that the board is doing what it should in overseeing risk?

The key strategic questions

A. Strategic planning and ERM

1. How do we integrate ERM with the organization's strategic direction and plan?

The strategic plan is about maximizing the opportunities in the business through its assets, knowledge, capital resources and people in order to thrive and grow in the market place. Sometimes organizations move into new and profitable business opportunities, discontinue unprofitable ones and consolidate other business operations. Taking managed risk involves considering the financial viability of new initiatives and investments, as well as assessing the implications of internal and external opportunities and threats for the organization as a whole.

Recommended practices:

With a thorough understanding of the business risks that may affect the achievement of the strategic objectives, the board contributes to the development of strategic direction and approves the strategic plan.

The organization's core competencies, its goals and objectives and the strengths, weaknesses, opportunities and threats it faces need to be taken into account in the strategic planning process as well as forecasts and assumptions made by the management team. ERM activities should be integrated with the development and implementation of the organization's strategic plan.

The organization should develop key performance indicators and matching KRIs based on the balance between threats and opportunities.

There should be active consideration of a range of scenarios that includes the worst-case as well as the best-case.

2. What are our principal business risks both coming from the strategic plan and those that threaten (enhance) that plan?

All organizations will have a range of strategic threats and opportunities that are core to success. Directors must know what those major threats and opportunities are and should be provided with suitable intelligence from management, such as risk dashboards and a risk report.

Recommended practices:

The board should mandate management to provide a framework for identifying, monitoring and managing the organization's business threats and opportunities. They should expect management to provide regularly scheduled, understandable and concise reports on ERM to the board on which it can take decisions.

The board should step back from these reports and challenge the results against past performance, expected performance and other ERM information that may have a bearing on strategic planning.

3. Are we taking the right amount of risk?

Managed risk taking and risk-based decision making are closely related to an organization's objectives, values and the expectations of its owners or key stakeholders. It is important that the board and management have a common understanding of their risk appetite levels and base them on the organization's tolerance and capacity for risk. The board and management should appropriately balance 'value protection' with 'value creation' when agreeing upon the organization's overall risk appetite levels.

There is a continuum of risk taking that runs from day-to-day routine tasks such as bidding on or procuring major contracts, making individual investment decisions, etc, to major new investments and initiatives that change the strategic direction of the organization. The board should be satisfied that the organization has processes to ensure that all risk-related decisions are properly made. However, the board must be directly involved in major decisions and should ensure that the associated risks receive the weight they deserve.

Organizations with a large appetite for risk pursue opportunities that could pay off handsomely – or fail to repay the investment. Other organizations may have a smaller appetite for risk and place a higher value on preservation of reputation and service delivery. The capacity to take risk is also related to the organization's financial position and the scale of investment in proposed ventures. Successful organizations understand risk appetite and take risks intelligently.

Recommended practices:

The strategic planning process should take into account the organization's appetite and capacity for risk and use techniques such as risk and sensitivity analysis to determine its exposure to risk. The impact of individual risks should be minimized, where cost-effective, by the use of specific risk management techniques such as insurance, partnering or outsourcing, which address timing and financial factors.

Organizations might measure their risk appetite in terms of and number of value drivers, corporate goals and possibly strategic risks. Wise organizations will set their risk appetite levels for each of these areas, and might have corporate thresholds of risk appetite as well as departmental thresholds so that risks at departmental level that exceed the threshold at that level can be escalated to the corporate level.

There should be clearly defined processes in place for setting, approving, monitoring and communicating risk tolerance levels for all major types of risks and ensuring that business strategies are compatible with them. The board should knowledgeably approve the broad risk appetite limits for the organization along with the types of risks that it can or cannot take.

Risk appetite levels should be regularly reviewed and adjusted to prevailing external conditions, and the financial capacity and current objectives of the organization. There should be processes to ensure that people in the organization operate within the risk appetite levels approved by the board.

4. Do we know which risks, if managed well, will increase or decrease the value of and results for our organization?

Not all risks are equal in terms of their impact on the organization, their likelihood and their proximity to the business plan – when they are going to happen and how fast they are changing.

Recommended practices:

Once the board is assured that the strategic risk register contains the right list of risks for the organization, there should be an assessment as to which of them are most important by evaluating the likelihood, impact and proximity or velocity of the risks.

The risks should then be presented in order of importance for review by the board and questions on the level and type of controls (for threats) and enhancers (for opportunities) should be posed.

B. Risk management processes

5. How effective is our process for identifying, assessing and managing business risks?

Boards need not be familiar with the many individual risks that face their organization, but they must be satisfied that it has comprehensive and effective risk management processes and that major risks are escalated to them for consideration.

Identifying, assessing and managing the risks that an organization faces can be a complex and challenging job. There are, however, a number of techniques and guidelines that can save time and help identify, assess and manage business risks. The objectives of identifying, assessing and managing risk are valid for every organization. The processes and practices they adopt will depend on their size, nature and complexity.

Recommended practices:

The board should ensure that the organization has:

- A well-defined process for categorizing risks that covers strategic, operational and corporate reporting risks – both financial and non-financial. The classification framework is developed in sufficient detail to enable management to use it as the basis for establishing and maintaining risk management policies and processes.

- A well-defined risk management programme that clearly identifies and records the principal risk factors for the organization's specific businesses, objectives, processes and activities.

- A well-defined and executed escalation process for risks that are key to the organization as a whole so that these risks are actively considered and actioned at board level.

6. How do we ensure that risk management is an integral part of the planning and day-to-day operations of individual business units?

Organizations need to provide clear direction and use consistent language on risk management to ensure consistent performance. Consideration of business risk should be a regular part of day-to-day operations rather than something that employees need to pay attention to separately.

Recommended practices:

There should be a comprehensive and well-articulated set of risk management frameworks, policies (including thresholds for acceptable levels of risk) and programmes, appropriate approvals and regular reviews to ensure ongoing relevance.

Business unit managers should integrate risk management activities with business strategies and the business unit/function planning process that produces the budget and includes their performance targets. Business plans at all levels of the organization should identify business risks and opportunities and incorporate the appropriate level of resources for managing risk.

7. How do we ensure that the board's expectations for risk management are communicated to and followed by the employees in the organization?

Strategies are more likely to succeed if everyone in the organization knows what those strategies are and how to contribute to achieving them. Boards should ensure that there are processes in place to communicate a consistent message.

Recommended practices:

The organization should have a programme of communication and training on risk that includes promoting a risk-aware culture and providing guidelines on policies and procedures for individual employees. Risk awareness in the business units and functions should be regularly monitored using such techniques as internal audit reviews, risk and control self-assessment workshops and employee surveys.

8. How do we ensure that our executives and employees act in the best long-term interests of the organization and its stakeholders?

The chief executive is responsible for ensuring that the conduct of senior executives and other employees is appropriate and can withstand public scrutiny. The challenge is to act ethically while striving to meet the goals of maximizing value and achieving performance targets. This requires that the people concerned have a common understanding of what it means to act in the best interests of the stakeholders and the organization for the long term. It also means that employees are compensated and rewarded for actions that benefit the organization and its stakeholders.

Recommended practices:

The organization should have a written code of conduct and governance, review it annually and require key employees to provide a signed annual statement of compliance. The chief executive should monitor the actions of senior executives and act on breaches of the code. The corporation's compensation and reward systems should explicitly recognize positive actions and success by senior executives in achieving targets for managing principal business risks. The systems should also recognize and respond to failures to effectively manage risks.

Corporate executives should establish the risk management 'tone at the top' and demonstrate leadership by setting an example for others to follow. This should send out the clear message that the organization seeks to only make 'good' or 'sustainable' profits for the long term.

9. How is risk management coordinated across the organization?

Every business unit in an organization plays some part in risk management. In most cases the managers and staff are responsible for the risks directly related to their day-to-day activities. There may also be specialists who handle particular aspects of risk such as insurance, health and safety and environment. The chief executive must make sure that all the risk management activities are coordinated and that no major risk area is overlooked.

Recommended practices:

The organization's strategic and operational planning processes should coordinate the risk management processes of line management and the departments that specialize in specific risks.

Larger organizations may have a designated risk manager or other senior executive, reporting through the chief executive to the board of directors, who is responsible for coordinating risk management across the organization.

10. How do we know that we are getting the most from our ERM strategy?

The outputs from the ERM programme should result in clear benefits both in terms of improved taking and seizing of opportunities and in minimizing and mitigating threats.

The board's oversight role includes reviewing regular and timely information about the organization's performance and the performance of controls over the risks that could affect the achievement of its strategic and business objectives.

Recommended practices:

The board should request regular dashboards and reports on the outputs of all aspects of risk management. These should include not only the cost of investments in the risk controls and risk management structure, but also the savings achieved, increased opportunities gained, costs of risks avoided and improvements in compliance and governance.

C. Risk monitoring and reporting

11. How do we ensure that the organization is performing according to the business plan and within appropriate risk appetite limits?

Monitoring performance against key targets is an essential business practice. boards need assurance that management at all levels does this and should understand in general terms what procedures are in place. This means that the organization has appropriate mechanisms to ensure that it is achieving its business objectives and related targets without taking undue or unmanaged risks.

Recommended practices:

The corporate information systems should incorporate reports on performance against risk appetite levels, key performance targets and related KRIs.

Managers throughout the organization should receive regular reports on performance and provide explanations of variances and planned corrective action.

12. How do we monitor and evaluate changes in the external environment and their impact on the organization's strategy and risk management practices?

Strategic plans incorporate assumptions about factors in the external world that can change at any time and significantly affect the business plan. Some factors are relatively easy to monitor – exchange rates, commodity prices, interest rates, etc. Others, such as political, regulatory and social trends, are harder to quantify and assess.

Recommended practices:

There should be processes for identifying and monitoring changes in the external environment and responding as appropriate. There should be clearly assigned responsibility for collecting and sharing information on the external environment.

The board should review with management how the strategic environment is changing, what key business risks and opportunities are appearing, how they are being managed and what, if any, modifications in strategic direction should be adopted.

13. What information about the risks facing the organization does the board get to help it fulfil its stewardship and governance responsibilities?

Board time is limited and agendas tend to be full, so risk reporting should be focused and scheduled. Since strategy and risks are closely intertwined, the board should allocate sufficient time to review and discuss all the risk-related issues.

Recommended practices:

The board's agenda planning should include regularly scheduled documents to the board or designated committees on the following areas:

- Events and trends that impact strategic plans, principal business risks or the continued validity of underlying assumptions. Briefing material should include the results of sensitivity analysis that show the range of probable financial and other outcomes. The board can then exercise oversight over the adjustment of plans to take advantage of new or changed opportunities and risks.

- Specific operational risks, with presentations by the managers responsible for key functions such as finance, internal audit, human resources, health and safety, credit, legal, production, research and development, and environmental protection.

- Preparedness for predictable emergencies such as the sudden death or incapacity of the chief executive, major fire, extensive product recall, facility failure, natural disasters, and terrorism.

Management should provide prompt documents to the board on:

- Incidents that have significant financial implications or the potential to damage the organization's reputation, for example by causing injury or death. Such incidents can be addressed in a timely telephone conference call and followed-up at the next regularly scheduled board meeting, along with the actions taken, the lessons learnt and an estimate of value lost.

- Serious breaches of the code of conduct.

- When called upon to approve a specific proposal or action the board receives a balanced picture with information about the potential risks and opportunities, the alternatives that were rejected as well as the proposal being advanced, the worst-case scenario, and management's apprehensions and uncertainties as well as its optimistic expectations.

The information derived from the analysis can be recorded in a risk register or series of linked risk registers.

14. How do we know that the information the board gets on risk management is accurate and reliable?

Boards rely on management for much of the information they get on risk and need assurance that it is complete and accurate. This typically involves a combination of formal reports and opportunities to meet and hear from a number of sources in addition to the chief executive. Regardless of the source, board members should demonstrate healthy scepticism and ask themselves if the information they get is consistent and rings true.

Recommended practices:

The board should receive information from a cross-section of knowledgeable and reliable sources in addition to the chief executive, such as executive and financial managers, internal and external auditors and external advisers.

The board should periodically request a formal review and report on the effectiveness of the risk management process from an objective and independent source outside of senior management (internal auditor, external auditor, consultant, etc).

15. How do we decide what information on risks we should publish?

Boards are responsible for overseeing the organizations' external reporting and should be aware of any applicable legal requirements for the contents and approval of annual and other reports. The requirements for including information on risk and controls/enhancers in annual reports and other external communications are set in legislation and regulations that continue to evolve.

Recommended practices:

In addition to reporting on principal business risks the annual report should include a statement of corporate governance practices that describes the board's governance role in the area of strategy and risk.

The board should obtain timely documents to confirm that public disclosures meet current reporting requirements.

16. How do we take advantage of the organizational learning that results from the risk management programme and activities?

Organizations that analyse their response to crises, problems and successes can profit from their experience, if they take advantage of the opportunities they identify.

Recommended practices:

The board ensures that:

- Management promptly reviews the most significant lessons learnt from each major business event, surprise and disaster and how it has responded to these findings.

- Management has a process for reviewing the organization's response to crises and takes action to improve the handling of similar events in the future.
- Management has put in place effective knowledge transfer processes, so that significant findings and lessons learnt (both positive and negative) can be transferred quickly and effectively across the organization.

The board should take time to define its role in risk management. It should make sure it is organized to meet its responsibilities for ensuring that the corporation's risk management policies and programmes contribute to sustainable value creation for the owners and other stakeholders.

17. How does the board ensure that at least some of its members have the requisite knowledge and experience in risk?

Stock exchanges, institutional investors and other regulatory bodies are increasingly demanding that boards include directors who understand the organization's business and its inherent risks.

Recommended practices:

The board's nominating practices should recognize the need to include directors who are familiar with a broad range of risks, including those risks are specific to the organization's industry. The board takes steps to raise the awareness and understanding of risk among directors by:

- Scheduling training sessions on risk issues and processes.
- Using internal and external experts to advise the board and committees on specific risk issues.
- Ensuring that the board collectively and individually uses the appropriate techniques to make risk-based decisions.

D. Questions directed at the board itself

18. How do we, as a board, help establish the 'tone at the top' that promotes a 'risk aware' culture?

Effective boards play an active role in reinforcing an organization's approach to risk taking and risk management. They do so when they participate actively and lead by example. The biggest challenges in developing strategy and identifying risks are denial and unwillingness to think the unthinkable. Most people are reluctant to contemplate the possibility of major stock market crashes, executive fraud, war or terrorist acts. Chief executives are often optimists who may discount the risk of failure or loss. Directors can contribute to discussions of strategy and risk by providing a tough-minded 'reality check'.

Recommended practices:

The board should play an active role in discussions of strategy and risk and ask tough questions that challenge assumptions and focus on the interests of owners and other key stakeholders. The board's actions should be compatible with and reinforce the organization's stated objectives, values and risk tolerance in such areas as:

- the choice of chief executive;
- the selection of directors;
- the strategic plan;
- the code of conduct;
- executive compensation.

Risk management issues should be included as regularly scheduled board agenda items.

The board should review and approve the compensation package for the chief executive and senior executives.

19. What are our priorities as a board in the oversight of risk management?

The board must decide how to make best use of its limited time for overseeing risk.

Recommended practices:

The board should establish its priorities and determine the scope, depth and timing of its involvement in risk management. This may take into account:

- The nature and status of the organization, the business it is in, how long it has existed, etc.
- The board's level of trust and confidence in the chief executive.

- The degree and rate of change in the industry and other aspects of the external world.
- The extent to which the organization needs to change its strategy to anticipate and respond to external opportunities and threats.
- The effectiveness of the structures and processes that the board has established to handle its responsibility for oversight of opportunities and risks.

20. How does the board handle its responsibility for the oversight of opportunities and threats?

Wherever possible, the entire board should participate in the oversight of risk. Because some areas of risk management have technical aspects that can be complex and time-consuming to review, boards may delegate the detailed work of overseeing certain aspects of risk to one or more committees, such as the audit committee. In such cases the board must make sure that it is fully informed of the findings of the committees and that no significant aspect of risk is overlooked, and that the significant risks to the business are regularly and actively reviewed at top level.

Recommended practices:

The board and its committees should have written policies and procedures on governance issues related to risk. Where the board elects to delegate specific risk-related responsibilities to board committees, the committees should be required to report their activities to the full board at least annually. Key risks should be actively considered and actioned at top level.

21. How satisfied are we that the board is doing what it should in overseeing risk?

Effective risk management integrates and coordinates the activities of people across the organization through strategic planning, organizational culture, and policies and procedures. The board is typically involved with committees, reports, presentations and discussions, each of which complements the overall process of risk oversight. Boards need to take time to satisfy themselves that all the pieces are coordinated and collectively support a conclusion that risk is properly managed and that the board has fulfilled its stewardship obligations.

Recommended practices:

The board should regularly schedule time to assess how effective it has been in meeting its responsibilities for the oversight of risk and what corrective action it needs to take.

Summary

The expectations on directors are vast. When these expectations are combined with the myriad of information and the level of demand for a response, it can be very stressful to be in a senior position in any organization.

Enterprise risk management should *not* add to that burden; rather, it should assist senior management in assembling and organizing the priorities that need to be attended to in order to maximize value creation and to balance that with value protection. Successful ERM achieves a balance of value creation and value protection.

These 21 questions should provide some logical order and sense to the apparently complicated world of enterprise risk management.

APPENDIX 1
Examples of corporate governance and ERM regulations

The January 2013 Guidance from the Office of the Superintendent of Financial Institutions Canada (OSFI)[1] sets out what it calls its five lines of defence for Federally Regulated Financial Institutions (organizations) including:

1 Corporate Governance for organizations

- Defining Corporate Governance;
- The Board, Senior Management and the Oversight Functions.

2 The Role of the Board of Directors

- Board Responsibilities
- Board Effectiveness
- Board Skills and Competencies
- Board Independence
- Board Chair
- Interface between the Board and Senior Management
- Interface between the Board and the Oversight Functions
- Board Oversight of Internal Controls.

3 Risk Governance

- Risk Appetite Framework
- Oversight of Risk
- Board Risk Committee
- Chief Risk Officer.

4 The Role of the Audit Committee

5 Supervision of organizations

- The Role of Corporate Governance in OSFI's Supervisory Process
- OSFI's Supervisory Assessment
- Changes to the Board and Senior Management.

There is an interesting parallel with the UK Code of Governance where issues of board collective responsibility, of leadership, effectiveness and accountability including ERM are developed. UK listed companies (including, but not limited to, financial institutions which are subjected to much more rigorous risk management requirements) are expected to comply with the Code or explain why they do not or cannot comply. The main aspects are summarized in Appendix 2.

Note

1 http://www.osfi-bsif.gc.ca/app/DocRepository/1/eng/guidelines/sound/guidelines/ CG_Guideline_e.pdf

APPENDIX 2
The main principles of the UK Code of Governance, October 2012

Section A: Leadership

- Board collectively responsible for the long-term success of the company.
- Clear division of responsibilities at the head of the company.
- Chairman responsible for leadership of the board and ensuring its effectiveness.
- Members of a unitary board and non-executive directors to challenge and help develop proposals on strategy.

Section B: Effectiveness

- Appropriate balance of skills, experience, independence and knowledge of the company.
- Appointment of new directors to be formal, rigorous and transparent.
- Directors to allocate sufficient time.
- Induction and ongoing training for directors.
- Information supplied to board to be timely and sufficient.
- A formal and rigorous annual evaluation by board of its own performance and that of its committees and individual directors.
- Re-election at regular intervals for all directors, subject to continued satisfactory performance.

Section C: Accountability

- A fair, balanced and understandable assessment of the company's position and prospects presented by board.
- The board is responsible for determining the nature and extent of the significant risks it is willing to take in achieving its strategic objectives.
- The board should maintain sound risk management and internal control systems.
- The board should establish formal and transparent arrangements for considering how they should apply the corporate reporting, risk management and internal control principles and for maintaining an appropriate relationship with the company's auditors.

Section D: Remuneration

- Levels of remuneration should be sufficient to attract, retain and motivate directors.
- Link rewards to corporate and individual performance.
- Policy on executive remuneration and for fixing the remuneration packages of individual directors to be formal and transparent.

Section E: Relations with shareholders

- The board as a whole has responsibility for ensuring that a satisfactory dialogue with shareholders takes place.
- The board should use the AGM to communicate with investors and to encourage their participation.

The Organization for Economic Cooperation and Development (OECD) defines corporate governance as:

a set of relationships between a company's management, its board, its shareholders, and other stakeholders. Corporate governance also provides the structure through which the objectives of the company are set, and the means of attaining those objectives and monitoring performance are determined. Good corporate governance should provide proper incentives for the board and management to pursue objectives that are in the interests of the company and its shareholders and should facilitate effective monitoring.

APPENDIX 3
Summary COSO guidance

The 2013 consultation version of the COSO Framework sets out 17 principles representing the fundamental concepts associated with each component. Because these principles are drawn directly from the components, an entity can achieve effective internal control by applying all principles.

All principles apply to operations, reporting, and compliance objectives. The principles supporting the components of internal control are listed below.

Control environment

1 The organization demonstrates a commitment to integrity and ethical values.

2 The board of directors demonstrates independence from management and exercises oversight of the development and performance of internal control.

3 Management establishes, with board oversight, structures, reporting lines, and appropriate authorities and responsibilities in the pursuit of objectives.

4 The organization demonstrates a commitment to attract, develop, and retain competent individuals in alignment with objectives.

5 The organization holds individuals accountable for their internal control responsibilities in the pursuit of objectives.

Risk assessment

6 The organization specifies objectives with sufficient clarity to enable the identification and assessment of risks relating to objectives.

7 The organization identifies risks to the achievement of its objectives across the entity and analyses risks as a basis for determining how the risks should be managed.

8 The organization considers the potential for fraud in assessing risks to the achievement of objectives.

9 The organization identifies and assesses changes that could significantly impact the system of internal control.

Control activities

10 The organization selects and develops control activities that contribute to the mitigation of risks to the achievement of objectives to acceptable levels.

11 The organization selects and develops general control activities over technology to support the achievement of objectives.

12 The organization deploys control activities through policies that establish what is expected and procedures that put policies into action.

Information and communication

13 The organization obtains or generates and uses relevant, quality information to support the functioning of internal control.

14 The organization internally communicates information, including objectives and responsibilities for internal control, necessary to support the functioning of internal control.

15 The organization communicates with external parties regarding matters affecting the functioning of internal control.

Monitoring activities

16 The organization selects, develops, and performs ongoing and/or separate evaluations to ascertain whether the components of internal control are present and functioning.

17 The organization evaluates and communicates internal control deficiencies in a timely manner to those parties responsible for taking corrective action, including senior management and the board of directors, as appropriate.

The following is an extract from COSO regarding the implementation of enterprise risk management:

1 *Seek board and senior management involvement and oversight*
   a Set an agenda item for the board and executive management to discuss ERM and its benefits.
   b Agree on high-level objectives and expectations regarding risk management.
   c Understand the process to communicate and set the tone and expectations of ERM for the organization.
   d Agree on a high-level approach, resources and target dates for the initial ERM effort.

2 *Identify and position a leader to drive the ERM initiative*
   a Identify a person with the right attributes to serve as the risk management leader; does not have to be a CRO (Chief Risk Officer).
   b Use existing resources.
   c Set objectives and expectations for the leader.
   d Allocate appropriate resources to enable success.

3 *Establish a management working group*
   a Establish a management working group to support the risk leader and drive the effort across the organization.
   b Have the right, key people in the group – sufficient stature; 'C-suite' representation; business unit management.
   c Look at using cross-functional teams.
   d Agree on objectives for the working group.
   e Build ERM using incremental steps.
   f Define some sought-after benefit to evaluate each step.
   g Establish reporting process for management and the board.

4 *Conduct an initial enterprise-wide risk assessment and action plan*
   a Focus on identifying the organization's most significant risks.
   b Look for risks at the strategic level.
   c Consider risk factors beyond just probability and impact, eg velocity of risk, preparedness, other factors.
   d For the most significant risks: assess exposure to the risk; assess adequacy of existing risk mitigation or monitoring; identify opportunities to enhance mitigation or monitoring activities.
   e Develop action plans to enhance risk management practices related to the risk identified: identify actions to implement the opportunities identified above; establish target dates

and responsibilities; develop process to monitor and track implementation.

5 *Inventory the existing risk management practices*
   a Identify and inventory existing practices.
   b Identify gaps and opportunities.
   c Consider initial completion of the risk management alignment guide.
   d Develop specific action steps to close gap.
   e Produce and implement action plans to close gaps and manage risks.

6 *Develop initial risk reporting*
   a Assess adequacy and effectiveness of existing risk reporting.
   b Develop new reporting formats: consider extensive use of graphics and colours; consider developing a risk 'dashboard' for the board.
   c Develop process for periodic reporting of emerging risks.
   d Assess effectiveness of new reporting with stakeholders and revise as appropriate.

7 *Develop the next phase of action plans and ongoing communications*
   a Conduct a critical assessment of the accomplishments of the working group.
   b Revisit the risk process inventory and identify next processes for enhancement.
   c Identify tangible steps for a new action plan including benefits sought and target dates; review with executive management and the board.
   d Implement with appropriate resources and support.
   e Schedule sessions for updating or further educating directors and executive management.
   f Assess progress and benefits of ERM initiative against objectives and communicate to target audiences.
   g Continue organization-wide communication process to build risk culture.

APPENDIX 4
Case study: Applying a more granular mathematical model to a risk for a non-financial organization

Here's a list of threats and opportunities for a fictitious animal feed manufacturer. It has 20 manufacturing units spread across three countries in the EU. It has high borrowing levels but also owns all its own assets. It is listed on three stock exchanges and shareholders expect, and have received over the last 10 years, consistent dividends of around 4 per cent yield as well as price appreciation.

The main value drivers in the business are:

- *Formulations:* consistent, innovative, safe quality and delivery of superior results for the customers; maintained confidential.
- *People:* skilled people working on the formulations and providing advice; management and sales people having great local relationships with farmers and farming communities; planners, designers and project management incentivized to deliver excellent results; unit managers and area managers loyal and incentivized.
- *Logistics:* efficient and safe.
- *Return on capital employed:* above 10 per cent for all units.
- *Borrowing levels:* below 20 per cent of overall assets.

The stated strategic goals of the business are to become the market leader for provision of animal feed in the EU and a major provider of animal feed and related farming solutions on a global basis. Initially, let's start with a simple assessment of low/medium/high for the likelihood and impact; see Table A4.1. The highest of the threats is the increase in the cost of grain.

The business would turn to a model to calculate and forecast the cost of grain and might, as a result of the analysis, opt to forward-buy some

TABLE A4.1 Assessment of likelihood and impact

Threats	Likelihood	Impact
Increase in cost of grain	High	High
Increase in cost of other raw materials/additives	High	Low
Increase in cost of energy	Medium	Medium
Cross contamination in one of the units	Low	Low
Loss of use of one unit	High	Low
Change in regulations requiring re-engineering of all units	Medium	Medium
Aggressive takeover bid by main competitor	Low	High
Takeover of small business with two units fails	Low	Low
Current project to build new unit fails	Low	Low
Cost of borrowing increases	High	Medium
Opportunities	**Likelihood**	**Impact**
Decrease in cost of grain	Low	High
Decrease in cost of other raw materials/additives	Low	Low
Decrease in cost of energy	Low	Medium
Takeover of small business with two units succeeds	High	Low
Main competitor opens itself up for takeover	Low	High
Current project to build new unit succeeds	High	Low
Cost of borrowing reduces	Low	Medium

grain on the market, or even enter into direct contracts with farmers to give assurance of supply and price. The further option of buying farming land and engaging farmers to manage the land for the organization is open to it, depending on the analysis of the risk (threat and opportunity) and capital availability.

APPENDIX 5
Capital and risk considerations for US insurers, from NAIC ORSA Guidance

Table A5.1 is a summary of the considerations, methodologies and examples of the elements of the US own risk and solvency assessment (ORSA).

TABLE A5.1 Summary of the US ORSA

Considerations	Description of Methods and Assumptions	Examples (not exhaustive)
Definition of Solvency	Describe how the insurer defines solvency for the purpose of determining risk capital and liquidity requirements.	Cash flow basis; balance sheet basis
Accounting or Valuation Regime	Describe the accounting or valuation basis for the measurement of risk capital requirements and/or available capital.	GAAP; Statutory; Economic or Market Consistent; IFRS; Rating Agency Model
Business Included	Describe the subset of business included in the analysis of capital.	Positions as of a given valuation date; New business assumptions
Time Horizon	Describe the time horizon over which risks were modelled and measured.	One-year, multi-year; lifetime; run-off

TABLE A5.1 Summary of the US ORSA (*continued*)

Considerations	Description of Methods and Assumptions	Examples (not exhaustive)
Risks Modelled	Describe the risks included in the measurement of risk capital, including whether all relevant and material risks identified by the insurer have been considered.	Credit; market; liquidity; insurance; operational
Quantification Method	Describe the method used to quantify the risk exposure.	Deterministic stress tests; stochastic modelling; factor-based analysis
Risk Capital Metric	Describe the measurement metric utilized in the determination of aggregate risk capital.	Value-at-risk (VAR), which quantifies the capital needed to withstand a loss at a certain probability; Tail-value-at-risk (TVAR), which quantifies the capital needed to withstand average losses above a certain probability; Probability of Ruin, which quantifies the probability of ruin given the capital held
Defined Security Standard	Describe the defined security standard utilized in the determination of risk capital requirements, including linkage to business strategy and objectives.	AA solvency; 99.X per cent 1-year VAR; Y per cent TVAR or CTE; X per cent of RBC

(*continued*)

TABLE A5.1 Summary of the US ORSA (*continued*)

Considerations	Description of Methods and Assumptions	Examples (not exhaustive)
Aggregation and Diversification	Describe the method of aggregation of risks and any diversification benefits considered or calculated in the group risk capital determination.	Correlation matrix; dependency structure; sum, full/partial/no diversification

APPENDIX 6
Sample terms of reference for a board risk committee

1. Duties

The board risk committee should carry out the duties below for the company, major subsidiary undertakings and the group as a whole, as appropriate. The committee should also undertake periodic environmental scans to gauge any possible impact on the risk profile of the company. The committee shall:

a advise the board on the company's overall risk tolerance and strategy;

b oversee and advise the board on the current risk exposures and future risk strategy of the company;

c in relation to risk assessment:
   - keep under review the company's overall risk assessment processes that inform the board's decision making;
   - review regularly and approve the parameters used in these measures and the methodology adopted ; and
   - set a process for the accurate and timely monitoring of large exposures and certain risk types of critical importance.

d review the company's capability to identify and manage new risk types;

e review the organization's capacity to take on risks even if the threats are realized to their worst possible extent;

f before a decision to proceed is taken by the board, advise the board on proposed strategic transactions, focusing in particular on risk aspects and implications for the risk tolerance of the company, and taking independent external advice where appropriate and available;

g review reports on any material breaches of risk limits and the adequacy of proposed action;

h keep under review the effectiveness of the company's internal controls and risk management systems and review and approve the statements to be included in the annual report concerning the effectiveness of the company's internal control and risk management systems;

i provide advice to the remuneration committee on risk weightings to be applied to performance objectives incorporated in executive remuneration;

j review the company's procedures for detecting fraud, including the whistleblowing policy (if any). The committee shall ensure that these arrangements allow proportionate and independent investigation of such matters and appropriate follow-up action;

k monitor the independence of risk management functions throughout the organization;

l review promptly all relevant risk reports on the company; and

m review and monitor management's responsiveness to the findings.

2. Membership

a The committee shall comprise at least (three members).

b A majority of members of the committee shall be independent non-executive directors who have the relevant experience. In addition, the committee may co-opt from time to time persons who have the relevant expertise to assist it but who may not be directors.

c Such persons may be associate members or invitees of the committee but shall have no decision-making powers or voting rights.

d Members of the committee shall be appointed by the board, on the recommendation of the nomination committee in consultation with the chairman of the committee.

e Only members of the committee have the right to attend committee meetings. However, other individuals such as the chairman of the board, directors, the chief executive officer, and representatives of the risk function, compliance, and internal and external audit, may be invited to attend all or part of any meeting as and when appropriate and necessary.

f The board shall appoint the committee chairman who shall be an independent non-executive director. In the absence of the committee chairman, the remaining members present shall elect one of themselves to chair the meeting.

3. Quorum

a The quorum necessary for the transaction of business shall be [insert appropriate number] members.

b A duly convened meeting of the committee at which a quorum is present shall be competent to exercise all or any of the authorities, powers and discretions vested in or exercisable by the committee.

4. Frequency of meetings

The committee shall meet at least [appropriate frequency], or as and when circumstances or events merit it.

5. Notice of meetings

a Meetings of the committee shall be called by the secretary of the committee at the request of any of its members.

b Unless otherwise agreed, notice of each meeting confirming the venue, time and date together with an agenda of items to be discussed, shall be forwarded to each member of the committee, any other person required to attend and all other non-executive directors, no later than [appropriate number] working days before the date of the meeting. Supporting papers shall be sent to committee members and to other attendees as appropriate, at the same time.

6. Minutes of meetings

a The secretary shall minute the proceedings of all meetings of the committee, including recording the names of those present and in attendance.

b Draft minutes of committee meetings shall be circulated promptly to all members of the committee. Once approved, minutes should be circulated to all other members of the board.

7. Annual General Meeting

The committee chairman should attend the general meeting of shareholders to answer shareholder questions on the committee's activities, role and scope of responsibilities.

8. Reporting responsibilities

a The committee chairman shall report to the board on the committee's proceedings after each committee meeting.

b The committee shall make whatever recommendations to the board it deems appropriate on any area within its remit where action or improvement is needed.

c Taking into account the company's reporting obligations (pursuant to, as applicable, relevant rules and regulations), the committee shall produce a report of its activities and the company's risk management and strategy to be included in the company's annual report.

9. Other matters

The committee shall:

a have access to sufficient resources to carry out its duties, including access to the company secretary for assistance as required;

b be provided with appropriate and timely training, in particular in respect of risk management expertise, both in the form of an induction programme for new members and on an ongoing basis for all members;

c give due consideration to laws and regulations and the provisions of the applicable rules, as appropriate;

d oversee any investigation of activities which is within its terms of reference; and

e arrange for periodic reviews of its own performance and, at least annually, review its constitution and terms of reference to ensure it is operating at optimal effectiveness and recommend any changes it considers necessary to the board for approval.

10. Authority

The committee is authorized to:

a seek any information it requires from any employee of the company in order to perform its duties;

b obtain, at the company's expense, outside legal or other professional advice on any matter within its terms of reference; and

c require any employee to be in attendance at a meeting of the committee as and when required, and to respond to the committee's questions and/or to provide the committee with any other assistance.

Example of roles of CRO and ERM team

Enterprise risk management roles and accountabilities

The dedicated team is focused on coordinating the ERM process across the organization. This team is responsible for conducting the following:

- Communicating the goals and objectives of the group risk policy and its supporting ERM programme.
- Managing the implementation, maintenance and continuous improvement of the organization's ERM programme on behalf of the risk advisory group.
- Managing and driving the use of the risk management information system to support the ERM process and programme.
- Delivering consistent and accurate reports to the risk advisory group, group executive management, risk/audit committee and board to support risk-based decision making.
- Continuously improving the delivery of consistent risk management information to key internal and external stakeholders.
- Reviewing the risk profiles created in the context of events and external environmental factors to identify new or emerging risks throughout the organization.
- Defining risk appetite and tolerance levels for authorization.
- Proposing allocation of risk appetite and tolerances.
- Evaluating the potential for risk combination through the impact of multiple risk events.
- Developing techniques for modelling a range of risk exposures to allow the assignment of appropriate levels of capital to risk exposures.

- Monitoring and reporting on risk exposures against agreed risk tolerance levels.
- Managing and analysing the reporting of risk events and near misses using consistent reporting processes.
- Providing coaching and support to managers across the organization in their roles within the ERM programme.
- Working with HR to develop and implement training and development programmes focused on driving behaviour and culture change to create a risk-aware culture across the organization.
- Reviewing with and reporting to the board and HR the risk and capital inputs that would affect remuneration at all levels of the organization.

FURTHER READING

James A Belesco and Ralf C Stayer (1999) *Flight of the Buffalo: Soaring to excellence, learning to let employees lead*, Replica Books, informata.com

Peter L Bernstein (1998) *Against the Gods: The remarkable story of risk*, Wiley, New York

Spencer Johnson (1998) *Who Moved My Cheese? An amazing way to deal with change in your work and in your life*, Vermillion, Random House, London

David Spiegelhalter (2009) *A Worrier's Guide to Risk*, http://understandinguncertainty.org/rules

Nassim Nicholas Taleb (2007) *The Black Swan: The impact of the highly improbable*, Penguin, London

INDEX

Note: notes and questions for chapters are indexed under 'chapter notes' *and* 'questions' page; numbers in *italics* indicate figures or tables

Against the Gods: The remarkable story of risk 2
appendices
  capital and risk considerations for US insurers 294, *294–96*
  case study: applying a more granular mathematical model to a risk for a non-financial organization 291, 293, *292*
  examples of corporate governance and ERM regulations 283–84
  enterprise risk management roles and accountabilities 302–03
  main principles of UK Code of Governance (October 2012) 285–86
  sample terms of reference for a board risk committee 297–301 *see also subject entry*
  summary of COSO guidance 287–90 *see also* COSO guidance
Apple 55, 56
Asia 73–74
l'Association pour le Management des Risques et des Assurances de l'Entreprise 207
audit in ERM 208, 210–11, *209*
  Effective Internal Audit in the Financial Services Sector (IIA, 2013) 208, 210–11
  and lack of transparency 208
Australia
  as dependent on Asia's growth 74
  as risk-hungry 73–74

Basel II 53, 220
Basel III 227, 229–30
  Accord 53
  regulatory requirements for banks under 9
Basel Committee on Banking Supervision on banks and global financial crisis 181, 234
benefits of well-managed enterprise risk management 7–8

Bernstein, P L 2
Bhutan, Kingdom of 239–40
The Black Swan: The impact of the highly improbable 8, 157
Bow Tie analyses 249–51, *250, 251*
blame 98–99 *see also* ERM culture, blame, boundaries
BP and Deepwater Horizon crisis 165–66
business continuity management (BCM) 156–61
  for innovation, streamlining and saving costs 159–61
  for mediating the business's expectations 159
  in summary 158–59
  and testing the plan 161, *162*
  as vital for health of business 156–58
    see also case examples
business and risk 2–5 *see also* case examples

Canada
  Canadian Institute of Chartered Accountants 215
  and CoCo 215–16
  Guidance from Office of the Superintendent of Financial Institutions (OFSI) 283–84
capital and risk considerations for US insurers 294, *294–96*
case examples (for)
  business continuity management (BCM)
    author's experience 160
    business continuity in practice 156–57
  business and risk 3–4
  conduct risk: Financial Conduct Authority (FCA) 110
  conduct risk: PPI scandal in the UK 109–10
  corporate social responsibility: the Rana Plaza collapse 167
  embedding ERM 129–30
  ERM, owned 125

case examples (for) (*continued*)
  ERM, top level leadership in 25
  ERM cultures and the blame culture: JP
      Morgan Chase 99
  ERM information systems : author's
      experience 191–92
  governance, risk and compliance: Barings
      and Bugatti 37
  identifying risk: Deepwater Horizon oil
      spill 28
  managed risk: from author's experience
      103–04
  managed risk: Meredith Vaughan 101–02
  resilience and sustainable habits: business
      continuity in practice 156–57
  risk: Lufthansa and Adidas 46
  risk as both opportunity and threat:
      minimizing threats in demolition 42
  risk of not taking a risk: Coca-Cola 82–83
  risk as uncertainty: Large Hadron Collider
      (LHC) 44
  risks that cannot be valued: Gross
      National Happiness and Gross
      National Product 239–40
  senior management: BP and the
      Deepwater Horizon event 165–66
case study (on)
  applying a more granular mathematical
      model to a risk for a non-financial
      organization 291, 293, 292
  risk appetite 100–101
chapter notes (for)
  conformance, performance, roles,
      responsibilities and regulations 242
  deliverables from quantitative ERM
      approaches 242
  embedding and integrating ERM 138
  enterprise risk management (ERM) 38
  ERM and performance management
      synergies 264
  ERM culture, blame, boundaries and
      elephants in the room 117
  ERM tools for senior management 254
  introduction 14
  learning and communication 196–97
  maturity in enterprise risk management 154
  resilience and sustainable habits 174–75
  risk as opportunity/threat 57–58
  risk attitude, risk propensity and risk
      appetite 95
China 73–74 *see also* KFC business
      objectives
  and demand for Australian exports 74
cloud computing 42 *see also* risk as
      opportunity/threat
Coca-Cola 82–83

conduct risk 108–13, *109 see also* case
      examples
  statement adapted from ERM COSO
      Application Techniques 111–13
Code of Governance (UK, 2012) 285–86
  accountability 286
  effectiveness 285
  leadership 285
  relations with shareholders 286 *see also*
      definitions
  remuneration 286
communication 68–70, 121, 126, 158–59,
      203, 207, 288 *see also* learning and
      communication
  crisis 158, 161
  external 194
  risk 178, 196
conformance, performance, roles,
      responsibilities and regulations (and)
      199–22
  compliance requirements *see* risk
      management compliance requirements
  governance for ERM *see* enterprise risk
      management (ERM)
  managing conformance vs performance
      200
  role of boards in ERM *see* enterprise risk
      management (ERM)
  role of internal and external audit in
      ERM *see* enterprise risk management
      (ERM)
corporate social responsibility (CSR) 155,
      166–68, *169 see also* case examples
  Daily Finance report on (2012) 171
  EU definition of 168
  EU strategy (2011–14) for 168
  and honesty 172
  ISO 26000 Guidance Standard on 168,
      170, *169*
  and opportunities for improving the
      business 170–72
COSO Framework 213–14, *214*
  and COSO Consultation (January
      2013) 214
COSO guidance (on) 287–90
  control activities 288
  control environment 287
  implementation of enterprise risk
      management 289–90
  information and communication 288
  monitoring activities 288
  risk assessment 287–88

definition(s) of
  corporate governance (OECD) 286
  near miss (*Risk and Regulation*) 185

deliverables from quantitative ERM
approaches *see* quantitative ERM
approaches

elephant in the room *see* conduct risk
embedding ERM 121–28, *122, 123, 124*
16-step plan for 128–29
and conscious/unconscious competence
127–28
driven with energy 126
led from the top 121–22
measured 126–27
owned 123–26 *see also* case examples
wider aspects of 127
embedding and integrating ERM (and)
119–38 *see also* case examples
main aspects of embedding ERM
see embedding ERM
meaning of embedding 119–21, *122*
the three lines of play/defence 130, 135,
131–35
Enron and corporate irresponsibility 172
enterprise risk management (ERM) (and)
15–38
essential attributes for delivering value and
capacity 23–24, *24*
evaluating and prioritizing risk
see subject entry
governance, risk and compliance
36–37, *36*
governance (through) 203–04, 206–07,
205 see also reports and extracts
appointment of chief risk officer 207
board risk committees vs audit
committees 206–07
identifying risk: types of risk, risk lists and
taxonomies 26–28, *27, 29*
and risk classification systems 26–28,
27 see also case examples
implementing the programme for
20–22, *21*
IT systems 177
the process of 22–23, *23*
risk management 16–17, 20, *16, 18, 19,
20 see also subject entry*
role of boards in 200–201, 203,
201, 202
role of internal and external audit in 208,
210–11, *209 see also* audit in ERM
roles and accountabilities 302–03
top level leadership 24–25 *see also* case
examples
ERM culture, blame, boundaries (and)
97–117 *see also* risk appetite
elephant in the room and conduct risk *see*
conduct risk

ERM cultures and the blame culture
98–99 *see also* case examples
link between managed risk taking, mice,
Maslow and Herzberg 104–08, *105*
see risk, managed; Maslow, A *and*
Herzberg, F
managing risk 101–04 *see also* risk,
managed
in the public interest: whistleblowing
113–14
ERM information systems 177, 188, 190–93
see also case examples *and* reports
and extracts
internal communication and dashboards
192
and RASCI principle 192–93
ERM and performance management
synergies 255–64
performance management 256–58
and research from PwC 257–58
performance management methods
258–63 *see also subject entry*
risk management alignment within the
organization 256
ERM tools for senior management 243–54
macro and micro risk management
252–53
triangle of risk – trigger, environment,
strength or weakness 244–47, *244,
245, 246, 248*
real life example of 246–47
using cause and consequence analysis to
transform risk approach 249–52,
250, 251
advantages of 251–52
Bow Tie analyses for 249–51,
250, 251
European Insurance and Occupational
Pensions Authority (EIOPA)
guidelines 220
European Union
audit for public interest entities 216 *see
also* legislation (EU)
strategy for corporate social responsibility
(2011–14) 168
evaluating and prioritizing risk 29–31, 34,
31, 32–33, 34, 35
governance, risk and compliance 36–37,
37 see also case examples
proximity or velocity of risk 29–30
recording and reporting risks 30–31, 36,
31, 32–33, 34, 35

figures
advantages of solid enterprise risk
management *16*

figures (*continued*)
 approach to risk from top down to
   bottom up *41, 81*
 the Bow Tie for analysing causes and
   consequences (1) *250*
 the Bow Tie for analysing causes and
   consequences (2) *250*
 the Bow Tie for analysing causes and
   consequences (3) *251*
 chart of performance against risk attitude
   75
 classic safety pyramid showing ratio of
   near misses/'incidents' to more serious
   events *186*
 core roles in the 'three lines of play' *209*
 COSO Cube as at January 2013 *214*
 data, information, knowledge, learning
   triangle *180*
 diagram of responses to threats and
   opportunities *51*
 example of completed maturity matrix
   144
 example of matrix to show output of an
   ERM maturity assessment *141*
 example of matrix for showing relative
   change in threats, indicating velocity
   or proximity *228*
 example of matrix for valuing threats
   (assuming maximum loss of $40
   million) *226*
 fish-bone or Ishikawa analysis for
   risk *251*
 graphic representation of risks that are
   both threats and opportunities *34*
 hub spokes and wheel of types of risk
   management making up ERM
   programme *20*
 illustration of organization for ERM as
   laid out by FSB *205*
 illustration of risk and capital calculations
   for Solvency II *231*
 IRM model of culture: sociability vs
   solidarity *105*
 known knowns and known unknowns *109*
 main aspects of embedding enterprise risk
   management *123*
 model for three lines of play *135*
 process for enterprise risk management *23*
 programme for ERM *21*
 relationships between governance, risk
   management and compliance *36*
 risk classification system example *29*
 road map for implementing enterprise risk
   management *60*
 schematic of learning relying on both
   information and knowledge *180*

 schematic overview of ISO 26000 –
   Corporate Social Responsibility *169*
 supporting documents for embedding
   enterprise risk management *62*
 three-dimensional matrix to show
   likelihood, impact and time *229*
 the three elements of risk as applied to a
   fire *244*
 the three elements of risk as applied to an
   opportunity *248*
 the three elements of risk as applied to a
   threat *248*
 three pillars of ERM: design, structure and
   implementation *24*
*Flight of the Buffalo: Soaring to excellence,
  learning to let employees lead* 104

gap analysis 150
global financial crisis 181

Heinrich, H W *185*
Herzberg, F 104–05

implementing an ERM programme (by/with)
   59–71
 building capabilities 66–68
 understanding and applying ERM to
   areas of responsibility 66–68
 documentation for ERM 62, *62, 63*
 establishing the foundation – the operating
   model for ERM 59, 61–68, *60*
 improving capabilities: monitoring and
   communication 68–70
 language, oversight and governance
   63–65
Industrial Accident Prevention 185
Insurance Networking News (2013) on
   aligning remuneration to risk 107–08
Institute of Internal Audit (IIA) 208, 210–11
Institute of Risk Management (IRM)
 ABC approach: attitude, behaviour and
   culture 98
 framework 80, *81*
 model of culture change 104
ISO 26000 (Guidance Standard on Social
   Responsibility) 168, 170, *169*
ISO 31000 12, 20, 211
 and options for dealing with risk 46–47

Johnson, S *105*

key point for board risk committees vs audit
   committees 206
key strategic questions for senior
   management and boards 265–81
 questions (on) 268–81

directed at board itself 278–81
risk management processes 271–74
risk monitoring and reporting 274–78
strategic planning and ERM 268–71
recognizing risks *of* vs risks *to* the strategic plan (and) 266–68
questions directed at board itself 268
risk management processes 267
risk monitoring and reporting 267
strategy planning and ERM 266
KFC business objectives 84

learning and communication 177–97 *see also* communication; ERM information systems; the learning habit *and* reports and extracts
the learning habit (and) 179, 181–86, 188
leading and lagging indicators 188, *189–90*
learning from failure/near misses 184–86, *186, 187–88*
learning from risk events 183–84
turning data into knowledge, knowledge into learning 179, 181–82, *180*
legislation (EU)
Directive 2006/43/EC: 8th EU Company Law Directive on Statutory Audit 216
ERM requirements of 216
Solvency I Directive 73/239/EEC (1973) 219
Solvency II 9, 219–20, 227, 229–30, 232
legislation (South Africa)
Municipal Finance ManagementAct (2003) 217
South African Companies Act (2008) 217
legislation (US)
COSO 36, 213–14, 287–90
Foreign Corrupt Practices Act 10
Sarbanes Oxley (SoX) 36, 214–15, 217

managed risk *see* risk, managed
Maslow, A 104–05
maturity in enterprise risk management (and) 139–54
action plan stages for measuring and tracing performance 143–51, *144, 145, 146, 147, 148, 149, 150, 151*
1: set the target 143, 145
2: adapt the model 145
3: get inputs from wide range of people 145–47
4: analyse the output 147, 149
5: conduct gap analysis and plan 149
6: communicate output and plan 150
7: implement action plan 151
8: run it again 151–152
9: benchmark 152

advantages/disadvantages of measuring risk maturity 142–43, *143*
how risk maturity enables managed risk taking 139–43, *141*
Millward Brown 55, *55–56*
minimum capital requirement (MCR) 230
Monte Carlo simulations 228, 242
myths about risk 8–12
black swans 8–9
emerging risks 9–10
perception of risk 10–12

NASA *25*, 183–84
and Rogers Commission 184
Netherlands 217, 220

opportunity/ies 47, *48–49, 51, 50–55*
see also risk as opportunity/threat
and COSO ERM executive summary 40
four Os of managing 47
internal controls for 47, *50*
own risk and solvency assessment (ORSA) 220, 223, 230, 294, *294–96*
NAIC – US insurance companies 215
under SII 232–33

payment protection insurance (PPI) scandal 109 *see also* case examples
performance management methods 258–63
Kaizen/Lean Six Sigma 260–61
lean processes 260–61
Six Sigma 258–60
General Electric description of 259
total quality management (TQM) 261–63
see also risk assessment tools

quantitative ERM approaches (and) 223–42
measuring risk 223–24
models for valuing risk and capital 229–32, *231*
the financial sector 229–30, *231*
working capital in non-financial services organizations 231–32
own risk and solvency assessments (and) 232–35
calculating a risk-adjusted return 234–35
return on risk-adjusted capital (RORAC) 234
risk-adjusted return on capital (RAROC) 233–35
risks that cannot be valued 239–40 *see also* case examples
stress testing and reverse stress testing 235–39
combined approach for 237, 239, *238*

quantitative ERM approaches (and)
(*continued*)
  valuing threat 224, 226–28, *225, 226,
    228, 229 see also* threat
questions (for) *see also* key strategic questions
    for senior management and boards
  conformance, performance, roles,
    responsibilities and regulations
    240–42
  deliverables from quantitative ERM
    approaches 240–42
  embedding and integrating ERM 136–37
  enterprise risk management (ERM)
    37–38
  ERM culture, blame, boundaries and
    elephants in the room 114–17
  ERM and performance management
    synergies 263–64
  ERM tools for senior management
    253–54
  implementing an ERM programme 70–71
  introduction 13–14
  learning and communication 194–96
  maturity in enterprise risk management
    152–55
  resilience and sustainable habits 172–74
  risk as opportunity/threat 57
  risk attitude, risk propensity and risk
    appetite 93–94

RASCI (responsible, accountable, supported,
    consulted, informed) principle 192–93
reports and extracts (from/on)
  the American Red Cross (*Forbes*, 2012)
    182
  causes of Fukushima disaster (TEPCO) 79
  connection of risk and performance (PwC
    research, 2008) 257
  CSR (*Daily Finance*, 2012) 171
  Financial Stability Board (2013) 203–04
  industrial accidents (Safety 101 website,
    2012) 185
  Kodak (*The Street*, 2013) 190
  McKinsey, 2013 (extract) 4
  NASA (Columbia Accident Investigation
    Board) 183–84
  near misses (*Risk and Regulation*, 2010)
    186
  risk communication (*Harvard Business
    Review*) 178
  role of directors and senior management
    (*Harvard Business Review*) 7–8
  Six Sigma (General Electric) 259
  summary of survey of 217 companies in
    Europe (*Harvard Business Review*)
    193

research on risk and performance (survey by
    PwC, 2008) 257–58
resilience and sustainable habits 155–75
  business continuity management 156–61,
    162 see also subject entry
  corporate social responsibility 166–68,
    169 see also subject entry
  role of senior management 161–66
    see also senior management, role of
risk
  averse 3
  and business 1–5
  capacity (or appetite) for taking 12–13
  communication 178
  culture 98
  difference between managed and
    unmanaged 5–6
  as effect of uncertainty on objectives 44
  evaluating and prioritizing *see* evaluating
    and prioritizing risk
  managers: 'Professional reference tool'
    document (AMRAE) 207
  managed *see* risk, managed
  measuring 223–24
  myths *see* myths about risk
  as threat 44–45
  as uncertainty 43–45
risk-adjusted
  capital (RORAC) 234
  performance metrics 258
  return on capital (RAROC) 233–34
  returns, calculating 234–35
  Sharpe ratio formula for 234
risk appetite (and)
  applications of a risk appetite tool 76–77
    four key factors for development of 77
  frameworks 78–81
    ability to control and enhance threat
      and opportunity 80, *81*
    current performance 81
    maturity 78–79
    risk propensity and culture 79–80
  organization behind setting of 88–90
    embedding risk appetite in the
      culture 90
    key features of risk appetite
      statement 88
    and risk limits 88–89
  statements (of a) 90–91, *92*
    global insurance company 91
    healthcare organization 90
  using as tool to destroy blame culture
    99–101
    case study for 100–101
  value drivers (and) 83–85, *86, 87*
    key control indicators 85

key risk indicators/STAFFS 84–85
risk assessment tools 261–62
  checklist 262
  control/Shewhart chart 262
  fish-bone/Ishikawa diagrams 261
  the five whys 261
  flowcharts 261
  HAZOP and FMEA approaches 262
  histogram 262
  inspection and audit 262
  Pareto chart 262
  questionnaire and checklist 262
  run chart 261
  scatter diagram/scatterplot 262
  SWOT and PESTLE analyses 262
  timeline analysis 261
  workshop and brainstorming 262
risk attitude, risk propensity and risk
    appetite (and) 73–95
  applications of a risk appetite tool *see* risk
    appetite
  developing risk appetite frameworks *see*
    risk appetite
  examples of risk appetite statements (of)
    90–91, 92
    a global insurance company 91
    a health care organization 90
  organization *see* risk appetite
  risk appetite and value drivers *see* risk
    appetite
  risk aversion vs risk hungry 73–75
    and determining risks 74–75, 75
  risk capacity vs tolerance 77–78
  risk of not taking a risk 82–83 *see also*
    case examples: Coca-Cola
    and stakeholder expectations and
    appetite metrics 83
risk, managed 101–04 *see also* case examples
  encouraging people to take 101
  example of buffaloes and geese
    leadership 103
  and mice, Maslow and Herzberg
    104–08, *105*
    and links to remuneration 106–08
  and risk-based decision making, setting
    boundaries for 98–99
risk management 16–17, 20, *16, 18, 19*
  and ERM, difference between 17, 20, *20*
risk management compliance requirements
    (for) 211–20, *214*
  Basel II and III – banks and investment
    entities 219
  CoCo framework (Canadian Institute of
    Chartered Accountants) 215–16
  COSO Framework 213–14, *214*
  Dodd-Frank 212–13

  EU Audit – for public interest entities 216
  NAIC ORSA – US insurance companies 215
  New York Stock Exchange Code 212
  Sarbanes-Oxley – US listed companies
    214–15
  Singapore Corporate Governance Council
    218
  Solvency II – all EU insurers and reinsurers
    219–20
  Switzerland
    SIX Exchange Directive 217
    Swiss Code of Best Practice for
      Corporate Governance 218
  South African entities – King III 217
  UK Code of Corporate Governance
    218–19
risk as opportunity/threat (and) 39–58 *see
    also* case examples
  as both opportunity and threat 42
  differentiating between objectives,
    strategic goals and value drivers
    51–53, 55–56, *54, 55, 56 see also*
    value drivers
  opportunities and threats 39–43 *see also*
    opportunity/ies *and* threat
  as uncertainty 43–45
Risk and Regulation 185
Royal Society for the Prevention of
    Accidents 3

sample terms of reference for a board risk
    committee 297–301
  Annual General Meeting 300
  authority 301
  duties 297–98
  frequency of meetings 299
  membership 298–99
  minutes of meetings 299–300
  notice of meetings 299
  other matters 300–301
  quorum 299
  reporting responsibilities 300
senior management, role of 161–66 *see also*
    case examples
  communication in event of crisis 161
  and key areas for communication in event
    of crisis 161–65
Six Sigma/Lean Six Sigma 255–56, 259–61
  and Motorola 258
SMART objectives 150
solvency capital requirement
    (SCR) 230
Spiegelhalter, D 10
strengths, weaknesses, opportunities and
    threats (SWOT) 6 *see also* SWOT
    analysis

surveys (of/on)
  links between executive compensation and
    risk management (Towers Watson,
    2013) 107–08
  maturity level of risk management
    practices (EY, 2011) 140
  senior executives (Economist Intelligence
    Unit, 2012) 26
Switzerland
  Six Exchange Directive 217
  Swiss Code of Best Practice for Corporate
    Governance 218
SWOT analysis 6, 44, 262 see also risk
  assessment tools

tables
  aspects of successful and unsuccessful
    efforts in embedding ERM 122
  assessment of likelihood and impact 292
  conformance versus performance drivers
    for ERM 201
  data for risks that have both positive and
    negative values 35
  description of elements for the
    documentation of ERM 63
  example of risk appetite statement 92
  examples of key performance indicators,
    risk appetite metrics, key risk
    indicators and key control indicators
    87
  examples of key performance indicators,
    risk appetite metrics and matching
    key risk indicators 86
  examples of leading indicators for
    forecasting threat and change in
    threat 187–88
  examples of leading indicators for
    opportunities 189–90
  five aspects of exercising a business
    continuity plan 162
  forecast of changing likelihood for an
    event over time 31
  insurable and uninsurable threats, list of
    225
  key attributes and principles of integrating
    ERM 124
  key success factors for embedding ERM
    131–34
  list of advantages and disadvantages of
    qualitative and quantitative aspects of
    risk management 238
  litigation and optimization techniques for
    threats and opportunities 34
  matching changing impacts to changing
    likelihoods over time 32–33

options for control of a threat and an
  opportunity 50
principal risks: KPMG survey 27
risk analysis of business survival 19
risk analysis of getting to work 18
risk maturity, advantages and
  disadvantages of various levels
  of 151
risk maturity: handling risks and outcomes
  of risk 149
risk maturity – inputs and outputs, seven
  aspects of 143
risk maturity: leadership in risk
  management 144
risk maturity: outcomes from ERM 160
risk maturity: partnerships and resources
  147
risk maturity: people aspects of
  ERM 146
risk maturity: processes for ERM 148
risk maturity: programme for ERM 145
summary of roles of board and senior
  management in maximizing
  performance 202
summary of the US ORSA 294–96
the three elements of risk for a fire 245
the three elements of risk for fraud 246
top 25 brands by brand value (2013)
  55–56
working out the options for control of a
  threat 48–49
Taleb, N N 8, 157
threat 44–47
  dealing with 45–47
  four Ts of 45–46
  and opportunity management 45
  stress/reverse stress testing for 235–37,
    239, 238
  valuing 224, 226–28, 225, 226, 228, 229

United Kingdom
  Code of Corporate Governance 218–19
  Code of Governance (2012) see Code of
    Governance (UK, 2012)
  Combined Code (2010) 217
United States (US) 232 see also legislation
  (US)
  Bankers Trust (New York) 233
  COSO Framework 213–14
  Dodd-Frank: Title XI – Federal Reserve
    System Provisions, Governance and
    oversight 212–13
  NAIC guidance on Own Risk and
    Solvency Assessment 215
  New York Stock Exchange Code 212

Sarbanes Oxley – US listed companies
214–15

value drivers 51–56, *54*
  capital 52–53
  cash flow and liquidity 53, 55

good will/reputation 55, *55–56*
knowledge 52

whistleblowing 113–14
Who Moved My Cheese? 105
A Worrier's Guide to Risk 10–12

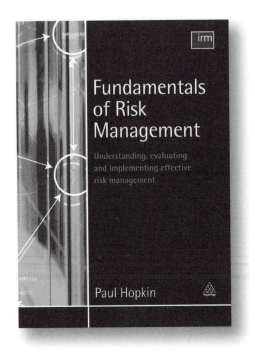